Hitters, Dancers and
Ring Magicians

D1565430

*to Lee and Diane
with best regards*

Kelly

Hitters, Dancers and Ring Magicians

Seven Boxers of the Golden Age and Their Challengers

KELLY RICHARD NICHOLSON

Foreword by DAN CUOCO

McFarland & Company, Inc., Publishers

Jefferson, North Carolina, and London

LIBRARY OF CONGRESS CATALOGUING-IN-PUBLICATION DATA

Nicholson, Kelly Richard.
    Hitters, dancers and ring magicians : seven boxers of the
golden age and their challengers / Kelly Richard Nicholson ;
foreword by Dan Cuoco.
        p.   cm.
    Includes bibliographical references and index.

    ISBN 978-0-7864-4990-3
    softcover : 50# alkaline paper ∞

    1. Boxer (Sports)—Biography.   2. Boxing—History—
19th century.   3. Boxing—History—20th century.   I. Title.
GV1131.N525   2011
796.830922—dc22 [B]   2010039582

British Library cataloguing data are available

Front cover: The amazing George "Kid" Lavigne, circa 1896

Manufactured in the United States of America

McFarland & Company, Inc., Publishers
  Box 611, Jefferson, North Carolina 28640
  www.mcfarlandpub.com

A special shout-out
to Frank and the gang —
Jess, Taylor, Christopher, Beacher, Suzy, and Liz —
at Franky and Johnny's Island Park
on Rte. 46 in New Jersey.

Thanks for good times,
hospitality, and encouragement
in a place where good friends did meet.

Acknowledgments

This book deals with athletes who thrived in what some have called a golden age, an age when American boxing came to maturity in a setting that still had in it some grit and taste of the old frontier. It is devoted to several men — founding fathers, one might say, of a modern sporting nation — who provide flesh examples of the age and its spirit.

In completing a project of this size, one becomes indebted to a fair number of folk; the present instance is no exception. As was the case with my first boxing book *A Man Among Men*, there are several individuals who deserve special mention for their generosity. Thus again I give thanks to Tracy Callis, an eminent boxing historian and an admirer of the early fighters, who in recent years has rekindled my interest in that era. Tracy is one of the most discerning individuals on the sporting scene, not to mention a text reader and a researcher of fact whose attention to detail is unmatched. Once more, as well, I am indebted to Harry Shaffer of Antiquities of the Prize Ring for his priceless store of materials on the game at the turn of the century, and for his painstaking helpfulness on more than one occasion.

I wish to thank also Clay Moyle, owner of the greatest boxing library that I have seen, and a man helpful in the extreme when it came to obtaining rare and difficult source material. From Clay I obtained plentiful information, much of it from the marvelous *Fight Stories* magazines of the prewar era. From Monte Cox, another historian with the International Boxing Research Organization (IBRO), I obtained a number of items regarding the career and fighting merits of Joe Gans, about whom Monte has written with keen-eyed admiration. David Jack and Tom Scharf provided little-known facts respectively about Bob Fitzsimmons and Terry McGovern. Christine Lewis, in recent months, has gone the extra mile to obtain for me details regarding George LaBlanche. Finally is the contribution of Dan Cuoco, current director of the IBRO, who has penned a foreword to this book, and who ranks as one of the game's premier sources of integrity and information.

Integrity? How often do we hear that boxing needs it? Corruption, long rife in the sport's bloodstream, abounds to this day. Yet were boxing, I submit, in the hands of men and women like these, the situation would be different. In the ranks of the IBRO are some of the best individuals whom I have met, in the sport or out of it, and whose friendship does me an honor. So, in short, I say thanks to these individuals for help, intelligence, and plain "old school" courtesy, and for insight in many cases that I would otherwise lack. Whatever merit this book has owes something to each. And whatever the problems of the sport, however much character it may lack, I declare that integrity, too, presently lives in this great and bittersweet science.

Table of Contents

The muscles of the shoulders play the most important part in the delivery of a hard blow. Take any boxer who has finely developed back and shoulder muscles and you will find that he is a stout hitter.

Bob Fitzsimmons

… stiffen the arm and push the shoulder forward; the force of the blow should not be ended the moment it lands — keep it going.

Dick O'Farrell, *How to Box*

Ain't no secret. All I do is put my hips into them punches.

Sam Langford

Foreword
by Dan Cuoco

In reading this manuscript, I am reminded first and foremost of one thing: that of all the pleasures given to sports fans, nothing compares with an absorbing good tale of heroes from boxing's "golden age"!

The stars of this work were men known largely for their punching power. They were men like Sam Langford, Bob Fitzsimmons, and Stanley Ketchel — two-fisted terrors who became famous for the way that they visited sudden disaster on their opponents. Were they truly the hardest punchers of their day? It is a subject laden with controversy: Any selection of a few men as being the best or the most destructive of their time will invite argument. On this point the author does not pretend to have the final word. The controversy, he realizes, will endure. But this book is not merely about punching power, nor merely about boxing talent. It is about heart and soul, and the raw stuff that makes great fighters in any era.

In *Hitters, Dancers and Ring Magicians*, which follows his biography of James J. Jeffries, Kelly Nicholson again delivers a wallop of his own, putting on display a cross-section of the best and bravest in the annals of the game. As a leadoff, he provides an historical context, succinctly tracing high points of the sport from earliest recorded times to the late 19th century. In the process, the reader gets an acquaintance with such figures as James Figg, Jack Broughton, and other pioneers who helped to take boxing from its crude beginnings to its current state. The following seven chapters, effectively mini-biographies, are devoted to fighters who exemplified the strength and spirit of the game in the era of 1890 to 1910, a time for which the author has an obvious affinity. In these chapters the reader learns of men, some of them largely forgotten, who were among the best that the sport has ever seen. Featured on center stage of this discussion, along with stars just noted, are George "Kid" Lavigne, Barbados Joe Walcott, Joe Gans, and Terry McGovern. In all, a worthy seven they make, men in every case who bestowed value on their sport and paved the way for fighters who have climbed the steps since.

The description of their exploits is first-class. Enriching each chapter are accounts of each man's greatest ring battles and insightful looks at some of his chief rivals. Kelly does justice to his subjects by examining what made each an immortal — a desire to succeed, an ability to dish it out, and in some cases an astounding capacity to take it in return. The result is a lean and flavorful piece of drama for which the true fight fan hungers.

Dan Cuoco is a boxing historian and director of the International Boxing Research Organization.

Introduction

"I am sorry that prize-fighting is gone out," remarks Dr. Samuel Johnson, late in the eighteenth century, in a conversation with his friend James Boswell. Every art, he contends, "should be preserved, and the art of self-defence is surely important."[1] Such an art "made people accustomed not to be alarmed at seeing their own blood or feeling a little pain from a wound."

While he preceded them by a century, Johnson would have admired the athletes who appear in the pages ahead. They were men equal to a challenge, men who were used to seeing blood, and to shedding it, in a time when spirit and muscle were forged in a hard school. There were no million-dollar paydays then, and young ring aspirants often were steered less cautiously in their ventures than they are today. The man who gave his all and came up short in a brutal fight might weep openly at its end — not from weakness, but from the sheer depth of his virile emotion. Competitors had to go it often, perhaps several times in a month, and two men who made a good show could get to know each other well in the years coming. Off nights were inevitable, and win-loss ledgers less pristine.

This is the story of heroes and wayfarers, of artists and proto-scientists, if one may stretch words like *art* and *science* to include what goes on within this arena. As its name suggests, it is about men who could punch, as well as men who excelled in creativity. The main subjects of this work do not exhaust the talent that can be mined from their era; another volume could spotlight contemporaries (some noted herein) arguably just as deserving. But the current selection constitutes a worthy sample.

By way of setting, I felt it appropriate, in the early going, to cover again some ground from *A Man Among Men*, which traced the life and career of heavyweight champion (1899–1905) Jim Jeffries. Thus certain topics noted there — boxing in ancient times, its development in the eighteenth and nineteenth centuries, the rise of the modern style — receive again their due. But in these sections I try also to shine light from new angles, avoiding flat repetition for the sake of readers who have passed this way before.

As to the merits of old-timers versus those of fighters more recent, I offer comment toward the end as I did in the Jeffries volume.[2] Could these bygone heroes hold their own with the best of today? In some cases, I believe, the answer is yes. But arguments can be made on each side, and in the last tally, greatness is probably best gauged according to its era. And surely boxing greatness is found across the ages: Present-day excellence in the prize ring, as in every field, has a seminal tie to the genius that precedes it.

The structure of the present work is as follows—it begins with discussion of the game's development up to the late nineteenth century, then a chapter is devoted to each of seven fighters George "Kid" Lavigne, Bob Fitzsimmons, Joe Walcott, Joe Gans, Terry McGovern, Sam Langford, and Stanley Ketchel—during the period of about 1890 to 1910 (extending, in Langford's case, a bit further). A brief afterword follows, noting subsequent developments in the sport and the perspectives of several ring historians on the men featured herein.

* * *

"I am not a prize fighter," remarks Bob Fitzsimmons, shortly after winning the middleweight championship. "I am an athlete, and I box for prizes. I belong to the new school, and not the old, and I therefore cannot be styled a prize fighter."[3] It is clear, in reading this comment, that boxing was then a sport in transition, moving from the bare-handed turf wars of the 19th century to what is seen on weekly telecasts of today. Some of these men knew what it was to fight with bare knuckles, or with gloves skin-tight; some fought in virtual marathons, wars of attrition that lasted two or three hours.

Well into the 20th century, a feature bout might be scheduled for 20 or more rounds. For this reason, men of the time were accomplished at body punching, a tactic that pays dividends in an extended battle. Less attention is given to this aspect of the game today, when fighters often spend years in the amateur ranks with a scoring system (generally, one punch, one point) that can turn a three-round bout into a fencing match. But punches downstairs, as experienced fighters will tell you, are more profoundly damaging. Get hit in the head, and you may be stunned; get hit below the heart, in that neural center known as the solar plexus, and you will think that your opponent has torn out a chunk of your soul.

The reader will notice also a sheer size difference between "big men" of that day and this. The reason for this difference is complex, but it owes in part to the fact that athletes now come from a much wider spawning ground than they did a century ago. At the upper end, they themselves are running larger. Boxing's heavyweight contenders at this writing are apt to scale some 250 pounds, and a specimen of 210 (quite good-sized even 30 years ago) is counted as small to average. For this reason the present reader may be taken aback when hearing, say, of "Irish Giant" Peter Maher, a late 19th century slugger standing 5'11" and scaling 178. These were, in fact, respectable figures in their day, and any man above middleweight (generally meaning the low to mid–150s) was in the open weight class. Not until the early 20th century did the sport see the adoption of a 175-pound "light heavyweight" division separating average-sized men from the dreadnaughts, and not until the 1970s was a "cruiserweight" level (190 or 195, and since nudged to 200) added.

Each of my main seven subjects was known for punching. There exist longstanding questions regarding this talent and its origins. Wherein does it reside? Is it a gift from on high, or can it be taught? Punching, like much indeed of human activity, is hard to capture in precise terms. It is tinged, when all is said and done, with some element of mystery. Some fighters do damage with blows that look ordinary; others, just as big, tee off with shots that look as good, yet lack the effect. How is it that one man has "heavy hands" while another does not?

One of the few to address this question in recent times is James Carney, in "What's the Power Source for Boxing's Big Hitters?" Among the factors that seem to be relevant, notes Carney, are strength, speed, timing, concentration, body type, and perhaps others, present in various mixtures in those who merit note as punchers. While there is some positive correlation between raw strength and punching power, there is no less "a whole contingent of rather scrawny guys who [can] knock your brains out."[4]

On this point the old-timers had their ideas, as well. "It is not only the hand and arm that are used in striking," recalls Fitzsimmons during the latter part of his great career. "The legs, body, and shoulders also come into play.... A blow, to have force, must have the 'send' of the legs and the swing of the body with it."[5] In truth, many words could be expended on the subject without saying more. Maybe there is an analogy in sports like golf and baseball. Hitting of every kind is applied force, an execution of bodily physics wherein balance, leverage, and coordination yield their product. In boxing, as elsewhere, a novice must learn something about rhythm and alignment. He may need to be guarded against a natural tendency to "kill" the target by swinging in roundhouse fashion, or drawing back to gain (so it may seem) punching momentum. A blow from the ordinary hands-up position can pack surprising power, and its impact may be increased dramatically by slight alterations in delivery, as for example by "riding" one leg or the other, or by getting the hips into the act. (A slight clench of the hand or snap of the wrist at the moment of impact, say some, is also vital.) By the same token, punching is not altogether one thing, for *how good* a puncher you are will depend in some measure on the opponent that you are facing.

* * *

However one may assess this knack, these men certainly had it. Yet a full century now separates us from most of their exploits; how much can we know about what happened back then? Sources, in fact, are more plentiful than one might imagine. Motion picture footage, some of it remarkably clear, dates from as early as 1894. As to literature, newspapers and magazines of the day were thick with commentary on approaching bouts and blow-by-blow reports of their transaction.

In years since, there has built up an accretion also of related material, some of it supplied by eyewitness memory, some by reports secondhand. Such accounts, flavored often with the blood and sap of mad beast and crashing timber, are testament to the love that their authors bore the sport. Even so, the reader must be wary. Penned often in what has been called a "half-blinded by his own blood, he swung from his heels" style, these accounts are a joy to read, but they reflect more, at times, of the writer's imagination than of the event itself. One source may have two men, at bout's end, practically knee-deep in each other's blood, while another, closer to the scene, remarks that "no great damage was done"! A man with ruptured ear tissue, by the same token, fights on with the organ "hanging by a shred." Stricken by a right hand, he may do a mid-air flip and land (apparently doing a one-and-a-quarter turn) flat on his back. Here, as elsewhere, time breeds magnification. In some cases this enlargement owes to willful yarn-spinning by author or fighter, in some merely to that natural "morphing" of recollection, over time, to which human beings are prone. All things equal, the earlier account (usually also the more conservative) is the one toward which I lean. The inquiring reader will find numerous chapter notes to allow checking of sources firsthand.

There is also a minor issue as to how some of these men sounded when they spoke. Here, too, sources vary and writers embellish. One scribe tries hard to render the *patois* of Afro, Caribbean, or British-based speech as it struck the ear, while another ignores it. (Of course, when the fighter is writing the words, or issuing a comment for publication, no such effort is made.) Overall I follow the lead offered, maintaining a quote as it is given.

As to the books cited, the veteran reader will recognize some to which I am indebted. For information on the era's black prizefighters, there is the five-volume work *Black Dynamite* by Nat Fleischer, founder and editor of *The Ring* magazine, a periodical that began publication in 1922. (Especially of use from this source were the third and fourth volumes, titled *The Three Colored Aces* and *Fighting Furies*.) While this work contains exaggeration, and is sometimes careless in its details, it is unmatched for spirit and for sheer volume of information on its subject. (Fortunately, the reader may want to note, a new level of excellence has begun in this area during the past few years with the first volumes of a multiple work by Kevin Smith.)

Regarding Bob Fitzsimmons, the classic biography is the one by Gilbert Odd, which had its first printing in 1971 and stands to this day as a model of balance, patience, and editorial scrutiny. Fitzsimmons fans have benefited of late also from the large-format pictorial *Fitzsimmons — Boxing's First Triple World Champion* by Christopher Tobin and *Prize Fighter: The Life and Times of Bob Fitzsimmons* by Dale Webb. More recently we have the massive project of Adam J. Pollack, a multi-volume sequential work detailing the exploits of heavyweight champions from John L. Sullivan forward, the third volume of which is *In the Ring with Bob Fitzsimmons*. And recently, too, there is *Lanky Bob*, a thoroughgoing work just released as of this writing, by Keith Robinson. For summaries of Ketchel and McGovern, Fleischer is a ready source, and a veritable one-man repository of insight and anecdote. Here again, one has to maintain a critical distance, as Nat was prone to accept stories at face value, particularly where his own heroes (who were often his personal acquaintances) were concerned.[6] Thus checking with independent sources is advised.

Other stars noted in this book, such as Lavigne, Gans, and Langford, are deserving no less of separate volumes, though few such volumes are to be found. A new book by Clay Moyle on Langford has done much to remedy the situation in regard to one of these men. A rewarding biography of Joe Gans, by Colleen Aycock and Mark Scott, has recently appeared. Most of the boxers found within these pages still await their due, and with the revived interest in boxing history among historians and scholars of all stripes, one hopes these men will soon receive the attention that they, their sport and their times rightly deserve.

I

The New Game

They used to fight real vicious,
And went right in to maul
Outside of bites and gouging
No holds were barred at all;
Each milling cove was reckless
And often would abuse
The other fellow's feet with
The spikes upon his shoes!
> Popular refrain, celebrating the advent
> of the Marquess of Queensberry rules[1]

"No other thrill in the world of sports," writes Alexander Johnston in a classic text, "can equal that which comes from watching two men engage in combat with no other weapons ... but those with which old Dame Nature has provided them."[2]

It is nothing new, this combat. Primal song tells of men who compete with their fists for prizes and admiration. An episode late in Homer's *Iliad* describes two who "toe to toe, let fly at one another." Epeios, we are told, "leapt out with a long left hook" (it is a nicely current rendition of the Greek) that dropped Euryalos flat on his back.[3] Virgil's story of Aeneas, legendary founder of Rome, has in it a kindred scene, in which aging pugilist Entellus dons the gloves against a young hitter named Dares. Swinging wild at one point, the veteran misses and falls to the ground. Rising, fueled by shame and pride, he goes at Dares with both hands, his blows "thick and fast as hail ... drumming on roofs," to win the battle.[4] Reference is made, in this story, to a pair of massive gauntlets, seven layers of ox hide loaded with lead and iron, once worn by Dares's brother in his fatal bout with Hercules. (A horror even to Dares himself, they are stained, it is said, with blood and brains from bygone use.)

Figg, Broughton, and the London Prize Ring

Boxing was the rage also in modern England. In 1723, during the reign of George I, a "ring" (a wide spot of ground encircled by railings) was erected for the purpose in Hyde Park. The game's modern lineage is said to commence with James Figg, a fighting expert who rose to fame on the strength of multiple talents. Figg, described by historian Bob Mee as "belligerent, happy-go-lucky, shrewd, and illiterate," was discovered by the Earl of Peterborough when displaying his skills in boxing, fencing, and the quarterstaff on a village green. The Earl brought him to London, where he achieved celebrity status.[5]

Six feet and 13 stone (182 pounds), with shaven head and bull neck, Figg dished out lessons in democratic fashion to anyone who had the fee. Figg's Academy held about a thousand people on the ground floor with room for 300 more in an elite gallery. At the center of the hall was a 40-foot stage where James and his pupils showed their stuff. Indeed, any who went to Figg could expect rough instruction. Captain Godfrey, a sporting gent and contemporary chronicler, is quoted as saying of his experience in Figg's school, "I have purchased my knowledge with many a broken head, and bruises in every part of me. I chose ... to go to [Figg] ... partly as I knew him to be the ablest master, and partly as he was of a rugged temper, and would spare no man, high or low, who took up a stick against him."[6]

What was "boxing" in those days? The rise, in recent years, of so-called mixed martial arts is sometimes conceived as an expansion of boxing of the conventional kind. In fact, where history is concerned, the sport as we now have it descends from a broader discipline. In the seventh century before the Common Era, Greek Olympians mixed it up in *pankration* ("all powers"), a term that has been revived in recent "mixed marital arts" competition that combines strikes with assorted holds and takedowns. In Figg's day, boxing was a bruising endeavor that involved likewise bare-handed punching, holds, and throws to the ground. One index of its roughness might be gleaned from the fact, mentioned by Elliot Gorn, that in one fight Figg was caught in a stranglehold by an opponent and was all but killed before finally breaking free.[7]

An advance in the sport's civilization owes to Figg's protégé Jack Broughton. Born around 1704 in a small village near Bristol, Jack suffered the loss of his mother at a young age. In time, fleeing an abusive situation that developed, he and his sister Rose, ages 12 and 10, left home and found work in the city. (As Mee notes, a departure at this age "was not an uncommon thing" for children in this lower social stratum. Rose, as it turned out, married well, and Jack was a noted athlete even in his mid-teens. Rarely, however, did such refugees meet with any good end, and Jack and Rose might be gauged as being luckier than most.) In about 1725 he crossed paths with Figg, possibly at one of James's traveling fairs. It is said that a scrape between Jack and the winner of a bout on a Figg program convinced James to hire him at the academy.

Standing 5'11" and scaling 14 stone (196 pounds), Broughton was a find. Intelligent, possessed of fine sense, he was intrigued by things that ranged from methods of combat to the wondrousness of flowers. His aptitude found expression in the ring, where he learned to use his full reach, and to catch and parry what came his way until he was nearly untouchable. He also made use of a punch to the short ribs, a target that became known in his honor as Broughton's Mark. Testament to his genius is offered by ring historian Pierce Egan: "Broughton, like all great performers, generally exhibited something new in every performance, and those pugilists who had witnessed his contests ... expecting to find that he would fight upon the *old suit*, were most terribly deceived; as, contrary to most other boxers, he did not depend upon any particular blow, although he was distinguished for giving some remarkable hits, which were [not to be] forgotten."[8]

Broughton's real contribution to the sport was occasioned in early 1741 by his fight with George Stevenson, a tough comer who had issued an open challenge to the 36-year-old celebrity warrior. Jack, hampered of late by illness, did not fancy the challenge, but accepted it as a matter of honor. In short order, he took command. The fight, which lasted 39 minutes, was brutal even by the standards of the day. A relative novice, Stevenson went headlong at Jack and was sent crashing several times to the wooden floor. Beaten and bloodied, the Yorkshire challenger fought back gamely until at last, backed against a ring post, he fell from a blow beneath the heart.

As George lay still, Broughton wondered aloud if he had killed him. Stevenson eventually regained his senses, but two of his ribs had been broken and greater damage had been done to his internal organs. He lingered for a month before succumbing, developing a friendship with Broughton during that time and eventually dying with Jack at his side.

Deeply moved by the loss that his hands had inflicted, Broughton devised a new fighting code, imposing on the sport a greater clarity and making it less savage in the bargain. Written up by his friend Captain Godfrey, it was published in August of 1743. Broughton's Rules, as they were called, required a chalked three-foot square in the middle of the stage, to which each man went, or was led by his second, for the start of a round. Failing this, a man was *knocked out* of the contest. Likewise, by this new code, "No person is to hit his adversary when he is down, or seize him by the ham, the breeches, or any part below the waist; a man on his knees [is] to be reckoned down." Jack introduced also the use of "mufflers," gloves that could be worn in sparring sessions when training for full-fledged combat. Contained in a London newspaper of 1749 is an announcement of the opening of Broughton's academy in Haymarket:

> For the instruction of those who are willing to be instructed in the mystery of boxing, where the whole theory and practice of that truly British art, with all the numerous stops, blows, cross-buttocks, etc., incident to combatants will be fully taught and explained and that persons of quality and distinction may not be debarred from entering into a course of these lectures they will be given with the utmost tenderness and regard for the delicacy of the frame and constitution of the pupil, for which reason mufflers are provided that will effectually secure them from the inconvenience of black eyes, broken jaws and bloody noses.[9]

This code held sway until introduction of the rules of the London Prize Ring, drafted by the British Pugilists Protective Association in 1838.[10] By London rules, a fallen man had to make it back to the scratch-line unaided. The rules also made explicit a requirement, already acknowledged in principle, that a fighter must not fall without being hit. Butting was disallowed, and it was stated that "in picking up their men, should the seconds or bottleholders willfully injure the antagonist of their principal, the latter shall be deemed to have forfeited the battle on the decision of the referee." The new code made provision, as well, for certain contingencies, such as the fall of darkness in a fight held outdoors.

The New Rules

Modern boxing is sometimes divided into eras by the style prevailing. One might thus be marked by the heyday of Figg and Broughton, another by the London style. The next is the one that has endured. In 1858 John Sholto Douglas became the Marquess[11] of Queensberry, a village in the greater London area. Seven years later, J.G. Chambers, a prominent member of the Amateur Sporting Club, composed a set of rules that markedly changed the face of the sport. Credit for their authorship is generally given to the Marquess, from whose station they get their name.

Chambers, it appears, was satisfied with this situation for a couple of reasons: Since Douglas's father had been an amateur pugilist with ties to the prizefighting world, authority in this area would better emanate from the Douglas line. A man with title, by the same token, carried more weight with the sporting public than did a commoner, and so increased the chance that the new rules would find acceptance. And the Marquess was a man who commanded respect from those who met him: "Sailor, soldier, amateur boxer, [and] lover of fair play"—so was Douglas described by an acquaintance who counted his 1888 introduction to the man as being "the proudest memory of my life."[12] He was a man faithful to his own conviction, one whose regard for justice extended beyond the sporting arena and addressed such things as religious intolerance and hypocrisy. His rules caught on, and are essentially the ones that now govern the game.

First intended for amateurs, the Queensberry rules were finding their way into the professional arena by 1872. They called for a square ring, bordered by ropes, preferably 24 feet on a side; a round was now defined not by a knockdown, but by a fixed three-minute limit, with one minute's rest between. Gloves were mandatory, a provision that lent to the sport a measure of civility, even if they were of such small size (in some cases, but a couple of ounces) that they served only to lessen damage to the hand that struck the blow. Further, when a fighter was down, he gained no automatic respite. At the count of ten, he was done.

* * *

Upon this scene arrived John Lawrence Sullivan like an exploding comet, capturing public fancy as had no man before. While other men might spar for an advantage, it was said, Sullivan fought from the opening second. In short order, he transformed the game "from contests of endurance into dazzlingly quick and skillful performances, characterized by a new kinetic style in keeping with the up-tempo spirit of the age."[13]

After sparring with John L., renowned veteran and boxing teacher "Professor" Mike Donovan remarked that being hit by him was like being kicked in the head by a runaway horse. Such was the force of Sullivan's right hand, Donovan would later remark, that on those occasions when he got through with it to the top of the veteran fighter's head, "his blows made me see stars of different colors."[14] In 1881, Sullivan met John Flood, a prominent slugger known as the Bull's Head Terror. In eight one-sided rounds, he left Flood lying all but comatose with blood running from one ear.

Against champion Paddy Ryan the next year, fighting under London rules, he won in blazing fashion. Half a minute into the going, said one witness, "Sullivan let go his terrific right hand, and Ryan went to grass like a shot, face downward, from a blow on his left jaw."

All that John L. did, he did big and loud. When with his chosen companions—plain folk, in the main, whom he preferred to higher society—

he laughed, ate, drank, and carried on in ways unforgettable. He would sing, recalled acquaintance Arthur T. Lumley, with a thundering voice "that almost cracked the ceiling."[15] At times he would stomp his feet in time to a ballad, practically shaking the building. Sullivan could adorn a steak with a whole bottle of Tabasco and down it like a savage. On occasion he would put away three large steaks and polish them off with dessert besides. His own concoction of Irish stew, which he proclaimed to be (what else?) the best in the world, was likewise saturated with enough hot sauce to wilt anyone who shared it with him.

So dominant was Sullivan in the ring that competition at the highest level, some observers imagined, was effectively over. After nine rounds, and less than eleven minutes, Ryan had been destroyed. "Mr. Sullivan," it was remarked, "has probably put an end to heavyweight prize fighting. It is altogether improbable that for many years a man will be found who would dare to face him in a prize ring. He cared nothing for Ryan's blows, and his own hitting is so tremendous that it seems beyond the power of man to recover from the shock of one of his hands let out from the shoulder."[16]

Not that John L. was any kind of role model — in a short time, he would be known as a philanderer and a tyrant, and a drunkard of phenomenal proportion. Before he was 30, the drink would land him at death's door. Such was his magnetism, however, that he remained a hero. He was also a voice in favor of the new rules, which bestowed some increase of dignity on both fighter and audience. The Queensberry setting, as he observed, was generally a hall with police supervision and a price that protected the going spectator from rougher elements. In a statement extolling Sullivan's ability, scribe John Boyle O'Reilly said that he could be credited also with uplifting the game. Not only had he taken on all comers, but he had made "a manly and most creditable effort to establish the practice ... of sparring [and] of fighting with large gloves."[17]

The Emerging Game of the Late 19th Century

Thus Sullivan, rough-cut and hell-bent, actually figured in the sport's refinement. Possibly, as more than one historian has noted, it had nothing to do with his own preference as to rules, but to his disgust with the problems — dodging the authorities, doing jail time and paying fines afterward, etc. — that attached to the old game. But the result was the same, whatever his motives.

Yet Sullivan was not the last word in the game's development. As to punching power, he was unmatched. But the advent of the Queensberry rules brought new emphasis on such things as footwork, defensive technique, and counterpunching. There came also increased participation in the sport by smaller fighters, and the establishment of weight classes wherein the lighter men could square off with one another.

The concern with speed and maneuver was not brand-new. Late in the previous century, Daniel Mendoza, a Jewish fighter of Spanish descent born in London, had improvised in that direction. Standing 5'7" and weighing about 160, Mendoza intrigued onlookers with his use of the whole ring, keeping his game at long range and darting in when he chose.

Daniel took a beating his first time out. After that, notes Fleischer, in an account that all but glows with the author's own ethnic pride, Mendoza devoted three years to developing an effective system of "guarding, side-stepping, and effective use of the straight left" before trying again.[18] Mendoza, remarks Bob Mee, has mention also in a book that lists in order the 100 most influential Jews of all time. (It appears, in fact, to be a tough field, with Moses ranking first and Jesus of Nazareth second, while further down are King Solomon at 29 and Harry Houdini at 81, with Mendoza two rungs below the great magician.)

Now, a hundred years later, fighters were getting the hang of this style. The coming shift may have had one presage in May of 1883, when John L. agreed to box Charley Mitchell in a sparring session with gloves. In that brief mix, Mitchell showed that a slugger, even a great one, could be made to look bad. Shifting and sliding, he actually paused and laughed openly at the champion at one point; he also managed to put Sullivan on his backside (John would forever swear that he was essentially *pushed* over when off balance), an indignity that had him rushing Mitchell crazily from that point forward. It was declared over when John L. caught the Englishman and hurled him mightily to the floor.

Several years later, the two met again, this time in bleak conditions, with rain falling so hard that by the 15th round the ground beneath the fighters was churned to mud. A nasty wind made things worse, and Sullivan was in distress by the 31st. In the 39th, after more than three hours, neither man was up to a sustained attack. The bout ended in a draw. Yet Mitchell, at this point, strolled about in relative comfort, while the champion, by contrast, "stood like a tired, snorting mammoth, out of his time and as if staring into a huge, unwelcoming future."[19]

The Marquess, as it turned out, lived until 1900, long enough to see his enterprise supersede the old one. In 1889 came the last London Prize Ring fight of any consequence, a war to the finish between Sullivan and

Jake Kilrain. It went 75 rounds before Kilrain's people declared a halt to keep him from being killed. Kilrain, in fact, was a beaten man as early as the eighth round, and was knocked out (by Queensberry standards) in the 14th and 16th rounds. In the 50th, a Sullivan left hand sent him backward in a somersault, after which he was the object of brutal target practice. Soon Jake's second Mike Donovan feared for the fighter's life. As rounds passed, Sullivan regained vitality and went on the upswing. In the 74th, Donovan pleaded with Kilrain to quit, and the challenger said that he would rather die.

Proud, vain, and immensely skilled — the one and only Gentleman James J. Corbett, who conquered John L. Sullivan and helped to move boxing from its bare-knuckle era into the age of strategy, footwork, and ring science (c. 1895).

In the 75th round, Jake was too weak to stand without spreading his legs for support, and he could not raise his hands. A Sullivan right hand to the body folded him, and Donovan, recalling that he had seen two men, in his time, perish in the ring, refused to let it continue. While the reality, staged in miserable July Midwest heat, was grittier than the image that endures (Kilrain sought a half-minute refuge in the dirt many times in the later going, and Sulli-van, gulping tea and brandy between rounds, started vom-iting in round 44), the bout stands as a grand closure on an era.

* * *

If boxing was on a scien-tific rise, James J. Corbett was its Galileo. Up to now, said trainer Joe Donoghue, "Good left-hand performers were rather scarce, especially among the big fellows."[20] Years after working with Corbett, he recalled how the fighter, while working as a clerk at a San Francisco bank, had noticed that his left hand had less strength than his right. He set out to correct the problem, using his left overtime in sparring matches with fellow employees, then practicing afterward on his own, with hair-splitting dedication, shooting that hand countless times into a cushion to improve his stamina and his accuracy. In time he would have a jab unrivaled.

In experimental fashion, Corbett also devised moves of his own, knowing that anything unusual in the sport was a subject of ridicule until its effect was proved. Feint, footwork, luring a man out of position and lowering the boom — all of this he set out to master. (In later years he regaled his stylistic heir Gene Tunney with stories of how he would literally map his game, diagramming on paper step-patterns that might lend themselves to ring situations.) He was also adept at getting inside the head of a prospective opponent and capitalizing on what he found. A revelation came in 1890 when he met John L.'s rival Kilrain. In a bout pitting James against a warhorse 20 pounds heavier than himself, onlookers caught sight of a rising star.

War, stated the Chinese sage Sun Tzu, is an exercise in rapidity and deception.[21] He might have enjoyed sitting at front row for this one: "As we met in the centre," notes Corbett, "I feinted Kilrain a couple of times. Then, too swiftly for the audience to count them, I hit him six punches right on the nose, and the spectators began throwing their hats in the air."[22] While Corbett's own recollection of this fight bears the mark of his pride, and is a mite loose in some details (for example, he recalls being a gawky 21 year old of 165 pounds, while the records show him to be a little older and probably further along in his development), it provides insight into the evolution of the game: Kilrain was thoroughly outmatched. In the second round, he was sporting a bad cut over his right eye, and in no time, every man present saw that this former bank window attendant could hit Jake however he pleased.

At the end of six, the audience hailed a new hero, hoisting James aloft and later opening cases of champagne to celebrate his victory at the smartest club in New Orleans. Afterward, notes Corbett, he wired his father with a message: "Won with hands down. Love to all," a message that the elder Irishman took with him all over San Francisco, pretending not to understand the figurative "hands down" phrase so that he could have it explained to him all evening long.

About six weeks after the Kilrain fight, James visited the renowned Professor Donovan at the New York Athletic Club, where he and Donovan boxed every day for a month as James lent a hand with the young pupils.

Corbett, Donovan saw, was the man to beat Sullivan. Repeatedly, the older man mimicked moves of the champion — slapping down an opponent's guard with his left hand, then heaving the right with cannonball force, or swinging the roundhouse right to land fist or arm on a man's neck.

It was the Professor, in large part, who made the young tactician a real fighter. In the early going, James was strictly a long-rage boxer. But soon he was able to get inside and land to the body with power shots. Throughout these sessions, Donovan would say, he demonstrated amazing aptitude. While he caught James often with punches to the body in the first week, "after that time it became almost impossible to reach him."[23]

Showing grit to go with genius, Corbett sought another bout with a bigger, more seasoned opponent. This time it was the most feared man in the division, Australia's great black heavyweight Peter Jackson. Again, it looked like the young dude had bitten off more than he could swallow, and early betting reflected it. Even his supporters were wagering on little but how long he would last.

Yet Corbett knew what he was doing. Not long after Jackson arrived in San Francisco, the two saw each other in passing. On meeting at the California Athletic Club, they had words. Jackson was onto the fact that Corbett had recently slighted his prowess after seeing him in action. Not one to mince, James confessed, he had thought Peter's effort, at that time, lacked something. To Jackson, an old-school sort who had lived through some lean years in his pursuit of Sullivan, this was a breach of tact. He replied that he was ready to give the upstart a lesson in manners when James was up to it. Then and there, they agreed to settle their differences in the one place where it mattered.

In the months that followed, as Jackson waded through more contenders in a futile attempt to secure a title shot, Corbett worked on strength and strategy. He knew also that however hard a fighter may work, the fight, when it occurs, is a product of *two* things — his own performance and the other man's, as well. For this reason he missed no chance to see the great Australian in the ring. When Joe McAuliffe was matched to fight Peter, Joe's people requested James as a sparring partner. He obliged, and on fight night he was in the audience. While Jackson won impressively, Corbett was not deterred.

"During the fight," he would recall, "I watched every move of the big negro's and figured out a system of fighting him by which I might have a 'look in.'" Soon after, he sold the directors of the club on a bout between himself and Jackson, for the biggest purse in boxing to that date, $10,000. He also attended a middleweight title bout in New Orleans between Nonpareil Jack Dempsey and lanky Australian middleweight challenger Bob Fitzsimmons. And he watched a Chicago stage production of *Honest Hearts and Willing Hands*, starring none other than John L. Sullivan.

Corbett had first seen the great man at 15, finagling his way into a theatre to see John L. when he was in his prime. Though awed at the time, he was soon thinking on another level. "Whatever put the idea into my youthful head," he would say later, "I don't know, but in my heart I felt that with agility, and science, and a certain system that could be worked out, I could beat him some day!"[24]

On this occasion, prior to the fight with Peter, Corbett received an invitation to meet John L. after the first act of the Chicago performance. Some fighters might have been overwhelmed by the meeting; others might have treated it as a confrontation. For Corbett it was a chance to gain insight.

A revelation it was, starting with the powerful handshake that greeted every new Sullivan acquaintance. The reigning king then wanted James to have a drink, something that he was not doing with so much looming ahead. The meeting turned nonetheless into a lengthy bar-hop, with Sullivan putting down enough for both of them, roaring always his stock challenge to "lick any sonofabitch" on the premises. Finally tiring of the routine, and of Sullivan's trumpeting of himself as world's greatest heavyweight, he announced to the reigning king that the whole display was a discourtesy to him as a fellow ringman.

For a moment it looked like fireworks would erupt, whereupon Sullivan said affably, "Aw, come on and have a drink!" For the rest of the evening, he behaved himself, revealing to Corbett something worth note: As a bully, John L. reigned supreme, but when called on his act, he was like a miscreant schoolboy whose bluff had been called.[25]

It is, according to the great fighter, "one of the most important things to get over in a fight: the short-ender should always try and convince his opponent that he himself hasn't lost heart and feels sure he will be the victor." About two weeks before meeting the Australian, James worked to get Jackson's goat, as he would put it, letting fall a disparaging word whenever a scribe came within range. He knew that Peter would read the words and would be unsettled by them. Before long, he had confirmation of success when W.W. Naughton, celebrated sporting editor of the *San Francisco Chronicle*, came to his camp. Relaying a terse message from the Jackson side, Naughton said that the "$3,000 to the loser" provision no longer held, and that the man who was defeated would receive only $1,500 of the ten-thousand-dollar purse total.

Going the veteran one further, Corbett replied that he would do it "winner take all" if Jackson agreed! Before the fight, he would get into Jackson's head again, refusing Peter's courtesy on a point of the rules (hitting in the clinches), saying that it could go how Jackson wanted. (When the men entered the ring, he claimed later, he also tricked Peter into ducking under the ropes first, violating a Jackson ritual and adding to his pique.)

What followed, in any case, was an epic: 61 rounds of *give and take* before it was declared a standoff due to each man's exhaustion. At the end, the two best men in the world had provided an enduring testament to skill and courage. But only one man was going to improve from that point, and that was Corbett.

Sullivan, returning from a tour of Australia, announced that same year that any more defenses of his title would be fought with gloves and by Queensberry rules. He signed the following year to fight Corbett in New Orleans on September 7 according to the new format.

The champion, it was still believed, was immune to defeat. But on that night the death knell was sounded on an era when Corbett laid on Sullivan a boxing lesson. "Although people generally don't know it," Donovan would say, "the clash of minds has as much to do with winning fights as the crash of fists."[26] Here was a prime case, as Corbett entered the ring in a jovial spirit, tossing a gibe in Sullivan's direction as if the champion did not belong in the ring with him. Soon the point was proven.

At the opening bell Sullivan slapped his left hand several times on his thigh, then chopped with the left and let go a haymaker that missed.

Corbett, wary in the opening minutes, was drawing blood from John L.'s nose with his jab by the end of the third round. In the fifth, his right hand shattered that nose. By the end of eight, the champion was effectively done, as Corbett's jab continued to spear his face and gut, and an occasional right to the body sapped him more.

Fans were stunned. As the evening rain subsided, wrote biographer Donald Chidsey, an overhead canvas sheet was rolled back, and "in a square of blue-black sky the stars themselves hung appalled at what they saw."[27]

So the action continued until the 20th round, when only the bell ended the drubbing. A right hand dropped John in the 21st, and he went to his knees. With no surrender in him, he struggled up and took another right that finished it.

* * *

At this point, a new game was established, with new heroes on the rise. Among them was middleweight terror Bob Fitzsimmons, who had fought his first four professional bouts by the old rules. In Fitzsimmons's mind, it was a change for the better — the new method was safer, more dignified, more intelligent, than the old way of letting go with abandon. "If you want to make a success in life," he would say, "always hit when you see the chance; do not draw your arm back; hit from where your hand is, and you have got him."[28] Like many of his day, he believed also that boxing was a healthy sport, one that instilled in a young learner endurance and a sense of fair play.

How, they once asked him, would the bare-knucklers have fared against the new crop? The rough and tumble boys, he answered, were game. But they were strangers to "the leg qualities" (essentially what we today call footwork) of current professionals. Their idea of strategy was to abuse a man repeatedly around the eyes, inflicting swelling to the point of blindness.

Then again, said Fitz, gloved fighters did not know how lucky they were compared with those who mixed it with "the raw 'uns." Often, in the old-style scuffle, a fighter might suffer a broken arm. "You 'ad to look out for yourself more than with the mitts," he recalled of the London style, "because there was a 'undred little ways of trickin' a man with fouls that the referee wouldn't be likely to get on to."[29]

And, he added, "there was them spikes in the shoes!" The old wars were waged on turf, where men could wear metal studs that helped their footing. These projections were three on each shoe, two at the wide portion of the foot and one at the heel. They could be up to $\frac{3}{8}$ of an inch in length, and as little as $\frac{1}{8}$ of an inch in diameter at the end. A seasoned fighter could employ his footwear to great effect, in the heat of action, in ways that looked accidental. Even if his tactic were declared a foul, it took repeated warnings before he was apt to be disqualified.

The new system had more order. A London-style fighter could drop from a grazing blow to get the 30-second respite, and while this fake was a foul, the rule was hard to enforce. The older men were also short on science. Though great in their day, they were no match for fighters of the new era. "To tell the truth," said Fitzsimmons, "I do not think they realized that the jaw was the vital point." Pitted against one of them, he maintained, "I would simply go at him with the science and hitting powers I possess, and put him out, perhaps in the first round."

II

The Saginaw Kid:
George "Kid" Lavigne

Mista Tom, this boy ain't human. I cain't hurt him.
Welterweight Joe Walcott, to his manager,
between rounds against George "Kid" Lavigne

"What a pity," notes an authority who knew him well, on the event of his passing, "that we have no Kid Lavignes in the ring to-day!"[1] He had a right hand like a mallet, remarks another, "and he never gave up — never."[2] Old-timers of stature, writes columnist Louis E. Chiesi, "insist that this fierce little man from along the Saginaw, a product of the tag end of the lumber days, qualifies yet as one of ... two or three of fistiana's best."[3]

The son of French Canadian emigrants who moved to the Saginaw Valley of Michigan, George Henry Lavigne was a 5' 3½" fighting machine who scaled, at his peak, between 125 and 135 pounds. Fair, mild of manner, with smooth features to go with his diminutive stature, he had a schoolboy look that carried well into his career. Early on, he was known as "Kid." Indifferent to danger in the ring, he fought and defeated men much bigger; in gameness, grit, and sheer vitality he had scarcely an equal. Before he was done, he would climb into the ring with Joe Walcott, Jack McAuliffe, Young Griffo, Johnny Griffin, Dick Burge, George McFadden, and Tommy Ryan.

Nearly always conceding height and reach, the Kid was a puncher who broke down his opposition by going first to the body and then to the head. In the pioneering manner of his day, he employed a short, jolting right hand in place of the haphazard swing. Often he confounded an opponent by staring at the man's feet, rather than his face, when setting up his attack. He was, as the accounts testify, a rusher, forcing the action, yet awkwardly clever, with a formidable jab, even if he was not a stylist. For several years, and despite his hatred of training camp regimen, Lavigne was a vanquisher of foes. It was said that men who fought him were never the same again.

Rise to Prominence

Hailing from Quebec, the Lavigne family settled in the hamlet mill town of Melbourne, Michigan, and established a boarding house that became the den of area lumbermen. It was not a place that indulged weakness. George, born in Bay City on December 6, 1869, was preceded in boxing by his older brother Billy.

Down on Tuscola Street in Saginaw was a barbershop run by C.A.C. Smith, an accomplished black heavyweight who tutored interested students during off-hours in a back room. When Billy found the place, he was hooked. One day he brought home a pair of boxing gloves, and George got his first lesson. Soon the younger Lavigne was giving Billy what-for when they mixed it up, and by September of 1886, in a contest billed for legal reasons as an exhibition, 16-year-old George took on Smith's prize student Morris McNally. George stopped Morris with the first good shot that he landed. When he flattened another neighborhood prospect named Bill White, more offers followed.

By early December, George had racked up eight wins in the Saginaw vicinity. In an era that abounded in good little men and let them go at it, in the parlance of the day, till the cows came home, he became known for a crushing right hand and a body attack that knew no finish. During these years, he worked many hours also as a cooper on the riverfront, an exercise that inured him to the demands of a long day's work. The lesson soon had application, for in 1889, when George was not yet 20, he went 77 rounds to a draw with the formidable George Siddons at a Saginaw hotel.[4] Less than two months later, at the Kid's insistence, they met again and went 55 more, in a bout at Grand Rapids, billed as being for the featherweight championship of Michigan. While this one was more hotly waged, it ended likewise even.

At this point not many men in the area wanted a go with Lavigne, and he fought seldom in the next couple of years. Finally he talked Billy into going west, where California might offer room for advancement. While there weren't many bouts handy for the taking, George did attract notice in 1891, in San Francisco, when he beat highly regarded Joe Soto in 30 rounds. In Brooklyn, on September 17, 1894, he took on his toughest opponent to date, seasoned ringman Jerry Marshall, a black fighter who had gained the featherweight championship of Australia.

Taller and rangier than the Kid, Marshall figured to be a handful. Yet in the first round, George held his own. Action continued, nip and tuck, through the second, when Lavigne struck. Nailing Marshall with both hands, he drew the crowd's roar. By round seven, it was obvious that nothing Marshall threw could faze him. When the announcer voiced referee Dominick McCaffrey's decision in George's favor at the end of ten, there was no argument.

Another test came at Coney Island on October 29 against Johnny Griffin, a 5'5" redhead touted as one of the toughest young comers in the division. The bout was held at the Seaside A.C. (a common designation at the time, signifying Athletic Club), where each man, a scribe noted, had already put on shows "pretty enough to tempt an epicure."[5] It was a spirited clash, and soon the pace and the punishment started to tell on Johnny. After seven, his eyes were nearly closed and only his savvy kept him in it. In the 14th round a blockbuster right hand sent him down. At the start of the next frame, police stopped it.

Thus did 1894 see Lavigne make a climb. On December 14, he would score another resounding win, though one that would end in tragedy, when he met Andy Bowen in Bowen's native New Orleans. A hard-hitting mulatto (a term then common, signifying half–African ancestry) with endless staying power, Bowen had engaged in bouts of amazing length in the past year. On April 6, 1893, he had gone 110 rounds to a draw with Texas Jack Burke, the fight lasting seven hours and nineteen minutes. Late in the following month, he had beaten Jack Everhardt in 85.

The two men were close in weight, the Kid entering the ring at 135 and Bowen two pounds lighter. But strength was another story. After some modest skirmishes in the first couple of rounds, Lavigne entered the fray in earnest. In the fourth, his right hand found its mark. Bowen staggered.

By the seventh, it was evident that Andy was outmatched. From the tenth round on, it was all Lavigne, and in the fifteenth, only the bell saved Bowen. In the eighteenth, now a trudging persona of defeat, the Louisiana fighter went to ring center one last time. When Lavigne landed a left to the heart and a right hand on the jaw, Andy fell like the proverbial oak, his head cracking the floor with a terrible sound. Carried to his dressing room, he lay unconscious for nearly half an hour. He was later taken to his home where he died the next day.

Back then, certain boundaries were less clear than at present. While there was not the proliferation of "champions" that one sees today, it was often a matter of debate who was the real division champion. Weight class limits were also uncertain, and were sometimes specified on a per-fight basis. And anything could happen. There is no way that the Bowen contest, for example, would have lasted to its end today, even were contests set for the long distance. Yet other fights, depending on where they were staged and the rules in force, were cut short when they became too violent! And criminal liability was an issue when a fight turned tragic. After Bowen's passing, a charge of manslaughter was filed against George, though within two weeks it was dropped.

In April of 1895, Lavigne boxed eight rounds in a return with Marshall, a fight that was called even, by earlier agreement, when each man finished on his feet. On May 30, he fought highly regarded Jack Everhardt at the Seaside A.C. at Coney Island. Attendance was scant, owing not to low expectation, but to a fear that since each man was a gamester with a punch, the fight might get too "sluggy" and be stopped.

In fact, two of the evening's prelim bouts did end this way, but not the feature. In a battle deemed "worth twice the price of admission,"[6] George and Jack went 20 frames, to the satisfaction of all. The opening round saw each man connect with heavy fare, Lavigne getting in a right hand to the chest and Jack landing a left-hand wallop on the nose that had George feeling the appendage as if to be sure it was there. More hard exchanges followed, and at the end of round six, the Kid got across a blow that sounded through the hall. On it went to the close of 18, when Everhardt staggered to his corner. In the twentieth, when Jack summoned the ginger to plant his left hand a couple of times on the Kid's face, the crowd cheered his gameness. The verdict went to Lavigne.

Now there was growing recognition of George as world lightweight champion. On August 26, 1895, he faced young New Jersey up-and-comer Jimmy Handler. Jimmy was a protégé of Bob Fitzsimmons, who had reigned as middleweight champion of the world since 1891 and who was now casting a glance upward to the heavyweights.[7] While each man came to Maspeth, Long Island, in splendid shape, it was a disappointment to those who fancied Jimmy as a coming titlist. In the early going, Lavigne's right hand landed on the heart with telling impact. In the fourth, the Kid drew blood from Handler's mouth, and in the fifth, his right hand provided the finish.

The Australian Wizard

"There he is, Hype. The only thing that could hit him squarely was death itself."

The man making the statement in this New York funeral parlor was James J. Corbett, former heavyweight champion of the world, who had shocked the sporting world by knocking out John L. Sullivan some 35 years before. He spoke these words to renowned fight columnist Hype Igoe of the *New York Journal*.[8] On this date, December 9, 1927, they were standing over the casket of Albert Griffiths, known in his fighting days as Young Griffo, a little pug out of Australia whose talent and eccentricity had made him a legend.

Hype agreed. "I thought George Dixon was great," added the writer, "until I watched Griffo pick Tommy White apart in Chicago."[9]

Had Griffo a knack for something more delicate, such as the piano, he would have been deemed a *savant*. Neither bright nor educated, he had one talent: In the ring, it seemed, he could sense what an opponent was thinking, and could react in the bat of an eye.

Corbett, who saw Griffo perhaps eight times in action, judged that this aptitude was inborn, for no amount of instruction could have produced it. The former champion recalled when Griffo had shown up at his camp, years earlier, weighing perhaps 120 pounds and standing 5' 4". Corbett wanted Griffo to get in the ring and work with Steve O'Donnell, a hefty tyro who served as Jim's sparring partner. Griffo insisted that Corbett would owe him three drinks, beer and ale mixed, in return for the task. Corbett agreed and a show was on. Soon O'Donnell was looking foolish, and his nose was bloodied when the session was done.

Bob Fitzsimmons's nemesis Jim Hall, center, around 1895 at the Seaside A.C., together with assorted fight followers and what might politely be termed local business folk of every stripe. The shorter man in the dark hat to his right is Young Griffo.

As Corbett said now, "I ... prided myself on being able to figure out ways of checkmating any fighter after watching him box, but in Griffo's case I was lost." He and Igoe agreed that if this odd little duck had been a puncher of any note, he would have ruled four or five weight divisions. Former lightweight champion Jack McAuliffe, also present on this occasion, had boxed Griffo some 33 years earlier. He admitted that in his day he never ceased to be glad Griffo was lacking in that department.

He was, by historian and publisher Stan Weston's account, short-armed and knock-kneed, with a constant smile and wide black eyes that "gave him the appearance of a good-natured goblin." His staying power, seemingly inborn and without limit, gave him an added resource, and may have accounted for his success on nights when he entered the ring with little training.

Such nights were frequent: Griffo remained a mental child for all of his 58 years. He could not save a dollar once earning it, and much of his money went either to whiskey or to panhandlers. "His gymnasium," according to Stan, "was the nearest bar." On occasion he would enter a ring under the influence, cop swigs between rounds, and head for a tavern when the bout was done.

Probably Griffo did not even fathom the arithmetic that a dollar involved. "'*U-ey*," he would say to manager Hughey Behan, at a bout's close, "gimme some *pelf* so's I kin toike the lads out for a good time." He would then hold out an old Derby, which Behan would fill with small bills, and head to a neighborhood establishment where he would dump the contents on the mahogany, telling the barkeep, in that brogue thick as Queensland cheddar, to keep drinks coming all around until the "'atful of pelf" was gone. He was not above mischief of a juvenile kind, even when he had established a reputation as a fighter. His idea of a clever businessman was a good pickpocket.

One time, alleges Weston, he landed in an Indianapolis jail for drunk and disorderly conduct, and received, on the judge's insistence, a psychological examination. The results gave indication of "an unbalanced and possibly dangerous ape." Joe Humphries, who came to Griffo's rescue on this occasion, found him in good spirits. On greeting Joe through the cell bars, claimed Humphries, Griffo bet him "a fiver" that he could catch a fly in his thumb and finger and furthermore release it unharmed. Joe swore that he took the bet, and lost.

Born in the waterfront section of Sydney on April 15, 1869, Griffo— Albert Griffiths—was the son of a hard-drinking coal heaver and spent his youth in poverty. As a child peddling papers, he found his share of scrapes in the neighborhood, and soon learned that he could hold his own with bigger boys, dodging blows in ways that had them confounded. In time, he came to the attention of Larry Foley, Australia's premier boxing coach, who saw in him a prodigy without rival.

Larry got Albert off the streets and soon he had him in the ring with experienced professionals. Griffiths had his first pro fights around Sydney and Melbourne in 1886. It was a rough business in that neighborhood — hitters met in gin mills and in barns; often they were rudely paired as to size and weight. Cops were on the prowl to break up bouts if they heard about them. In such an environment Griffo learned his trade, honing his skills on men like the renowned "Belfast Spider" Ike Weir, Young Pluto (a black fighter from South Africa, less known, but fearsomely tough, whom Griffo fought countless times), and Billy Murphy, each of whom ranked with the best in the world.

He was not, in the estimate of those who saw him, a classic boxer in the mold of Corbett, but he could alter his style to suit the occasion. Against a slow fighter, Griffo was in low gear; against a faster one he could step it up to no end. (Weir, who was renowned for his own ringmanship, said that the air seemed to be filled with flying gloves when Griffo went into high gear.)

Defensively, too, he was a marvel. He sometimes ducked punches, a tactic still handy against men who threw the roundhouse, but for the most part he slipped them, leaning back or to the side, making even seasoned fighters look ridiculous. In a time when rules were less tightly enforced, he might lay an open hand on an opponent's face and punch him with the other. Oblivious to social status, or to the company he kept, Griffo had a legitimate claim to a world title when he beat Murphy in 1890, but never pressed it, content to remain champion of Australia.

On July 1 of that year, the *Australian Bulletin* remarked that he would do well to emigrate, and to get free of the "push" (gang) that surrounded him. Eventually he was persuaded to try his luck in America. But he did not leave behind his ways. In the ring or out, Griffo was like nothing before or since. Checking into a hotel in the States, he might enter barefoot, and insist upon having his feet shined! Often he was out to the wee hours, entertaining bar patrons with his "handkerchief trick," spreading the clean white cloth on the floor and wagering that a man could not move him off it by throwing punches.

According to the *Bulletin* account, Griffo once bid good-bye from the ship's rail to a cheering throng, overcome with emotion and wiping his eyes with a handkerchief. When the crowd later went uptown to continue the festivity, whom did it meet but Griffo again, after he had slipped away unnoticed from the boat and headed to the bar! On another occasion, when on board a boat, the fighter suddenly leaped from the deck, fully clothed, and swam ashore. Before his bout with Jack McAuliffe, his trainers resorted to locking him in his hotel room to keep him out of trouble. They found him shortly afterward in a neighborhood saloon after he had made a rope of his clothes and climbed down from the window, swiping a swimsuit from a nearby bathhouse on the way to the establishment.

Following this escapade, notes Weston, Griffo's men convinced him that he needed a shave before he got into the ring. When he sat down, they wrapped him in a hundred yards of clothesline, and proceeded to work on him with hot and cold towels in an effort to get him sober. He ended up making McAuliffe look bad, albeit losing the decision. (Afterward, alleged Ed Williams, Griffo's trainer, the referee told them that he had two registering devices in his hands to keep track of the punches, and admitted that he "must have got the gadgets mixed" in order to award McAuliffe the verdict.)

In the summer of 1893, Griffo arrived on the west coast of the United States. Soon he made for the opposite shore, where more fights were available. Matched against Johnny Griffin, he put on a show to remember.

Johnny, at the time, had Griffo rival Billy Murphy as a chief second. After being trounced in their Australian meeting, Billy bore Griffo no good will. At the opening bell, recalled Nat Fleischer, "Griffo advanced flat-footed, erect ... the left advanced on a line about three inches above the waist. He seemed to glide toward Griffin, and then like a flash he shot out his left with the precision of a sharp-shooter and it struck his target — Griffin's nose."[10]

According to Nat, word at the time had it that Griffo actually bet James $1,000 that he could stand on a kerchief and keep a cigar butt in his mouth without Corbett knocking it out in three minutes. (While Corbett, said Nat, never admitted to taking the wager, neither did he deny it, and thus the outcome, if any, was never known.) Either way, the remainder of the bout saw Griffo duck, slip, or parry practically everything that Johnny threw, and by the third round most of his effort was going into a trade of taunts with Murphy. Soon Griffo was actually telling Murphy his next move against Griffin, and then executing it! After eight frames, though it went into the books as a draw, the crowd had no doubt as to the superior fighter.

* * *

Griffo, as it turned out, would linger on the stage well after the booze had robbed him of his ability. As late as July of 1900, he made even the great Joe Gans look bad for several rounds before he folded. According to "Dumb" Dan Morgan, it was one of the few times that Griffo actually applied himself in training, and through five rounds, he had it all his way. But years of self-abuse by now had taken their toll on his constitution. He began to fall apart, and in the eighth round, on the end of a shellacking, he dashed back to his corner, hands in the air, pleading "Don't let 'im hit me."[11]

But for now, he still had it. On October 12, 1895, in a much-anticipated matchup of boxer and puncher, he met Lavigne at the Empire A.C. in Maspeth, Long Island. While the two had gone eight rounds to a draw the year before, this bout, scheduled for 20, figured to be more decisive. The mighty John L. Sullivan, on hand to witness it, was met with a powerful ovation when he took the stage before the main event. At the opening bell, there were 3,000 on hand, with few seats vacant.

Right off, Griffo planted both hands merrily on the face of his young opponent, scoring several times before taking a hard right on the ear. Lavigne landed that same punch in the second, but as rounds passed, he was finding little for a target. It was strength *vs.* savvy — time and again, the Australian landed his left on the Kid's face while getting back, every so often, a heavy shot to the body.

By the end of eight, Lavigne had bloodied Griffo's nose. In the 13th, now running red from the mouth, the Australian kept that pesky left hand working, and the Kid was showing wear of his own. In the 19th, Griffo rallied, and got across a few backhands for good measure. In the final frame, Lavigne was the stronger of the two, and general feeling was that he had prevailed, though the referee ruled it even.

A good many men would have raised a fuss, but George had no kick. "I never saw so many gloves in my life," he exclaimed, calling his little foe "too marvelous for words." The Kid added, "There were times when he just stood dead still in his tracks and I thought I had him and let one go that had 'finish' written on it. He would jump away or block. His timing was so perfect that he would just edge over an inch or two and the blow would miss. What can you do with a fellow like that?"[12]

The Battle of Maspeth

What George had in modesty, he had also in courage. Few contenders at this time were willing to take on the most feared man in the welterweight division, one avoided even by good middles. A squat, long-armed terror, little more than five feet in height, Barbados Joe Walcott had beaten men of every size, and his hitting power was fabled.

When Lavigne said that he was up to it, Walcott's manager Tom O'Rourke seized the chance. The matchup, declared O'Rourke to the *Police*

Gazette editor, was probably "too good to be true."[13] But if Lavigne was serious about trading with his man, said Tom, it was time to put up. Since George was not averse to fighting black opponents, any failure to follow through would owe to personal fear of Joe himself.

This statement prompted a hot reply from Sam Fitzpatrick to the same editor, and shortly the meeting was set. On December 2, 1895, Lavigne and Walcott met at Empire A.C. in Maspeth, Long Island. It was agreed that the decision would go to Lavigne if the bout went its scheduled fifteen rounds. It was also agreed that the weight limit would be 133, several pounds below Walcott's preference, but a condition accepted by O'Rourke.

Few fans today know of this fight. But as recently as forty years ago, it was the gold standard by which fights were measured. Those who wrote of it counted it as a testament to courage on the part of each man, and as the most savage fight they had ever seen.

Walcott, a 10–6 favorite, entered the ring a picture of confidence. The general feeling was that fighting this man, much less trading with him freely, was tantamount to craziness. Many thus figured Lavigne to play it safe, and rest content with going the distance. Yet an opponent in front of the Kid, O'Rourke would later say, "was like a red flag in front of a bull."[14] As a result, those present got something for the price of admission that they would never forget. From the opening bell, Joe and the Kid were warriors bound to the death. When either man landed, he did damage, and the other came back hell-bent.

Lavigne's intentions were clear in the opening seconds, when he planted a bold left on Walcott's chest and another on his face, getting a right hand to the heart in return. He scored with another left and then tried to take Walcott's head off with a right that missed. Before the round was over, he scored with a hard right to the ear.

George's bravery caused astonishment. Several bettors who had taken the long odds now rushed to his corner before the bell for the next round, yelling support. The second frame was still more spirited, with George nearly dropping Walcott to his knees with a right hand.

Already each man showed wear, and Walcott had taken a warning for his in-close "rabbit punch" behind the head. In the third, Lavigne got home a right to the ear and took a savage right to the heart. When they clinched, Walcott got in another stray right that brought a hiss from the seats. In the trade that followed, it was Lavigne getting the better, and when he landed a big right hand, the crowd began to erupt. In the fourth, neither man heard the bell, and referee and cornermen had to pry them apart.

In the fifth, even as Lavigne's left eye was becoming a mess, he continued to hold his own. In the sixth, an uppercut to the Kid's nose made the blood run. Over the next round, that uppercut continued to do grisly work before Lavigne, summoning strength from some deep source, got home a telling left to the face.

Each man was now splattered with red, most of it from the Kid. Believing that he could end it, Walcott came out strong in the eighth, but no sooner did he press his advantage than a right hand on the heart had him in trouble. Then, when Walcott's own right hand scored to George's ear, the organ swelled to awful proportion.

By every indication, Lavigne was near defeat. Never, O'Rourke would say, did he see a man take the punishment that the Kid took in these middle rounds. It was *soul-stirring*, a blood spectacle that came once in a century. Indeed, today "the modern sporting world would not stand for it." In the ninth, each man was dazed. In the tenth, Walcott again was up, yet at the close of the session, the Kid went to his corner with a look of grim resolution.

Lavigne's left ear, a constant target of Walcott's in-close abuse, had now swelled to obscenity. Walcott went after the bloated target in the eleventh, and suddenly the organ burst, showering blood down Lavigne's face and neck. In response the Kid buried a left in Walcott's midsection, making the Caribbean fighter groan with what might have been pain mixed with disbelief. Now, each time that Walcott would land, the Kid would heave back one of his own, and as he began to faze the Barbados terror in the twelfth, the crowd went into delirium.

In 1955, octogenarian Joe Woodman, images of the fight still etched in his mind, described the comeback of Lavigne after he had been practically cut to ribbons. The Kid, he said, "fought on, more viciously now than ever.... He landed ... punches with accuracy to Walcott's midsection and every blow made the Barbados Demon wince. [Joe] was ready to quit and would have done so had not [Tom] O'Rourke, a tough hombre of the old managerial school, threatened to horse whip him if he dared."[15]

"No man," Woodman wrote, "ever displayed greater fortitude" than did the Kid on this occasion. (By his recollection, O'Rourke also said to his man at one point, "If you quit, you'll never live to tell the story.") In the 13th, Lavigne came on with a vengeance. In the 14th, when Joe mustered one more assault, the Kid unloaded a right that sent him to the floor. He followed with a rally that had Walcott dead on his feet. In the final round, it was the Kid staggering Walcott again and again. (By some accounts, the round was actually shortened to save Joe from a knockout.)

* * *

So ended an epic bequeathed to Valhalla. Lavigne, though he would bear scars of that encounter evermore, kept a cheerful disposition afterward. In the first round, he admitted, a right hand on the ear had made him wonder if he would survive. He said also, with pure candor, that the weight limit had factored into his achievement.

On balance, history favors the view that weight indeed was much of Joe's problem. Interestingly, O'Rourke himself, years afterward, made a contrary admission. In truth, he maintained, the weight issue was a ruse, and Walcott was better below 135 than he was above it. He had wagered, shortly before the bout, that Joe would come in below Lavigne on the prefight scale. The evening before the fight, he claimed, a private weigh-in showed the Kid at 130½, and Walcott at 129¾![16]

George himself would recall, years later, that there was a moment, in the heat of the action, when Walcott actually aided him by his roughhouse tactics. It came at the point when his ear had suffered its worst swelling. Those middle rounds, he said, were "a whole comic opera chorus in my head going full blast, singing songs that sounded like the stuff you hear in the dentist's chair before you come up for air." But at a key moment, in close, Walcott had pulled the heel of his glove over the injured spot and the wound burst wide open. When the blood came down, it was enough to make even members of that hardened crowd woozy. But at that same moment, the pain and the noise stopped. Thus the Kid, all but beaten, had been convinced to stay in the fight!

McAuliffe, Burge, and Everhardt

It is likely that neither Lavigne nor Walcott was ever quite the same after, and if neither had fought again, each would still merit a place in history. But each did fight many more times, and Walcott would win belated honors as welterweight champion of the world some six years later.[17] As for Lavigne, there could be no doubt now as to his place among the lightweights. On March 11, 1896, he met former champion Jack McAuliffe, the heralded Napoleon of the Ring, who would eventually retire without a loss in his professional career. Jack was lucky on this night, when a police inspector entered the ring at the end of the sixth round in order to save him from defeat. After three rounds fought more or less evenly, Lavigne's right hand began to take a toll. By the sixth, the former lightweight king was on that fistic avenue called Queer Street. (The bout went into the record as either an exhibition or a "no decision.")

Again, championships then were less well demarcated — while McAuliffe once had been hailed as lightweight ruler, his best days were gone. A few days after the bout, a benefit was held for him at Madison Square Garden. When Lavigne was coaxed into the spotlight for an introduction, master of ceremonies John L. Sullivan bestowed on him virtual knighthood: "Friends and gents," intoned the great man in his rich baritone growl, "This is Kid Lavigne, the lightweight champion of America, now that McAuliffe's retired. Nobody's to say the opposite — and that goes!"[18]

Folks were not in the habit of arguing with John L., but regardless, George had established himself. On June 1 he fought Dick Burge, an English fighter who outweighed him by several pounds, and who was being hailed as a phenomenon after holding his own with bigger men in his home country. They met at the National Sporting Club in London in what British writers (had they heard about the Maspeth event?) figured to be the contest of the Kid's life.

It was indeed a contest. Through four rounds each man had at the other as the crowd raised a deafening yell. In the sixth, Lavigne got home telling shots downstairs while Burge, harboring in his soul no quit, continued to work his jab. But increasingly it was Lavigne. In the 16th, he put Burge on the canvas. The English fighter got up groggy, and went down again. In the 17th, body punches by the Kid set up a right hand that ended it.

This win gave Lavigne an international reputation. In its aftermath, he got an unexpected bonus. Prior to the opening bell, the local bettors, when sizing up the little Yank, had made Burge 3–1. In the ring, looking out upon this small, select crowd in its high-fashion dress, the Kid heard an onlooker yell "*One hundred* on Burge," to which he called back that he'd take some of that action himself!

"You're on, old chap," came the reply, "I like your pluck."

As Lavigne was departing, the vocal sportsman stopped him and shook his hand in heartfelt congratulations. He then extended payment that the Kid had "jolly well won." Counting the take, Lavigne said that the man had made a mistake, as the gold was worth closer to $500. "I made a terrible mistake in betting on Burge," said the cheerful loser, and it was only afterward that Lavigne realized that the "hundred" had meant *pounds sterling*, and not dollars.

While the Kid was still in England, a challenge was issued by the camp of Jack Everhardt for a rematch. It was accepted, and on October 27, they met at the Bohemian Sporting Club in New York, in a bout scheduled for 25 rounds. By the time it was over, scribes were saying that this little banger from Saginaw was the best man ever to compete at the lightweight level.

It was not a scientific affair — not, at least, from Lavigne's side, as he fought with mad aggression from the start. The first good blow of the fight was his patented right hand to the body, after which he scored with his left to the same area, and got back a sizzling right from Everhardt.

After a dead silence that lasted the round, there came fierce applause at the bell. Soon the Kid's hitting power, as always, was shaping the story. By 13, it was a question of how long Jack would last. Amazingly, he rallied, but in the 22nd the Kid had him reeling. In the next round a right hand had him out on his feet at the bell. In the 24th, when Jack staggered back half-conscious from another right, referee John Kelly caught hold of him and helped him to his corner, declaring the Kid the victor.

While the fight game, in that day, was a tough affair, it did not frown upon a show of feeling. It is common to find accounts from this era in which one contestant, giving his all and coming up short, weeps openly at the close. This is one instance. Tears flowed from Everhardt when he spoke with a *Police Gazette* interviewer in his dressing room, as he insisted, while casting no aspersion on the referee or on Lavigne, that he could have continued.

Often, too, fighters — no matter how ferocious in the heat of battle — were exemplars of tact. No matter how fierce a battle, it was never the Kid's way to downgrade an opponent, or to employ language outside civil bounds. Prodded by one scribe, he could only manage, "By gosh, he's the toughest game I ever went against in my life." He complimented Jack on his punching, and admitted that he himself had been stunned in the exchanges several times. The men shook hands afterward, the heartbroken runner-up extending congratulations while the Kid admitted that he was lucky to prevail.

Champagne was then served, and Everhardt lifted his glass, waiting for the Kid to do the same. After one effort, his hand discolored and smashed to the point of disuse, Lavigne set his glass down.

"I can't drink it, Sam," he said through bruised and still bleeding lips. "Feed it to me." Fitzpatrick responded by getting a tablespoon and obliging him.

* * *

On January 11, 1897, Lavigne went against Owen Ziegler in a six-round no-decision bout at the Quaker City Club in Philadelphia. At the end of six, Ziegler was glad to see it over, but he had done better than expected. While scribes had it unofficially in the champion's favor, it was a surprising show by a fighter who had figured to fold early.

Or was the Kid on the downslide? By now, it was apparent to those around him that he was losing his hunger. One account from this period ended with the ominous remark that he might soon "go the John L. Sullivan route," a reference to John L.'s prodigious affair with the bottle.[19]

There was no doubt as to what the champion had accomplished over his career — he was now approaching the status of a legend. Were he built on grander scale, remarked one source, "he would ... show the big fellows a thing or two never demonstrated by [newly crowned heavyweight champion Bob] Fitzsimmons."[20] This commentary notes with admiration Lavigne's ability to set up the kill with his attack to the body, adding that when a fighter "is whipped by Lavigne, he is whipped in all the term implies."

But the Kid's pace outside the ring was telling. On February 8, he went 25 rounds with contender Kid McPartland at the Broadway A.C. in New York. It was a rough contest, with the challenger landing often with left leads and getting back Lavigne's right hand underneath. After 20, the champion's rushes had taken most of his own energy, and the pace slowed. Late in the fight, Lavigne tried to end it but had to settle for a decision.

On March 8, he went six rounds with Charley McKeever at the Quaker City A.C. in Philadelphia. It was a bout in which McKeever, the taller and heavier man, relied on his reach, scoring cautious pokes to head and face. Lavigne could not apply the finisher, and at the end there was little dispute when it was ruled a draw.

After McKeever, George signed to fight 25 rounds with Eddie Connolly at the New York Broadway A.C. late in April. It was a spirited fight in which the Kid showed that for now, at least, he still had what it took. The New Brunswick fighter gave a good accounting for six rounds, but at the end of ten, he tottered to his corner. In the eleventh, Lavigne dropped him several times. Some last-ditch wrestling got Connolly through the round, but he had trouble finding his own corner. A yell went up from the audience to end the bout, and when the bell opened round twelve, Connolly's seconds jumped in front of him, tossing the sponge. (Dead game, this challenger, too, cried without shame, saying that he would have gone on, had it been his choice.)

The champion met with a surprise when he climbed back into the ring for a non-title return with Ziegler on May 17 at the Winter Circus Building in Philadelphia. It was a good show, each man looking ready for more at the close. But this time, while the bout was again a no-decision, some thought that Ziegler had gotten the better of it.

By now, the Kid was beset with bigger problems. He and Fitzpatrick were quarreling often. The relationship suffered added strain in the following month when Lavigne failed to show for a bout with Young Griffo at the Quaker

City club in Philadelphia. In the Kid's absence, Sam announced on the spot that his man had not been ready for the fight, a claim that George would hotly deny. (Griffo, said Lavigne, had quit in a show in Brooklyn shortly before, and so he doubted that this one would be worth the while, and told Sam of his decision beforehand.) In September, he and Fitzpatrick parted.

Walcott Again

Still, there was demand for a second go with Walcott, nearly two years after the brawl on Long Island. Now, in 1897, they signed to meet in San Francisco at Mechanic's Pavilion on October 29.

Lavigne, as noted, had no love affair with training. Trainer Biddy Bishop would say, years afterward, that keeping George off the bottle for more than a few days at a time was probably his greatest feat in all the time that they spent in the camps. But if the Kid had taken it easy in recent months, he shifted gears now. In morning hours he alternated running and horseback riding, with a rousing session of gym work in the afternoon. Shortly before the bout, a number of sportswriters descended on foot and in buggies down a dusty road to Blanken's Six Mile House, where the Kid had set up quarters.

Taken aback, on this occasion, by the turnout, Lavigne did his best to stay courteous. In response to the usual question "How do you feel?" he replied with conviction, "Like a winner." Spectators left impressed. The old energy was back, and the fighter was in high spirits. They were allowed to watch him hit the bag, in an upstairs gym, where he rained "trip-hammer blows" on the leather for ten minutes, followed by a short rest and another ten. After this, casual watchers were dismissed, and there followed a session devoted to the clinches, largely a wrestling match, between Lavigne and trainer Billy Armstrong, and a thousand revolutions of the jump-rope followed by a rubdown.

As the Kid was about to don his civs, he was asked again by several scribes about the coming battle. A punch on the mouth, it was said, might cost him something, as the Kid now had only four teeth in the upper front portion.

"Well," replied George in buoyant fashion, "if Walcott can land square on my mouth hard enough to knock my teeth out, I suppose they will have to come out. I know if he lands there as hard as he did on my ear in the seventh round of our last fight, my teeth don't stand one chance in a thousand of holding their places."[21]

But the Kid was not thinking in that direction: He pronounced himself to be in the shape of his life, and when the time came, it showed. In the first round, after some initial sparring, he caught Walcott with a left hook to the head and a telling hook to the body. Rushing the heavier man, he scored again with a left to the body and took a stiff left to the face. Then he unloaded right and left on the jaw, stunning Walcott, and the two were trading mid-ring at the bell. Joe went to his corner with blood streaming from the nose.

Throughout this fight, Walcott did bruising work with a left hand to the face, but Lavigne did better. The Kid's first big rally came in the sixth, when he landed several hard rights, three of them straight over the heart. Moments later he staggered Walcott with a right to the jaw, and he landed another on the chest as the gong sounded. In the seventh, Walcott was in distress, and soon he was holding at every chance. It appeared that Joe wanted to quit when he came limping to ring center in the tenth. When he backed to the ropes after a serious exchange, the crowd sensed a Lavigne win was in the offing.

In the twelfth, Lavigne scored with wicked shots to the body. At this point his own face was covered with blood, much of it from a cut near his hairline, probably from a clash of heads, that would need stitches later. Yet there was no doubt as to which man was up. At the end of that round, O'Rourke threw the sponge.

While it was Lavigne's fight, a number of ring observers were surprised at its one-sidedness. Some doubted that Walcott had given his best, and the cry of "fake" arose afterward. But the claim was repudiated by firsthand observers, among them Harry Corbett, brother of James. Representative of comments in the next day's *San Francisco Examiner* was one by police surgeon J.L. Zabala, who declared, "I have witnessed a great many fights, but never before have I seen a harder or faster contest than took place here tonight." No man, he maintained, would have taken the punishment Walcott took if the outcome had been prearranged. O'Rourke himself declared in a personal statement that Walcott was beaten when the fight ended (though on this occasion he did employ the weight excuse).

"It was the hardest fight I ever had," announced a jubilant winner in his dressing room,

> except the time I went against him before, but there was never a minute I did not think I would win. I felt sure I had him, even if he lasted to the limit of the twenty rounds. I wanted to get him good and sore about the body before I went for his head....
>
> I went into the ring at about 134 pounds, and I think Walcott must have weighed at least 140. I never got punishment from him that hurt me any, but

his weight in the clinches took some of my strength. The cut on top of my head did not amount to anything in itself, but ... the blood running down came into my eyes and I couldn't see.[22]

In a statement for the paper, he attributed the win to his blows to Walcott's heart region, a favorite tactic of men in that day. He expressed regret that he was unable to provide a more conclusive finish, which he believed he soon would have done.

* * *

In months that followed, there came more rumbles to the effect that Lavigne was "going the pace that kills" outside the ropes.[23] Nonetheless he signed for a 20-rounder against Jack Daly of Wilmington, Delaware, scheduled for March 17. "The fighting was fast and furious from the start," observed one eyewitness account, "but the contestants were so evenly matched that neither could gain an advantage over the other sufficient to get a decision in his favor."[24] It was indeed a hard fight, with vigorous action extending into the final round, but the Kid did enough to merit a draw verdict from referee Kid McCoy.

On September 28 of that year, Lavigne battled Frank Erne, who would score a victory over ring immortal Joe Gans about eighteen months later. Erne was not a rough-looking sort; his soft, rumpled hair and clean features would have looked more natural in a Sunday morning choir. But nowhere are appearances as deceiving as in the fight game. Lean as a young panther and just as quick, Erne was no easy mark.

Entering as a 10-to-3 favorite, the Kid found out firsthand the stuff of which Frank was made. Missing big in the first, he took one on the neck that spilled him on the floor. As the bout progressed, Erne showed himself to be a boxer of the first order, meeting his attack with poise and a punishing jab.

Going after Erne in straight-ahead style, Lavigne managed to reach the challenger a few times and had him hurt in the 16th round with a right hand to the jaw. In the late rounds the Kid pressed the action, but Erne did not fold. The verdict at the end of 20 was a draw.

According to one current source, that decision had been agreed upon beforehand, in the event that both men finished on their feet. It was also said that many in the crowd thought that Erne had fared better than the champion overall, and that the outcome might be a lesson to Lavigne that he would have to "get down to work now and prepare properly for the next battle."[25]

On March 10, 1899, in an over-the-weight fight, Lavigne went up against his personal friend, a formidable welterweight (see the chapter ahead on Joe Walcott) who went by the name of Mysterious Billy Smith. While George and Billy bore one another warm regard outside the ring, that feeling went out the door when action commenced.

Smith, known for rough tactics, landed often in the clinches, contrary to pre-fight agreement, and received many warnings. In the 13th and 14th rounds, the Kid found the range and had his man bleeding from the nose. But when a return volley made him sag, Billy Lavigne jumped into the ring, forcing the ref to stop the bout. (Hardly a sentimental type, Smith apologized afterward, offering the Kid his heartfelt condolences, and there was no animosity on either side.)

On July 3, Lavigne suffered a decisive loss to Frank Erne at the Hawthorne A.C. in Erne's hometown of Buffalo. This time Erne was yet sharper than before, and he won cheers for the fight that he waged. Again his jab was a factor, and in the late going, only the Kid's iron will kept him in the fight. After 20, it was Erne's victory, and his championship, without a quarrel.

The two men offered mutual good wishes before leaving the ring. While he had been hampered, said the Kid, by a rib injury sustained against Walcott and aggravated in the bout with Smith, he had praise for the new titlist: "I knew after my first go with Erne that he was no slouch.... He appears to be a decent fellow personally, and I bear him no ill will whatever."[26]

In months following, Lavigne claimed that he would return to the shape that had won him the title. Unfortunately, he never maintained the effort for long, and reports soon had him slipping off the deep end where drink was concerned. Late in the summer he rejoined with Fitzpatrick, who had guided him to the top. Against the protest of brother Billy, he signed to fight rugged veteran George McFadden in a 25-round bout at the Broadway A.C., to be held October 6.

On this occasion Lavigne took the beating of his career. McFadden turned him into a chopping block in the bout's later stages, thus ending the heyday of what one writer called "the best lightweight that ever put on a glove."[27] Cautious at first, George staggered the Kid with a right hand in the fourth round and had him on the defensive most of the way after. From the 15th on, Lavigne went to the canvas repeatedly, collapsing in the 19th for good.

Afterward Billy Lavigne said that his brother had been bothered by a rib injury ever since the fight with Smith. When he lost to Erne, said Billy, George had been warned by a physician to stay out of the ring for a year. He also blamed Fitzpatrick for letting George take such a beating late in this fight. His brother's fighting days, he supposed, were over.

In January, Lavigne sailed for Paris. Word came, months later, that he was "painting the town" in lurid fashion.[28] While there, he was accused also of assaulting a woman, who asked that he be deported. Shortly after, he was back in Michigan. Late in the year, the Kid signed to fight Terry McGovern. The bout never came off, for in early December, he suffered a fall when leaving his mother's house with Billy in Saginaw. Slipping on a frozen porch, he went down nine steps to the stone walkway, remaining unconscious from the impact for hours afterward.

Later Years

Now Lavigne was falling down in every way, and to those around him it was obvious. On December 12, 1901, he showed that he still had something left when he entered the ring against Australian Tim Hegarty in Oakland. Staggered in the third, he rebounded to flatten his opponent with a right hand in the round following. But this, for all intents, was his last hurrah. In the early hours of June 13, 1902, shortly after losing to lightweight contender Jimmy Britt, Lavigne was taken from a lodging house and brought to Stockton's Detention Hospital. Having been depressed for some time, he was now said to be insane.

Yet again, in September, by some miracle of recuperative power, he was out and looking well. Soon after, he was back in Paris, where he worked on the stage and ran a boxing school catering to locals and to American residents. Naturally bright, and fluent in the language, he seemed to take on new life. He remained there until returning home to visit his ailing mother late in the summer of 1905.

The following year, he took to the gym again. In January of 1907, he went against Young Erne and got a lacing until the referee stopped it in the sixth. The year after, he applied for admission to a community poorhouse. He gained one last shred of glory in January of 1911 when he boxed three rounds with Mickie Sheridan on a charity card benefiting veteran fighter Bob Farrell.

In June of 1912, he was charged with creating a disturbance in his home and was sent to St. Joseph's retreat in Dearborn for treatment of his drinking. Two years later, he was tending bar at the Burns Hotel in Detroit. Late in 1915, he was the recipient himself of a charity show at the Amsterdam Opera House in New York.

Like many old pugs, Lavigne held up his own generation against what had come since. Young Griffo, he alleged, could whip the best of the current day at most any weight; he also lamented the vogue of "no decision" fights that let a boxer coast through a bout in mediocre shape without fear of a loss. The next couple of years would see him repeatedly in trouble for spousal abuse and other alcohol-related misbehavior. In his last year, the Kid lived in modest circumstances while working as a night watchman at the Ford Motor Company plant. On March 9, 1928, following a brief illness, he died at his home in Detroit.

* * *

So ended the life of a man counted by some as the best at his weight who ever lived. His feats against Walcott and Burge, maintained columnist Robert Edgren, made him one of a kind in lightweight annals, and entitled him to first place in the division.[29] Maybe the supreme compliment was bestowed by his old Barbados rival, who stated in his memoirs, not long before Lavigne's passing, that he had fought himself out at Maspeth, and was never the same again. (Lavigne, too, had conceded that this fight was "the beginning of the end" where his career was concerned.)

Tough, game to the nth degree, with a heart inversely proportioned to his size, and — before alcohol got to him — a gentleman: Maybe a fitting epitaph for this athlete can be gleaned from a remark attributed to George himself after his fight with Dick Burge. In days following that fight, he and Fitzpatrick were watched with interest everywhere. One night, when they were dining at a prominent London hotel, the Kid's king-sized consumption made one patron go to his table with eyes wide.

"My word," said the Cockney, patting him on the shoulder, "but you eat quite a lot for a little fellow!"

Looking up in his boyish manner, the fighter replied, "I'm not as small as I look from the outside."

III

The Fighting Blacksmith: Bob Fitzsimmons

He played for keeps.
Tracy Callis, on the ring
mentality of Bob Fitzsimmons

The fight game's first three-division champion was born in the market town of Helston, Cornwall, on May 26, 1863. It was a hard, barren place, near England's rough south coast, where grey slate buildings stood cold and somber in the heavy air. Seven years later, the youngster sailed with his family to New Zealand. He was, in the phrase of contemporary ring scribe Richard K. Fox, "bright and interesting to those who enjoyed his confidence,"[1] though never strongly inclined to the classroom. More to his liking was the free outdoors.

An Odd Specimen

"A strange moral transformation," remarks William James in a timeless work, "has within the past century swept over our Western world." No longer do we count it as a virtue to bear pain, when it comes, with equanimity.[1] James's comment, now more than 100 years old, is pertinent today. The difference that he observes, between past and present, is like the difference between his day and ours. Life, in the late 19th century, was harder than today, and human capacity for taking loss in stride accordingly greater.

If this philosopher ever chanced to lay eyes on Robert James Fitzsimmons, he would have counted him as a welcome throwback. From childhood, young Fitz evidenced a trait he would carry with him all his life. "He

43

took everything," his sister Catherine would recall, "with a smile — victory, hard knocks, and a beating."[2] This capacity, she believed, stood him later in good stead.

At first glance, Fitzsimmons did not evoke admiration. He cut an odd figure as he strode to the ring, long, unmuscled legs descending from the

hem of his robe and seemingly unfitted to his broad back, a small knob head and thin neck giving accent to his peculiarity. He had a reddish face, with large ears and a small nose, and bright blue eyes that had at times a slightly bewildered look. It was enough to draw smiles from many who saw him for the first time.

The reaction did not bother him. Throughout his career, he would take life's accidents in stride. "It is not physical strength," he would one day write, "or even the cleverness that comes to an expert boxer, that wins battles. It is moral courage."[3] His own resilience, borne seemingly of innate pluck and long years of labor, let him begin fresh, at the start of a round, even in a fight that was going against him. Enormous recuperative powers, aided by an abnormal lung capacity, served him well in a distance effort of any kind.

Freddy Bogan, a featherweight out of California, once described going for a run with Fitzsimmons and campmate Joe Choynski when Bob was on the coast training for a fight with Billy McCarthy. Often, said Bogan, Fitz would go for a long walk, rather than a run, at the start of a day, which prompted him and Joe to invite Bob on a morning run to test his mettle. "Our idea," he recalled, "was to

Bob Fitzsimmons as he looked around 1891, when he challenged Jack Dempsey for the middleweight title. Fitzsimmons had the strength of a heavyweight and all but massacred most of his competition at that lower weight. Ring historian Tracy Callis ranks Fitzsimmons, pound for pound, no. 1 on his all-time list.

run at a rapid rate to the sea, about six miles away, and then come back as fast as we could until he cried "enough."... Choynski and I ... set the pace in turns, but we were beginning to feel the effects of the rapid rate at which we were running long before we reached the beach, and no matter how many sprints we put in, there was Fitzsimmons running along-side, showing no signs of distress or even heavy breathing."[4] Bob, said Bogan, asked casual questions, as they ran, about the landscape. Soon their answers got forced and brief. On reaching the water, he wheeled and started for home, which prompted Choynski to gasp for a rest.

"You ain't had enough, have you?" asked Fitz. Joe, fumbling for words, said that they just wanted just to savor the shoreline for a moment. Anxious to get back for the evening meal, Fitzsimmons shot off, whereupon the other two decided to stay with him. By the time that they made it to camp, Joe and Bogan were exhausted. Almost too spent to have dinner, they watched Fitzsimmons scour his own plate with gusto. Later Bob asked Choynski to put on the gloves for a sparring session. Joe, some ten to twenty pounds heavier, obliged, and while Fitzsimmons did not have his friend's ring elegance, according to Bogan, "he showed up very well against him and I never saw a prettier bout in all my life."

Early Years

At 14, Bob arrived from Britain with his family in New Zealand. Soon he entertained the idea of a tour at sea, which would toughen him, he imagined, for a ring career afterward. In April of 1877, he was ready to set sail with the captain of the *Isabella Ridley*, harbored at Timaru, New Zealand, when a storm half-wrecked the ship on the town's rocky shoreline. Soon after, he settled for a job as a carriage painter, a task at which he excelled, but more to his liking was a position as "striker" at the Parson and Andrews Foundry, swinging a sledge. Later he settled into a job shoeing horses with his brother.

Shoeing got Bob acquainted with some rough animals, and to this encounter he had no aversion — "It strengthens my arms and legs," he would say, "when I'm kicked across the shop and it helps develop the sand in a man."[5] Recalling his adolescence, Fitzsimmons would say, "I was a cadaverous-looking kid.... Even my ears were thin. The exercise of boxing, coupled with my work at the forge, soon developed my chest and shoulders. Nothing I would do seemed to put weight on my legs, so I let it go at that."[6]

Crazy for boxing at a young age, he missed no chance to mix it up with friends when a moment allowed. In his mid-teens, the rough company of older men in the smith shop moved him to learn some of the game's fine points. He absorbed much in the evenings from Dan Lea, once a regional champion in England.

The sport, as it has been noted, was then in transition, moving from a style favoring brute strength to one that emphasized prudence and physical economy. Fitzsimmons, again, is a kind of amphibian in this story, fighting his first several bouts under the old London rules. He was also an innovator who sought to take the game to a higher level than did his predecessors. Hitting, he believed, was a skill that practically anyone could learn, but one that few ringmen themselves had really explored. Few of them, even if they could hit, managed to get the whole body into their effort. He also advocated making contact not with the bottom three knuckles, as most fighters do, but only (like some Asian-style *karatekas*) with the first two, seeking to concentrate the impact of a blow into a smaller area.

And hit he could, even from the start. Long after the fact, a shop worker named Jack Temple recalled how Bob once mixed it up in a freestyle wrestling match at a sporting picnic with a local tough who outweighed him by some 45 pounds. When the going got rough, the bigger man tried gouging Bob's left eye. Clenching a fist, Fitzsimmons laid waste to him with a single shot.

The Timaru smithing business, it appears, provided frequent occasion for young Fitz to put his fighting skills on display. Often teamsters, needing their animals shod, would find the forge by way of the saloon, getting "a mixed ale edge on"[7] in the process. Generally in a quarrelsome mood, they would fight on slight pretext, and "moral suasion" was not always successful in discouraging them. Thus Fitz would have at them if they insisted. Over time, this situation turned out to be good for business, since those who got a taste of Bob's fists would faithfully come back, hoping to see another of their trade meet with the same misfortune.

A dispute with shop boss Mike Casey, a bare-knuckle hellion, gave impetus to young Bob's real-life pursuit when the two men met in a fight to the finish with a purse of five pounds. Though giving away weight and experience, Bob hammered Mike senseless in about four minutes. Not long after, he entered a tournament sponsored by England's renowned Jem Mace. Called by ring folk the Fighting Gypsy, Mace was a tactician who emphasized defense and taught his pupils to hit straight from the shoulder. On whipping a local dreadnaught called the Timaru Terror, Fitzsimmons gained notoriety.

Mace left Timaru some time later and returned the following year with a prospect he was grooming for an invasion of America — a tall Maori native who went by the name of Herbert Slade and scaled 14½ stone (or roughly

200 pounds). As before, Fitzsimmons made his way through the competition, stopping five men before he came at last to the brother of the Maori fighter.[8] Then, putting to use what he had learned, he thrashed the native, much to the chagrin of Mace, who refereed. Seeing that his own favorite was done, Mace stopped it. But when he refused to declare Bob the victor, the crowd erupted. Thoroughly peeved, the novice called out the great teacher himself, whereupon Mace began to strip for action! The prospect, however, was dampened by the reaction of the crowd, which had already witnessed one injustice and would not tolerate another.

Herbert Slade later arrived in America with Mace and made more money than he ever dreamed while in New Zealand. Bob, in the meantime, turned professional and picked up what action he could, gaining some ring wisdom in evening sessions from Mace himself, before taking old Jem's advice and heading for Sydney. Once finding work as a smith, he joined the Australian Athletic Club, run by Mace's friend Larry Foley.

In 1885 he married a former Timaru girl named Louisa Johns. The couple would have three children, two of them dying in infancy. From 1883 to the end of the decade, Bob was on the circuit, beating some of Australia's best middleweights. In the process he benefitted from the tutelage of Peter Jackson, who would later fight the epic 61-round draw with Corbett.

The time came to leave Sydney. There is, however, one entry on Fitzsimmons's early record that requires note, namely his February 12, 1890, go with Jim Hall in that town.[9] Hall, handsome and strapping at 6'1" had whipped big men, and he was being touted as the best middleweight in the country. He and Fitzsimmons seem to have met in the ring more than once during this time, with Bob having the upper hand.

In fact the two men, it appears, had met as many as three times before the bout in question. While accounts vary, it seems that Fitzsimmons had the better of it each time. They first crossed paths in a sparring session when Hall was being matched, in the public eye, with Australia's heavyweight contenders. Fitz, by the estimate of those present, made him look like an amateur. Some credit Bob with a first-round knockout of Hall in a later meeting, which has the curious date of February 10, only two days before the bout in question.

By the going accounts, Bob was in better shape for these fights than Hall, who had been enjoying the fruits of his success in recent months. Yet on this night Hall landed hard shots from the get-go, discoloring the New Zealander's left eye with his right hand. In his effort to end matters early, though, he wore himself out and was hanging on toward the end of the third. Yet in the fourth round, he landed a right hand over Fitzsimmons' extended left, and Bob fell in a heap. Timekeeper Jack Gowland counted to ten, and Bob's seconds dragged him to his corner.

What exactly had happened in this fight? Over the next few years, Hall would insist that this fight was on the level, while Bob would say that it was a put-up job.[10] Neither man was willing to concede the point, and bad blood would simmer until they settled their differences in the ring a few years later.

Hall, it appeared, would now get an earlier promised shot at middleweight champion Jack Dempsey. Yet fate struck when he gashed his hand in a bar brawl amidst celebration of his win over Fitzsimmons, forcing him to stay behind when his ship sailed to the States. From the American side, there was still room for a challenge from the outback, and so Fitz received, like a gift from on high, the invitation to set sail.

On hearing, early in the year, that New Zealand compatriot Billy Murphy had won a world title, Fitzsimmons had begun to view America as his promised land. Boxing was on an upswing in the States, where adoption of the Queensberry rules had lent the sport a new dignity and John L. Sullivan had captivated an entire nation. Major city papers devoted regular columns to fight action, and saloons and pool halls throughout the land enjoyed a connection to the latest results by way of the telegraph. Added to this was a thriving economy and waves of immigrants, always hungry, infusing the game with their blood and spirit. Bob set sail with the blessing of Sydney scribes, who hailed him for his character and his talent, saying that he was the best at his weight in the world.

An Unsung Genius: The Nonpareil

Practically everyone is familiar with the name of Jack Dempsey, a veritable ring animal who electrified the sporting world in the roaring decade that followed the Great War. In fact, when this fighter began his career, he was William Harrison Dempsey, and he took the name Jack in honor of a middleweight who preceded him by three decades.

When this later Dempsey became the heavyweight champion, his fame far exceeded that of his predecessor. But in his day, the first of these Jacks was accorded comparable respect by those who saw him. Called the Nonpareil ("without an equal") in acknowledgment of his skill, he was a ring genius. "His style and method of boxing," wrote biographer and *Police Gazette* founder Richard K. Fox, "has a neatness about it which is completely new and unknown. He stops blows aimed at him by his adversaries with so much skill, and hits his antagonist with such terrific force and comparative ease, that he astonishes and terrifies his opponents...."[11]

Further, he noted, this hero was indebted to nature for a countenance "open and manly" and "a keen, sharp and penetrating eye which gives a fine animation to his good-natured face." Born on the Emerald Isle in County Kildare on December 15, 1862, young John Edward Kelly came to America with his parents as a child and was raised thereafter in Brooklyn. At the age of 14 he was apprenticed to a cooper and became expert in the rigorous craft of pounding hoops onto barrels. Fond of sports, well versed in wrestling, he became taken with boxing in his teens and soon devoted all he had to it. When later he chose prizefighting as a career, he called himself Jack Dempsey, getting the last name from his stepfather Patrick, whom his mother had married after losing her first husband not long after their arrival in the new land.

By the estimate of Jack Skelly, Dempsey's contemporary as a fighter and a close personal friend, "Jack could step into a ring, look across at his opponent, and know exactly what to do. He had uncanny insight,

"Nonpareil" Jack Dempsey, middleweight champion and a pioneer of the new boxing style. Dempsey was a talented and dead game competitor who fought some of his greatest bouts in the era of the London prize ring rules (c. 1889).

almost psychic."[12] He would emerge in the next several years as an athlete of both courage and kindness, charitable to those less fortunate and a stranger to scandal. In the beginning, his chestnut hair and clean features made him a bit unlikely in the role of a fighter. But there was no disputing his gameness or his resources. His first recorded battle was a baptism by fire, staged on April 7, 1883, in a makeshift arena on Long Island.

Jack fought a stocky Irishman named Ed McDonald, a ready mixer who punished the young fighter the first time that he closed the distance. Yet the strength of Ed was offset by Dempsey's left hand, which found its mark time and again, and by his footwork, still a novelty in that day. Round followed round, neither man willing to quit, even as a chill wind off the bay threatened to freeze every occupant in that flimsy house. For most of the way, it was Dempsey's left against McDonald's right, but in the 27th frame Ed threw his favorite shot square into Dempsey's groin. With the crowd yelling "foul," the referee signaled that Jack had won by disqualification. While it was not a spectacular end, this marathon signaled the entry of an immortal into the paying ranks.

The situation regarding champions and weight classes, as has been noted, was less clear in those days than it would be in decades ahead. The middleweight division had been created in 1867, 16 years before Dempsey began his career. By some accounts, England's Denny Harrington was the first world champion, while some time later Tom Chandler won general claim to the honors. The outstanding fighter of that size in 1878 was Mike Donovan, who would gain his figurative title of Professor by conducting sparring classes during years when the game was moving in its new direction.

When Donovan left the scene, Canadian George Fulljames emerged as the best around, but now Dempsey was on the rise, and a showdown was brewing. They met at Staten Island on July 30, 1884, in a bout waged under the London rules. In this fight, Jack, at 140, proved that he was indeed without a peer. At the start, when the two men closed on each other, Fulljames landed to Dempsey's body and got back a rousing right hand to the face. Shortly after, George went down hard from a back-heel toss that ended the first round. The pattern continued, as Fulljames sought to get in close while Jack landed smartly with each hand. At the end of 22, it was Dempsey's fight with no hard feelings between the principals.

In years to come, Jack would outclass everything in his path, well earning his tag as the man with no equal. Yet two men on the scene felt entitled to the same consideration, these being Jack Fogarty and a squat Marine named George LaBlanche. Fogarty and Dempsey agreed to meet.

These, again, were different times, and the game thrived largely on bootleg fights in makeshift arenas. The Dempsey-Fogarty bout, on February 3, 1886, provides an example of how fans and promoters could then improvise. In a writeup two days later, columnist Edward Forbes would describe how interested folk had "moved Heaven and Earth to see the championship fight."[13] Having heard weeks earlier of the contest through the grapevine, Forbes and a friend joined other "sports" in midtown Manhattan early that evening. In threes and fours they hailed horse-drawn cabs that took them to the 23rd Street ferry, which gave them passage across the Hudson River to Jersey City.

Moving in a scatter, the travelers made it hard for police to track them, and the police would be powerless when everyone had reached the New

Jersey shore. Once all were on board, jugs of booze made for a rousing good time. By now the cops, convinced that the action was to take place on Jersey soil, had actually given up the chase. But the travelers, still in flight mode, raced along the river to another ferry that would dock at New York's Courtland Street. From there they rode to Clarendon Hall, where the bout was waged. There the arrival of Fogarty backers, who had come from Philadelphia, made for some torrid betting, and a few *gratis* "prelims" besides!

The bout was a showcase of Dempsey's talent. Fogarty, tough, ruddy, and heavily muscled, had a formidable look, but he could not contend with mobility and an educated left hand. Often a slow starter, the Nonpareil took seven rounds on this occasion before he saw how to wage the war. By the 27th, Fogarty was a mess, beaten hard and sick from the blood that he had swallowed. While the Nonpareil had marks of his own, and aching, swollen hands, he could have fought on without end. After more than an hour and a half (the rounds were timed, but with only 30 seconds, rather than the full minute, allowed between), he was an uncontested victor.

Next came the Boston Marine. Thick and powerful, George LaBlanche was now the only contender on the scene who figured to extend Dempsey. Hailing from Quebec, he was a product of far northern lumber camps and the Canadian military. His stint with the U.S. Marine Corps, from which he was discharged in 1884 as "unfit for duty" after serving but six months of a five-year hitch, gave him his fighting moniker. A dubious, hard-drinking type, he would see legal trouble aplenty during and after his career, being jailed for a number of offenses that included petty theft with drunks as his victims.

Jack and George met on March 4, just a month after the battle at Clarendon Hall, for a purse of $1,500 and the *Police Gazette* diamond championship belt. Originally slated for the Bronx, the site was moved to Larchmont, in Westchester County, where it was witnessed by no more than a hundred people.

This fight took on a pattern like Dempsey's last, with Jack shooting his left hand in meticulous fashion and getting back little in turn. At the end of the second round, he remarked to Jack Skelly, "He is tougher than Fogarty, but he's not as smart — it will be a long fight." Yet by the sixth, he was hitting LaBlanche at will, knocking out three of his teeth before the frame ended. In the thirteenth, a left under the heart made George gasp. A right hand dropped him cold.

On December 13, 1887, Dempsey met outstanding Brooklyn prospect Johnny Reagan for a purse of $2,000 with the *Gazette* belt at stake. It was another case of dodging the law, and all involved (in the circumstances, this meant only 20 men) went by tug at 11 P.M. from a New York area dock to find a site. Once the passengers had disembarked, the fighters stripped to their togs, each throwing his hat in ceremonial fashion into the ring. A debate then ensued over Reagan's shoes, which sported a prominent spike under the big toe, rather than on the ball of the foot. As the exchange grew heated, Dempsey cut it short by insisting that they get down to the action.

In the opening round, fears about the shoes were confirmed. After being jarred by a left to the face, Reagan charged, raising his leg and catching Dempsey below his left knee. Blood ran from the cut, prompting Jack to say, in his mild fashion, "Be a little careful."

But it was nothing compared to what came next. Charging again, Reagan used the tactic to open a gash some five inches long. Dempsey's cornermen yelled for a disqualification, but the exchange was ended by Jack's own insistence that he was ready to fight.

Somehow the leg held up, and Dempsey, awash in pain and blood, fought on, outboxing his man and sending him down with back-heel and hip tosses round after round. As it turned out, however, the site was in a marsh, and the fighters were up to their ankles in brine by the seventh. After some wrangling, a higher ground was agreed upon. The men changed into dry gear in the tug, with Jack's men desperately tending his leg with whiskey as disinfectant.

When action recommenced, Dempsey continued to have the upper hand. Several times he threw Reagan hard, and after 20 rounds, he was in total command. As rounds passed, the cracking left lead turned Reagan's face to meat. Beaten thoroughly, streaming blood from nose and mouth, he began to seek respite by slipping to the ground.

His animus finally aroused, Jack yelled at Johnny, "Get up and fight, you cur!"[14] Coming up for the 41st round, Reagan, still game, made the pathetic protest that he was no coward. In the 43rd, a bone-crushing slam to the ground by Jack brought from him a piteous sound, and in the 45th, Reagan was dead on his feet. His corner cried out that he was done.

"Johnny," said Dempsey, paying due respect at last, "I take back what I said about your being a cur." Reagan, heartbroken, could only weep.

Thus now, in three furious years of action, Dempsey was unbeaten. Yet on August 27, 1889, he encountered the one misfortune that would precede his bout with Fitzsimmons. Trainer Jimmy Carroll, a lightweight boxer who was also employed as athletic director of the California Athletic Club, took on the task of training LaBlanche for a Dempsey rematch.

Carroll had recently developed a nasty trick, one that he had hit upon by chance one day in the gym. Essentially it was a backhanded move, analogous to a *karate* wheel-kick, whereby the striker pivoted full-circle and landed a blow that could have fist, forearm, or elbow as a point of contact.

Now Carroll wanted to see it work in a championship fight. If things went according to plan, he figured to cash in heavily on house odds that favored the champion. As bait, he offered Jack $12,400, the biggest purse that Dempsey had ever earned, for a fight under Queensberry rules.

The stage was set for a different outcome, since LaBlanche was allowed a higher weight this time, and Jack, now satisfied that he could handle George, was a little off his form. This time, too, the fighters wore bigger gloves, which took something off Jack's punches. Still, there was no comparison between the men in skill. For some 30 rounds, the bout went like its predecessor. But in the 32nd, the surprise came. LaBlanche, following Carroll's advice, swung a left hand that fell short. It looked like a clumsy move, but then George, following through, whirled and slung his right arm in centrifugal fashion, crashing a full-weight blow to Dempsey's chin. The champion went down and out.

There were cries of "foul" but Carroll claimed that the punch was used up north, where, he said, his man had learned it. The referee, who had declared LaBlanche the winner, resisted cries from Jack's corner and from the crowd, which already felt that George had committed a breach when he tossed Jack, London style, in a previous round. As it turned out, while George was recognized as winner, he did not get the title, since he had come in (so it was ruled later, at least) just over the prescribed weight limit of 154. Thus the bout, possibly as a concession to Dempsey, reverted to non-title status, and Jack was still the champion, even if this euphemistically named "pivot blow" had cost him the bout. (One sequel to the fight, according to Fox, is that when Jack's second Jack McAuliffe, the reigning lightweight champion, found out later that Carroll had been the architect of the pivot blow, he gained some measure of revenge on his own. Matched with Carroll for his own title, he administered a beating to Jimmy, finally knocking him out in the 47th round. Looking down at the stricken fighter, he announced, "That's for my pal, y'bum!")

The Middleweight Championship

In May of 1890, Fitzsimmons arrived in San Francisco. He wasted no time. On the 17th, a week after his 24-day voyage across the Pacific, he was matched with a local middleweight named Frank Allen.

In the first round, he dropped Allen with a right hand. When the stricken fighter got to his feet, it was discovered that he had broken his wrist in the fall, and that a gold bridge on the left side of his jaw had been wrecked in the bargain. The fight was done.

Though brief, it was enough to convince observers that Bob had the goods. He was pitted against Billy McCarthy, who had held the Australian title before coming to America a few years before. On May 29, they met at the California Club in San Francisco.

As it often happened, there were guffaws when stork-legged Fitz made his way to the ring. But when he started punching, the laughter ended. It was his fight from the first gong, and Billy's men tossed the sponge after nine rounds.

The newcomer, raved a local columnist the next morning, "is undoubtedly a great fighter."[15] Dempsey, it was added, would have his hands full when the time came. Jack's people, in fact, wanted no part of Bob after seeing what the Australian had done to McCarthy. An odd bird this fellow from Down Under might be, but a god-awful dangerous one, as well. He was also a virtual heavyweight, whatever the scale said.

Contender Arthur Upham, meeting Fitzsimmons at the New Orleans Audubon Athletic Club on June 28, fared no better. While Bob, at 155, was but a fraction of a pound more than his opponent, his advantage was ridiculous. Felled in the opening session, Upham was down several more times before he collapsed in the ninth.

As in his last bout, Fitzsimmons was unmarked. And he was now in line for a shot at the title. He and Dempsey met on January 14, 1891, at a contracted weight of 154 pounds, for stakes of $11,000 at the Olympic Club in New Orleans.

Though each man was 29, there was a difference. By now Dempsey's succession of hard fights was taking its toll. Fitzsimmons, by contrast, was entering his prime. Jack's basic health, in fact, was seriously on the wane. While training for McCarthy, he had noticed a lethargy that would not leave him. In time it was learned that he had a catarrhal condition that affected his stomach, and that his lungs were going bad. Within a few years of this bout in New Orleans, he would be gone.

"Never was a sorer-looking crowd of sports congregated on this continent," announced one morning report, "as the Dempsey contingent at the ring side last night, after the great middleweight battle between the 'Nonpareil' and the New Zealander had been won and lost and Referee [Col. Alex] Brewster had declared the American boy the loser."[16] The American boy indeed had a rough night of it. While Dempsey, at 147, gave only 3½ pounds to the challenger, he was cruelly outmatched. When Jack, who had never seen Fitzsimmons pared, watched the Australian's robe come off, he vented a high note of surprise. There were more shocks to follow.

The first time he tasted Fitzsimmons' right hand, the champion went on the retreat. In the third, he was spilled by a right. In the fourth, he tried to mount an attack, but took a withering left to the body. A hard left smashed his nose like it was ripe fruit, and one more downstairs had him in peril.

Soon Jack was hanging in by his courage. By the end of six, he was woozy, and he must have known the outcome. Still he would not fold. Felled with a body shot late in the seventh, he would not have been permitted another round today. But in those days, men fought until carried out on their proverbial shields, and Dempsey would not have it otherwise. In the eighth and ninth, he still was swinging back.

The tenth round was a massacre, with Dempsey down three times and still climbing up. In the eleventh, Fitzsimmons implored the champion to quit. "Don't make me 'it you again, Jack," he said. "Chuck it. Wot's the use o' goin' on with this?" In the twelfth, the sand-dusted floor now mottled with Dempsey's blood, Fitz repeated his request. It was matched with a growing chorus from around the ring. In the thirteenth, Dempsey staggered under the impact of a right hand to the ear and sank.

Incredibly, he rose and put up a rally. A glancing left sent him spinning down, and he was up at eight. Torn between showing mercy and bringing it to an end, Fitzsimmons again asked Jack to quit. Instead, the champion gasped that he would accept no such offer, and would land a blow himself if he could. "Then look out," said Fitz grimly, unloading a right hand that brooked no argument. After helping move Dempsey to his corner, he was heard to say, "I never lifted a gamer man to his feet." Jack, heartbroken, cried without shame when he gained his senses.

"The Oregon man," it was remarked, "was clearly outclassed from the start but he stuck to it until Nature would no longer exert herself."[17] He never fought a significant bout again. And Fitzsimmons was without a remote equal in the division. In fact, it seemed pointless for him to ply his trade at middleweight any longer. The new champion, it was asserted, was a clean fighter, but still "a heavyweight sweated out and trained down to a requisite figure." The great trainer William Muldoon announced that with twenty more pounds on his frame, Fitz would be a fight for any man living, including John L. Sullivan himself.

In Quest of Bigger Game: The Irish Giant

At this point Bob very likely was a match for any man alive. After winning a couple of non-title bouts that spring, he had a chance to prove himself a *bona fide* heavyweight when he fought Peter Maher at the Olympic Club in New Orleans. Few today know Maher except as a side-note, yet in his day he was a force to rival any in the world. At the moment, as Richard Fox observed, he was "being boomed to the skies as the pugilistic marvel of the decade."[18]

Born on April 18, 1866, Maher had his raw beginnings in the village of Kilbannon. One of eight siblings, he entered the labor market at 14 and two years later was at work as a laborer for the Phoenix Brewery. Dubbed, in time, the Irish Giant, he was a sleek specimen, standing 5'11" and weighing, in his maturity, but a few pounds over today's light-heavyweight limit. A football star in his youth, he developed a reputation as a brawler with a killing right hand. He won an Irish national amateur title at middleweight in 1887.

Later that year the great Sullivan made a voyage to the Isle and helped to sponsor another competition, which Peter won in devastating fashion. Thoroughly impressed, John L. now urged his kinsman to seek his fortune in the States. In time it would happen, but first Maher sought to establish himself in London, Europe's boxing capital in that day. In February of 1891, he gained major notice when he met highly touted Canadian Gus Lambert at the city's Pelican Club.

A rugged former wrestler and weightlifter, Lambert was a stout 5'8" and in recent years he had beaten some of the best. At 186, he enjoyed 20 pounds on Peter. When Maher sent him crashing with a right hand in the opening round, a new star had risen on the scene.

In the fall of 1891, Peter launched into American competition with a series of wins on the Eastern seaboard. Over the next few years, in venues ranging from Philadelphia to San Francisco, he scored win after win in violent fashion. On November 11, 1895, he actually gained some fleeting recognition as world heavyweight champion when he knocked out James Corbett's stablemate Steve O'Donnell at Maspeth in the first round. For after that fight, Corbett congratulated the winner, one Irishman to another, and proclaimed him to be his successor.

"Any title which I hold," said James, "I confer upon you. My withdrawal from the prize ring is final. I regard you as a worthy man to hold the championship."[19] Of course, whether or not a champion had such a right was another question. And Corbett, as it turned out, was not finished. But now Maher was established as a contender of the first rank.

At 178, he had fully 15 pounds on Fitz when they met at the Olympic on March 2. Peter went at him at the bell, only to taste a left hand that put him on his back. Arising with a gashed lower lip, he sent the Cornishman sprawling into the ropes near round's end. He got the benefit of a minute's rest, in which cornerman Joe Choynski nearly bit a hole in his ear trying to enliven him.[20]

According to Gilbert Odd, Choynski actually saved the day when he darted into the ring past the timekeeper, kicking the gong as he entered in order to bring the round to an early end. (In another version of the story, notes this author, it was a saloonkeeper who had bet heavily on Bob that turned the trick.) In any case, Bob lasted the second round. He regained his poise. His straight left began to connect, fracturing Maher's nose and splattering blood down his chest. From that point, he was in charge. By the end of twelve, incredulous at Fitzsimmons's strength, the Irishman was beaten. "It's no use," he gasped to his corner, "that fellow's a *divil*." The two fighters exchanged congratulations on a hellacious fight and shared pulls on Fitz's hard cider flask.

* * *

Fitzsimmons rang up four more knockouts in fast order in months that followed. By now, it was clear, he had his eye on boxing's biggest prize. Yet there was one item of business to settle first. His old rival Jim Hall, still claiming that his win over Bob in Australia was on the up-and-up, was in San Francisco. And he was talking up another go. Unmoved, Bob maintained only that the fight back home had been a phony deal. "I don't know what Hall expects to do here," he had told reporters after concluding a stage exhibition in New York in February, "but I suppose he is looking for a match with me. He might better have stayed where he was if that's what he's after, for he knows I can lick him in three rounds any time."[21]

Public interest was aroused. Bob and Jim soon met to sign for a bout in St. Paul in July. There had been plenty of argument about their last bout, but when the two now stood face to face in their street clothes, it was clear that no mystery would attend this next ring outcome.

"*You*," Bob hissed at the challenger, "you know that I went down for you and that you paid me to do so."

As Hall tried to keep his composure, Fitz started to pace. He then hit a nerve when he said that he could name five men who had been purchased by Jim in the same way! Hall shot back that the champion had beaten "a lightweight" in Dempsey and that twenty men back home could have done as much. When Fitzsimmons offered to prove his point right there, the confrontation was broken up and the men were told to wait for the date on the paper.

When the Minnesota governor refused to allow the fight, it was put off, and the meeting did not take place until 1893. In the meantime, Fitz got a close look at the man whom he would face one day in the fight of his life. He was a keen observer when heavyweight challenger Jim Corbett rocked the world that September at the Olympic. Corbett, he took note, was similar in size and weight to Maher, and while more skilled, he was not as hard a puncher. Seeing the time — 21 rounds — that it took James to beat a sadly dissipated John L. Sullivan, he took heart. He said openly he could beat the winner.

Fitzsimmons and Hall met at last in New Orleans on March 8, 1893, at a building on Canal Street. It was, as it figured to be, a spirited affair. After three rounds, Hall was holding his own, and he started the fourth looking a mite cocky. But when he drew straight back from a feint, Fitzsimmons had his opening. He let go with a left, then exploded a right hand that sent James crashing.

Hall, by one firsthand account, "fell backwards like a log, his head striking the cork floor with a resounding thud." For a time, it appeared that the blow had been fatal, and more than twenty minutes elapsed before he was able to be removed to his dressing room.[22]

* * *

A new chapter began in Bob's life when on a theater tour he came across three fellow Australians, Martin Julian and his sisters Rose and Theo. Together the siblings formed an acrobatic trio called The Julians.

Owing, perhaps, to his attraction to Rose, who would become the love of his life, the fighter soon had Martin for his manager. And Martin, as it turned out, had an eye for Bob's present wife Alice.[23] In due time, the situation would resolve itself by Bob and Alice divorcing, Martin marrying her, and Fitz tying the knot with Rose! Bob and Rose were married in July.

Fitzsimmons's next bout of significance was a scheduled ten-rounder with his friend Joe Choynski in Boston. Five years younger than Bob at 26, Choynski was nonetheless well seasoned, and had fought professionally for some six years in the U.S., Australia, and England. Like Fitz, he had been strengthened by early work at the forge, and he could annihilate a man with either hand. Coming now off sixteen fights without a loss, the San Franciscan was one of the most feared men in the game. Several years earlier, he had fought terrific bouts with a young James Corbett and he figured that a win over Bob would set him at the head of the heavyweight line. He also prevailed on Fitzsimmons's sense of gratitude by maintaining that his quick thinking had saved Bob from a knockout in the Maher fight. (To which the middleweight champion is said to have replied, "You're a cunning bastard. If you would bring off a trick like that to save me, what would you [do] to take my championship?")

Like the Maher fight, staged on June 17, 1894, this one had a fine line between *win* and *lose*. For two rounds, Fitz sought to close the distance as hard jabs drew blood from his mouth. In the third, he walked into a right hand that sent him down and nearly out. But anyone who figured on a quick finish, notes Gilbert Odd, got a surprise when the Australian came up after the minute's rest "cool as a surgeon."[24]

Midway through the round Joe himself hit the boards from a right hand. Up at nine, he was down again, getting the impromptu benefit of a bucket-splash of water from his corner. Felled again, he was saved by the gong. In the next round, after he went down twice, an attending police officer intervened. The referee, to Fitz's consternation, called it a draw.

According to Choynski's supporters, the verdict was fair, since the third round, they claimed, had been cut short in order to protect Fitzsimmons. When the two men met the next day on the street, Fitz congratulated his opponent on the terrific shot that he had landed in that round. (Asked in turn how he himself had managed to survive, Bob answered, "I was thinking what Rose would say if I went home beaten by you. So I just had to get up.")

On September 7, 1894, heavyweight champion Corbett sparred six short rounds with Peter Courtney for Thomas Edison. (The match, while it looks like a playful slap fest, is partially preserved on film that makes for a quite vivid relic of both the fight ring and the camera.) In January following, Fitzsimmons made known his estimate of Courtney as a challenger when he offered to fight Peter, paying his expenses to any site acceptable and giving him $2,000 if he lasted two minutes!

By now, Corbett had ruled the roost for two years. There was interest in a fight between him and Bob. But onto the scene came a new player at Bob's weight, and a New Zealander, at that. Discovered in Sydney two years earlier by theater impresario Colonel J.D. Hopkins, Dan Creedon was currently acclaimed as Australian middleweight champion. He came to America with Hopkins, who fancied that he had under his wing the next middleweight champion. At 5'8½" Creedon was a heavily muscled animal, undefeated in some 23 bouts, who figured to present a challenge.

Fitzsimmons and Creedon met in the finale of a three-day boxing festival on September 26 at the Olympic Club in New Orleans. The purse was $5,000, with the winner to get 80 percent. So certain was Hopkins of his man's talent by now, that he had bought him a saloon in St. Louis as a further inducement to leave Australia behind. For good measure, a telegraph receiver was installed at the establishment to give patrons a punch-by-punch rundown of the action.

The first information gained by way of that wire was that Fitzsimmons, at 11 stone, 2 (156 pounds), was a pound lighter than the New Zealand visitor, though he was a book favorite at 3 to 1. When action commenced,

Creedon gave his rooters something to cheer about with a bold start that had him slightly up at the bell. That noise did not last long, however, as a right hand on the ear in the second made him stagger. Another right sent him down. Regaining his feet, he went briefly to one knee to take an added rest. Up again, he got a right hand that left him unconscious for five minutes.

After Fitzsimmons was declared the winner, the announcer read a cable from Richard K. Fox, offering $10,000 and a championship belt for a bout between Fitzsimmons and Corbett. It would be some time, however, before this fight would take place. At a meeting of the parties in the office of the *New York Herald*, William A. Brady, Corbett's manager, insisted that Fitzsimmons would have to earn the shot by meeting then up-and-coming Steve O'Donnell. [25]

While the meeting ended in a stalemate, Fitzsimmons was elated when Brady sent a cable two days later, agreeing to fight him, and to match the money that Bob's camp was offering as a side bet. Yet when the camps met

again, the Corbett side was upping the ante to $10,000. It was also essential that they meet no sooner than July 1, 1895. Still, Fitzsimmons left with the belief that his shot at James was soon to come.

Happily married, and with Rose expecting their first child, Bob was on top of the world. Tragedy struck, however, on November 19 when he entered the ring on a road show to spar four rounds with fellow Australian Con Riordan.

The usual routine on this trip was for Fitz to box four each with Riordan and Joe Dunfee, after which an invitation was made to anyone in the audience who wanted to try his luck. The show would end with Bob hitting the bag and the punch ball (a heavy sphere suspended on a rope),

Bob Fitzsimmons, boxing's first three-division champion, as he looked around 1890, one of the hardest punchers for his weight in the history of the game. Fitzsimmons would develop a fierce rivalry with heavyweight champion James Corbett that extended outside the ring.

often sending the object, in dramatic style, into the gallery with his final blow.

On this occasion Riordan, who was known to be jealous of his countryman's status, had been drinking heavily beforehand. Entering the ring in a ugly mood, he came out punching with conviction, and Fitz, taken aback, went into a retreat. By the end of the first round, however, Riordan had landed little, and his nose had been bloodied. Then, in the second, he connected with a right to the ear that sent his employer into the ropes. But when Con sought to apply the finisher, Fitzsimmons pulled his "shift," starting a right and ripping the left, for all he was worth, into the midsection.

When Fitz hit men like that, they were done. Riordan gasped, hands at his knees. A right to the jaw laid him cold. Fitzsimmons helped carry him to the corner and awaited his next partner. But when Riordan gained his senses, he still needed aid to leave the ring. The second sparring session, a tamer one, ended when Bob saw that Riordan, who had been left sitting on a chair, had slid to the floor. Ignoring a left hook from Dunfee, he turned in mid-action and waved a halt.

After Con was taken to the dressing room, they finished the show. On changing into street clothes, Fitzsimmons learned that Riordan had been taken to the hospital. Setting out for that destination, he was soon apprehended by police officers. He spent the night in custody. The next morning, he learned that Riordan had died, and that he would be charged with manslaughter. Soon afterward, however, in view of the evidence, it was decided that Riordan had entered the ring, by his own fault, in bad shape, and the death was ruled accidental.

Crushed no less by what had happened, Fitzsimmons vowed not to fight again. Rose, willing to support him either way, had no objection to his return to horseshoeing if he wanted. But Julian, still hopeful of a showdown with Corbett, persuaded him to go on another tour that would keep public interest alive.

Probably the key to Fitzsimmons's perseverance during this period was the acquisition of a brewery night watchman named Jack Stelzner, who could fight some, and who was willing to come aboard as a sparring partner. Durable as a mule, Jack soon had Fitz at work full-bore.

In April, Bob boxed a couple of exhibitions. Yet efforts to stage a Corbett-Fitzsimmons bout that year did not succeed, and Corbett, who was finally getting his fill of the ring, announced his retirement. It was a tentative move that would not last long. But in the meantime, on February 21, 1896, in Langtry, Texas, in a bout that had partial recognition as a heavyweight title fight, Fitz faced Maher again.

Boxing was illegal in the state, and from the start there was pressure to stop the bout before it began. Yet the notorious Judge Roy Bean, a cantankerous (if not psychotic) figure who owned Langtry, in his own colorful phrase, "from the sludge slit to the graveyard," had hopes that his town would one day rival the nation's big cities. "The Judge," notes one columnist, "was a renegade with brains and a natural ability to organize and control the meanest of bullies." Ruling his little burg with an iron fist, Bean had "decreed himself town judge, tax collector, federal marshal, [and] coroner, and to make sure that not a single silver dollar would avoid his greedy paws, he ran the famous Jersey Lilly saloon, the only licensed establishment in town."[26] He wanted the fight, and was willing to do what it took to keep it.

So, with Texas Rangers now milling around the area to enforce the going law, Bean and promoter Dan Stuart took note of a sandbar in the middle of the Rio Grande, a little no-man's land to which neither the U.S. nor Mexico had clear entitlement. Thus they set up a ring there in the open air and the Rangers, along with about 200 Mexicans from the other side, wound up attending.

The swarthy Irishman, a thick-haired, mustachioed contrast to his bald rival, again at 178, now had only seven pounds' advantage. Playing his best hand, Maher sought to end it fast. He nearly succeeded, getting home a hellacious right that split Fitzsimmons's nose. Then he landed another right in breaking from a clinch, prompting referee George Siler to threaten him with disqualification. After the men touched gloves, Bob banged both hands to the body. When he was short with a right, Maher countered with shots of his own. Seconds later, after they broke again, Maher landed a right hand to the temple. But when he missed a left, Fitz hooked his left with paralyzing force to the body. A right hand dropped Peter cold at a time of 95 seconds.

The Irish Sailor

On December 2, Fitzsimmons met a memorable foe in a scheduled ten-round bout at Mechanics' Pavilion in San Francisco. Tom Sharkey, a black-haired archetype of Gaelic warrior aggression, was molded of some of the sternest stuff ever seen in a ring. In a few years, he would engage Jim Jeffries in bouts of 20 and 25 rounds, the latter of which would be called the most savage fight ever waged for the heavyweight championship of the world.[27]

Born in Dundalk, Ireland, in November of 1893, one of nine children, he knew from his youth what it was to earn his keep. "The first work I ever did as a boy," he would say, "was aboard a ship. I used to run on small coaling vessels between my home town and ports in Scotland. I took my turn at the wheel and often went nineteen and twenty hours at a stretch without sleep. Later I shipped on larger vessels, and before coming to New York from Buenos Aires in 1892 I had traveled the world — to Alaska through the Indian Sea and to ports where no white man had ever set foot."[28]

On arriving in New York he joined the U.S. Navy and was soon stationed on the USS *Philadelphia*. While on board, he donned the gloves a few times. As yet, he did not know a jab from an uppercut, but by the time the ship put in at Honolulu, Tom had established himself as a fighter.

At 5'8" and 185, sturdy as a gunboat, Sharkey was a one-man sprawl of strength and spirit that would never find a fit in any of society's more civil compartments. Over the years, his lack of refinement would make for anecdotes aplenty. According to Stan Weston, the sailor's close friend Col. Harvey Miller, a one-time president of the National Boxing Association, had all the goods on Tom outside the ring. On one occasion, for example, Ship's Corporal Sharkey was given the task of lining up the crew on payday in alphabetical order. Trying to play his role to the fullest, Sharkey singled out one meek-looking fellow and asked his name. Told that it was Phillips, the corporal ordered him to "git the hell up among the F's."

On another (hopefully this one is apocryphal), a superior officer got married to a local girl in Honolulu. The best man told Sharkey to go into town and get rice, which the men would throw at the bride from under a gangway ladder as she descended. When the time came, said Weston, "Tom obeyed — and how! As the bridal procession came down the gangway, Tom let fly and a two-pound bag of rice hit the astonished bride square on the side of the head, knocking her stone cold. It was Sailor Tom's first TKO."[29]

One other time, it is claimed, when Tom took his first trip on a deluxe train across country, he and manager Tim McGrath gorged themselves on a full-course dinner and then retired to a drawing room. In about fifteen minutes, a porter making the rounds opened the door and yelled, "Second call for dinner!" Seeing Tom's pained expression, McGrath asked if anything was wrong. Whereupon the young fighter said, "Tim, you'll have to go. I can't eat another bite."

* * *

Despite the wedding mishap, real knockouts were on the way. During 1894 he rang up six wins, all by the fast route. He added three more the following spring when the ship *Australia* came into port. The rig's chief steward was Tom James, a fight buff who had with him Nick Burley, a calloused journeyman who had met some of the sport's big names. Word got out that the *Philly* had a hitter of her own, and a few nights later Sharkey stepped into the ring for his toughest fight yet.

In this battle the young gob had his introduction to some rough tricks of the trade. In the early going, a "LaBlanche" maneuver by Burley broke his nose and covered him with blood. But when that blow set loose the sailor's instincts, Burley got back what he dished out with interest. The men proceeded to bludgeon each other right and left, Sharkey's shipmates rousing their man with screaming adoration. In the eighth round, when Burley sank to the canvas, a contender was born.

However crude, Sharkey was a true ring animal. Matched with the 6'4" Jim Dunn, he leaped to ring center at the opening bell, sparred for an advantage, and let fly an overhand right that sent Dunn crashing. It was his 13th straight knockout.[30] Late that summer the ship put in at Vallejo, and soon Sharkey had a California following.

In 1896, after seeing Tom go eight rounds to a draw with seasoned veteran Alex Greggains, Joe Choynski vowed to stop the sailor within that distance or forfeit the decision. It turned out to be a tougher proposition than Joe had figured, as Sharkey, after absorbing some mean whacks in the early rounds, had Choynski in distress when the last bell rang.

Later that year, Tom gave an out-of-shape Corbett a tough go in a brief chaos that was called even after four rounds. As it often happens, the principals would have different recollections: By Corbett's reckoning, it was a contest of a master and a novice, of skilled ringmaster and half-trained bear, the only advantage to Sharkey being that James had been wined and dined in recent months until he was out of shape. Tom recalled otherwise.

Either way, and however brief, it did not lack for spirit, especially from Sharkey, who had idolized Corbett's rival John L. Sullivan. The two men agree that Sharkey suffered a bruise to his eye in the first round from a left hand by Corbett. (According to Tom, the blow was landed illegally on a break from a clinch.) They also agree that Sharkey went after the champion in mad fashion from that point forward. In the fourth round, when champion, challenger, and referee all went to the canvas in a wild tangle, the bout was halted by the police.[31]

A Rank Injustice

Now, anyway, there was no disputing one thing. Tom had box office pull. And yet still, while he was interesting, he was little more than a Neanderthal in style. For this reason, both Julian and Fitzsimmons figured that he was made to order for Bob.

At this time it so happened that legendary gunman Wyatt Earp was in town with a string of horses that he was racing at the Ingleside track. Shortly after his arrival he was offered the assignment as referee of the bout between Bob and Sharkey.[32] But even though Earp had presided over some rough-and-tumble contests in his time, he was hardly a world-class referee. For this reason Julian was unhappy. Fitzsimmons, however, did not figure that it mattered — here was a chance to do Corbett one better by flattening Sharkey.

As it turned out, Fitz was right on one point of his assessment: Sharkey, rough and dog game, furnished no surprise. From the start, he came to trade, and Bob found him easily with his left hand. When Tom got home a right to the head, he was upended by Fitzsimmons's right, and might have taken the count in the opening round had the bell (some thought that it rang early) not sounded. As rounds passed, Bob took charge. By the eighth, Tom was spent. When Bob caught him with his double hook, gut and chin, he was done.

But victory was another matter. When the timekeeper tolled ten, Earp announced, to the astonishment of all, that he was disqualifying Fitzsimmons for a low blow! Seeing the outcry, he retrieved the .45 Buntline Special that he had checked at ringside, thus stifling any argument.[33] Afterward there was indignation, even from Sharkey's admirers. Earp issued a statement defending the decision, saying that each man had fouled repeatedly, and that his ruling was fair. But accounts overall were on Fitz's side.[34]

Bob's own reaction was succinct and unembittered. "I was robbed, that's all," he said early the next morning, scarcely showing signs of battle. "I expected it, and I got it."

Declared Julian, "It was the worst steal I ever saw in my life.... Reliable sportsmen, men behind the scenes and in town, came to me as late as 8 o'clock last evening and told me the fight was fixed for Sharkey ... and that Earp was the man put up to do the job. I protested, therefore, at the ringside; but what was the use? I thought afterwards that the crowd would shame Earp into acting on the level, so I agreed to go ahead."[35]

In time, Fitzsimmons would set things straight with Sharkey. But a bigger prize was in the offing when negotiations that December at a New York hotel finalized a meeting of Fitz and Corbett at Carson City, Nevada, on March 17, 1897. The purse was to be $15,000 plus side bets, for a "finish" fight, meaning 45 rounds if needed. The bout captured the fascination of the whole country,[36] and Carson City was a madhouse as thousands — dude and tramp, businessman and whore, miner, peddler, Piute, and China-man — flooded her streets in days preceding.

A Deadly Rivalry

Fitz and Corbett: If ever two men in Western civilization were cut from different cloth, these two were. The Australian, open and affable, always ready for a laugh, and the facile "Gentleman," who reeked of vanity and enjoyed being one-up in every encounter.

As to Fitz, a minor yet revealing incident is reported in a news column several years after the fact. In the fall of 1892, Fitzsimmons was in the nation's capital while on a theater tour, and chanced to make the acquaintance of the Washington baseball team that was put up at a hotel there. Senators outfielder Dummy Hoy rode up to the hotel on a bicycle, and when he took a spill, everyone present got a laugh.

This fall prompted the middleweight champion to remark, "I can do better than that, and I never straddled a bloomin' bike." There followed a wager between Bob and Hoy, involving drinks for the gang, over whether Fitzsimmons could ride the contraption around the block in 15 minutes. Fitz, it is reported, "tackled the machine without waiting to strip and for the next 15 minutes ensued the greatest catch-as-catch-can wrestling match ever witnessed between a pugilist and a bicycle." After repeated slapstick failures to mount the thing, he got going, and managed, inside the appointed time, to arrive, coat and trousers torn, hat wrecked, his knees and elbows skinned in the bargain! Everyone was impressed, and Dummy made good on the drinks.[37]

Yet according to Jim Jeffries, who came to know Fitz well after their 1902 bout in San Francisco, there was nothing unserious about Bob's resentment of the pompadoured champion.[38] It had started, said Jeff, back in 1892, after Corbett had beaten Sullivan to win the heavyweight title. Fitz, who had attended that fight, was on his way to the new champion's dressing room to offer congratulations when he learned that a telegram for Corbett had arrived. Taking the message himself, he found the door locked. Climbing up, he tossed the item through a transom and called out his good wishes. When Corbett made a sarcastic reply, ill will began.[39] (According to Mike Donovan, who was present at the time, Fitzsimmons extended the message through the transom, actually singing out, in the manner of a professional herald, the news. Corbett said to Donovan, "Take the message from him, Mike. I wouldn't speak to that sucker." Fitzsimmons then dropped the note and left without another word.[40])

Now Bob and the heavyweight champion were each on tour. Yet while Corbett concentrated on the stage itself, Bob ended every show with the announcement that he was anxious to get James into the ring. Corbett's stock reply was that Fitzsimmons ought to "stick to his own class," that last word being laden with implication. Soon remarks were exchanged by way of the newspapers. On August 11, they met in Philadelphia, in the lobby of Greene's Hotel, where Corbett was staying.

Having heard that the champion was there, Fitzsimmons went to see him in person and to see if there was any late news about the promotion of their fight. Seeing Fitz at the reception desk, however, the champion took it that he was there to start something. Looking over Bob's shoulder, he remarked to the clerk that he'd have to accept a "mark" since Bob was unable to write his name. When a surprised Fitz turned to look at him, Jim added, "Are you looking for trouble? There's been a lot in the papers about you are going to do to me when we meet. So now, I'll do something." Catching hold of Fitzsimmons's nose, he gave it a brazen tweak, and a brawl would have erupted had not Joe Corbett, Jim's brother, grabbed Bob from behind as several onlookers got between the fighters.

Morning papers blared news of this confrontation, and it was agreed that the men would put on a show worth seeing if they ever got into the ring. By year's end, the war of words had escalated, and Julian was calling Fitz the rightful champion of both middleweight and heavyweight divisions. "Should Mr. [Dan] Stuart," he stated, "fail to drag Corbett out of the hole which he has so cowardly crawled into," his own fighter would meet any man living.[41]

Now, two years later, there was rough consensus as to each man's strengths. "No one," ventured one reporter in hours preceding the bout, "who has ever fought Fitz has ever had any trouble landing on him."[42] Yet real danger, he added, lay in Bob's ability to land a devastating shot when he himself was all but done. The prevalent feeling was that Corbett, bigger and younger, and a peerless ring general, had the advantage, and that his edge would be more pronounced as the bout lengthened.

"Corbett's leg action," declared one scribe, was a revelation of strength and grace; the challenger was a gawky sort at best.[43] Then again, no one doubted Fitzsimmons's punching power, and his ability — unusual, then as now — to end a fight suddenly with either hand. Readers were reminded that Bob had killed Con Riordan, and that Jack Dempsey (now deceased) had been finished after what he got in New Orleans.

In ring attitude, as in temperament, they were a study in opposites. Fitz, it was said, was a natural fighter with the instinct of a bulldog. Corbett, a man of hard sense, fought for "cold, clammy dollars." Fitzsimmons, again, made "no pretense to refinement and does not have any ambition to shine as an authority on social ethics." He claimed merely to be the world's best fighter, and beyond that, only "a first-class horseshoer."[44] In training, Fitzsimmons let sparring partners hit him, while Corbett worked with precision, making each session a trial run.

Fitz, throughout training, was ready for fun at any moment. His day's work, which in the past had featured a friendly tussle with his pet lion Leo, now might include an impromptu run-in with a stray dog or a wild chase through the hills after pigs. Yet he had no illusion as to what lay ahead. In his own way, he was getting ready for the task of his career. While he was not, it would be said later, a classic boxer, he was *a fighter*, "cunning and wary."[45]

He was also an oddity down to his core. Fitz, Julian would say, was "an abnormal man" who did not act or think by accepted standard. He was, confessed Martin, "the queerest man I ever saw, and although I have been with him for many years, I do not understand him at all.... He always has something up his sleeve and he has it now.... I just get along with him the best way I can and let the results take care of themselves."[46]

So it was with his plan of battle, which always contained a wild card. Said the challenger, "I have never fought any man on the same plan that I fought anybody before him, and I never try to tell myself how to fight before I begin. When the time comes, I go as my instincts tell me, and that is all I can tell about it."[47]

It may be that this eccentricity unnerved the champion in the days leading to the fight, and took from him the edge that he often gained as the hour approached. An incident, days before the bout, when the two men passed on the road one morning between their training sites, had folks in each camp wondering.

Halting, James and Fitz eyed one another. When Fitz extended his hand, Corbett refused it, saying, with a gesture in the direction of the ring site, that he would shake only there. After a terse exchange, Fitzsimmons yanked back his coat, declaring war on that very ground. But the action was stilled, and the parties went their ways.

Though Corbett defended his action later, it caused worry among his people that he was not in mental shape for what was ahead. That feeling was shared by men in Fitz's camp. According to Robert H. Davis, hired by William Randolph Hearst to cover the challenger in the weeks leading up to the fight, sparring mate Dan Hickey came running to him right after, crying, "Fitz just licked Corbett!" The moment that Bob had started to take off that coat, said Hickey, "Corbett knew that Bob wasn't afraid of him. From that moment defeat sat on Corbett's shoulders."[48]

Still, an attending physician found each man "in splendid condition" shortly before the fight. When he awoke at 7:00 on the morning of March

17, the champion was all smiles. Asked by trainer Charlie White how he felt, he replied, "Fine as silk, Charlie, old boy," and slapped his friend on the back. Two hours later, horse-drawn coaches were carrying each fighter out with his retinue.

Odds were running about 10 to 6½ on Corbett. Though weights were not announced, referee George Siler would say later that Corbett came in at 183, Fitzsimmons at 157½.(Some accounts have Fitz at 167.) When they met in the center of the ring, each man wearing five-ounce gloves, the champion extended his hand. Recalling that slight on the road days before, Martin Julian shot out, "Don't do it, Bob." Fitz pulled back.

"Have it your way," said Corbett, and he strode to his corner.

At five minutes past noon, the bell sounded. Much of what transpired in the ring is captured in extant film, available today on tape or disk. Corbett, it is clear, had the upper hand through the early rounds, and he looked like a winner at the end of six.

In watching, one may be reminded a little of cobra and mongoose, the reptile lashing out as its warm-blooded foe leans away, judging angles and waiting its chance. There is a popular notion that Corbett fought his greatest battles by dancing continually and flicking his jab. In fact, he did use the jab in this bout, and used it well, but diagrams published later, depicting each man from the waist up, show by dot placement that the champion went also to Fitzsimmons's body. (Footage of the bout shows him pasting the challenger downstairs with a stinging right hand on occasion.) Fitzsimmons, over the course, landed blows to the champion's head and jaw, but little directly to the face, where Corbett hated to be hit, and where Bob himself took some of James's best shots.

In the early going, it was Corbett getting most of the "dots"—in the second round, he planted a right hand on Fitzsimmons's jaw and made him groan with a right to the body. When another shot drew the same response, the champion's trainer William Delaney thought that things were decided. At round's end he declared, "The fight is over."

The end did now seem close. Bob was missing his best shots, and a right to the heart stunned him in the fourth. In the fifth, Corbett's left hand, held low, singing like an arrow, drew red as it had with Kilrain and Sullivan. As crimson streamed from Fitz's mouth, Delaney and White, following an old tradition, yelled out "first blood" honors for their man.

"There is a well-defined appeal to women," observed Gertrude Phillips, "in the sight of strong men in physical combat."[49] The presence of Rose Fitzsimmons at ringside, she believed, encouraged members of her sex to attend prizefights in greater numbers in the years to come. Certainly, in wife Rose, who detested Corbett, Bob had his staunchest ally, and perhaps also his most vocal. Wide-eyed at every move, she barked to his seconds that he needed to go to the champion's mid-section.

But so far, it was an uphill battle. In the sixth, it appeared, the end indeed had come. A crashing right to the Australian's nose brought blood running, and more shots put Fitzsimmons down, where he remained on one knee, the referee intoning numbers as Jim himself urged him to speed it up. Bob, taking advantage of the rest, got up unbowed and ready for more.

Though Corbett's men yelled at him to take his time, he could not contain himself. Fitzsimmons, once surviving the flurry, went to his corner unperturbed. "'E ain't hurt me yet," he said, his pluck starting to surface. "I can get 'im. 'E's fast — but wait." To Rose, he managed, as an aside, "Never mind the blood. *I've got 'im licked.*"

Here again, Fitzsimmons's staying power, his hard-rubber capacity for smiling at the worst moments, came to the fore. While Corbett kept the upper hand for the next few rounds, he was unable to do the same damage. A right and a left had Fitz's nose running red in the seventh, and several lefts messed the blood all over his face in the eighth. Yet he was undismayed. And every so often he was getting through.

By now the Mrs. was being heard above the whole crowd. "Keep your back to the sun," she shouted, urging her man to "hit him in the slats" — downstairs.

In this fight, one writer would say, recalling the attitude of the Australian, "I saw a face that will haunt me until time has effaced it from my memory.... It was a mixture of pathos and tragedy. There was no savagery in it, but some intelligence. There was a leer and a grin and a look of patient suffering and dogged courage. It was the face of a brave man fighting an uphill fight, with lip torn and bleeding...."[50] One could not compare this face with anything, he added, "for there is not another human countenance like Fitzsimmons' when he is fighting against odds." Meanwhile, Rose continued to shout, enjoining her husband to go to the body. "It's the only way," she cried, "to whip the hound!" To her husband's corner, she intoned with conviction, "Make him keep punching Corbett's wind."

As Fitz felt Corbett tire, he sank his teeth into the effort. In the eleventh, he was finding the distance, and the steam was leaving the champion's punches. In the 13th, in a clinch, feeling the impact of the trade, Corbett turned his head and spit a tooth. Now it was anybody's fight.

At the end of that round, by his own recollection, the champion made up his mind to draw a haymaker from Fitzsimmons and unload his Sunday punch. He came out strong in the 14th, banging Fitz on that bloodied nose.

After two exchanges of lefts, Fitzsimmons landed a ringing right hand on the ear. Then, as Corbett stepped forward and started a left hook, it happened. The blacksmith got home with all his rending power, a left downstairs with full leverage, and Corbett went straight down. The punch, as Corbett would say later, "landed on the pit of my stomach. Quicker than all this takes to tell, I sank to my knees. I was conscious of everything that went on, the silence of the crowd, the agony on the faces of my seconds, the waiting Fitzsimmons, but my body was like that of a man stricken with paralysis."[51]

Siler began to count. Corbett, unable to use his legs, tried to hoist himself up with the aid of the ropes. On his feet a couple of seconds after the fatal ten, he made a desperate effort to continue. Grabbed by the arm by his brother Joe, he broke loose and made for Fitz, managing to strike a blow before order was restored.

Siler announced, "Fitzsimmons wins." Corbett, devastated, felt (as he would even going to his grave) that the crown had been stolen from him by a whim of fortune. Sobbing over the "sneaking little punch" that had snatched away victory, he insisted that he would fight the Australian again. Finally the men were brought together for the formality of a handshake, and though Corbett offered congratulations, he demanded a rematch.

"I will not fight you again," stated the new champion.

"You will have to," came Corbett's animated reply. "If you don't I will get you in the street."

"If you tackle me in the street," said Bob, "I will kill you."

Afterward, Corbett paid a grudging respect. "I came out of the ring to-day," he announced sadly, "a beaten man. I believe in the main I fought as well as ever I fought in my life, but luck was against me. The blow which won the fight for Fitzsimmons was in a large measure an accidental one. It was a left hook and it caught me directly under the heart."[52]

Even so, he credited the new champion with an "infernally clever" manner of fighting. And Rose, still resentful of how Corbett had acted toward Bob over the past five years, was ecstatic: "I was greatly excited all during the fight, and I could not keep still a moment. I know it made people look at me when I jumped up in my seat and called to Bob to be careful and all that sort of thing, but I could not help it, even when Bob and Martin told me repeatedly to keep still. I knew the quickest way to kill Corbett was for Bob not to try at Corbett's neck. Corbett expected that. That is why I kept shouting to Bob to 'Hit him on the body!'... I knew Bob would win all the time."[53]

Oddly, some present thought that Fitzsimmons, in his own way, had been the more methodical of the two. He showed, by one account, "better judgment than Corbett" in the ring, and exceeded him in coolness and deliberation. While some men would have jumped up, still shaken, from that knockdown in the sixth, he had remained calm.[54]

Fitz himself compared the knockout — a double left, as he deemed it, to body and head — to the one he had scored the year before. "I just put it on him," he explained, "where I put it on Sharkey, and it came out the same way."[55] Soon the game had a new phrase, albeit for an old tactic. Talking with a physician after the bout, Bob's friend Robert Davis was told, "Yes, it took the wind out of him. It was a punch in the solar plexus region that ... paralyzed the nerve center."[56] Seeing a good story line, Davis wasted no time wiring his paper with news of a "solar plexus punch" that had beaten the champion.

It was a great fight, in the estimate of referee Siler, "the best contest I ever saw." Fitzsimmons got ample praise also from William Muldoon, who called him, when in action, "the most wonderful specimen of muscular development that I have ever seen." Further, noted Muldoon, he had "a cool and collected mind" that enabled him to rise above a crisis.[57]

When it was done, Fitzsimmons doubted that he would fight again. (By some accounts, he told Corbett later, "Jim, you gave me a licking, a bloody good licking. I will never fight you again."[58]) He had accomplished all that he could see accomplishing, and his bad feeling toward Corbett was finally abating.

Julian, like his sister, was less amiable. "We gave Corbett all the best of it," he explained, "...abandoning every complaint we [had] made. I did this because I knew Fitzsimmons could lick that cur, no matter how he might be handicapped by rules or conditions. I am dead glad that all this talking and boasting and heaping of insults on the part of Corbett is at last ended."[59]

In truth, the hard feeling of Corbett and Fitzsimmons for each other would never, in mortal life, be fully cleansed from their souls. Soon the Australian would decide to continue his career, and the former champion would hound him for a rematch — but one that would never occur.

Heavyweight Champion

In his account of the Carson City fight, Davis remarks of his friend, "There was always a touch of humor in Bob's contact with the public. He never did take himself very seriously."[60]

Plenty of stories attest to this claim, and to the fighter's willingness to laugh freely at others and at himself. On one occasion, noted Chicago scribe George Pardy, he pulled one of his favorite stunts on a friend named Jack McNamara. Receiving Jack at his home, Fitz "tripped" on his garden hose and fell, letting the hose jerk up and drench Jack in his Sunday best. (A week later, McNamara stalked up behind Fitzsimmons, dressed to the nines in his suit and top hat, on a pier, and sent him tumbling into the water. The fighter bore no malice.)

One time, Fitz got his comeuppance from Wallace Sawyers, a man prominent in the horse racing business, who had repeatedly been on the receiving end of the Bob's unvarnished comedy. On this occasion, Sawyers arranged to introduce the fighter to the celebrated William "Buffalo Bill" Cody in the lobby of a hotel. Before the introduction, Wallace stressed to his friend that the Colonel was quite hard of hearing, and that one had to practically shout in order to make him understand anything.

Unbeknownst to Fitzsimmons, Sawyers had imparted the same news *about him* to the great frontiersman! The result was that the two men spent a good piece of time in the lobby yelling mightily at each other, waving their arms for emphasis, before astonished onlookers, until the ruse was discovered. (Sawyers, by this time, had slipped off toward another town.[61])

On another occasion, after his New Orleans bout with Maher in 1893, Fitzsimmons was making his way to New York and stopped in Newark where he was the guest of a well-heeled sporting fan whom he'd met in New Orleans. After four days of sightseeing, this fan asked Bob if he would care to visit an insane asylum.

"I would like to," was Bob's innocent response, "I've never been in one and I should think that it would be an unusual experience."

Indeed it would. The fellow, as it turned out, had phoned the house physician at the asylum, and told him that he was bringing a relative to the place in a few hours. "The chap is a little off," he had explained, "he has hallucinations. *He thinks that he is Bob Fitzsimmons*, and I'd like to have you keep him overnight and examine him."

Within an hour, Fitz and his host were at the hospital. "Meet Bob Fitzsimmons," said the sportsman, as if humoring his companion in the delusion. Feigning admiration, the doctor asked about the fights with Dempsey and Maher. Then he conducted a tour, presenting Fitz with a chance to test the reliability of one of the cells. When Fitz walked in, they slammed the door and vanished! After several hours, Fitzsimmons *was* close to insane, and had incited bedlam among the real residents of the place.

Some six hours later, the sportsman called the physician and told him that the whole thing was a joke. It was with great difficulty that the doctor finally convinced Fitzsimmons that he had not been a knowing party to the trick. The fighter, it seems, left the asylum with bad intentions toward this friend, and that outcome is unknown, except that Bob never went near an asylum again.[62]

Fitz, it appears, had only one notable fight in the following year, a confrontation of an odd kind with a challenger (some identify this man as one Lew Joslin; some wonder if it happened at all) in the town of Leadville, Colorado. It occurred when Bob was on tour and taking all comers who tried to collect a one-hundred-dollar prize for staying four rounds with the new champion. According to Davis[63] (whose description verges upon the surreal), placards were displayed around Leadville declaring the invitation.

The following day, seated in a chair near a hotel window, the writer was approached by a hulk of 6'4" and about 260 pounds who was game to try. "Any penalty for killing a man in the ring?" asked the big man. Assured by Davis that if all rules were followed, it would be ruled an accident, he expressed relief. He had never, he confided, hit a man with all his strength. But tonight, he ventured, "I'm going to let myself go."

Asked for his name, he replied simply that he was "the blacksmith of this here town of Leadville." As to the question about death in the ring, he explained, it was nothing personal, but he had friends in the town who wanted him to go for broke.[64] Benches were carted into the town hall, a building some 30 feet wide and 80 feet deep, as "miners, gamblers, Mexicans and Chinese, with a slight leaven of the local gentry filled the place to suffocation." Following a hurdy-gurdy pianist, a wrestling match, and an exhibition of boxing and bag punching that featured the champion himself, the "all comers" invitation was announced.

When "time" was called, the challenger bolted from his corner, swinging and hitting only air. But near the end of the round, the smithy caught the champion with a right hand, and Fitz staggered like he'd been hit with a rail tie. He made it to the next "time" and sat stunned in his corner as the challenger yelled out to all what he would do to Fitz in the next round.

Money changed hands in near chaos as odds suddenly shifted. At the start of the next round, Fitzsimmons went straight at his target, feinted with his left, and unleashed an uppercut — a punch, alleges Davis, starting "from the neighborhood of the floor," and producing a sound "as though someone had hit a cake of ice with a sledge hammer; a crackling, sickening sound that reverberated throughout Leadville."

The blacksmith, hit soundly, landed on the canvas, his head splashing water from a container on the ring apron. Half-conscious, he sought to "swim" to the nearest shore. Finally pulling himself to his feet with the aid of a ringpost, he is alleged to have said, "Gentlemen, having licked this freckled bum ... I now challenge anyone in the world." Then he turned and saw Fitzsimmons, who had a sympathetic hand on his shoulder, and fell unconscious to the floor.

When Fitz did meet a real contender, it was one of the most formidable in ring history. At 6' 2" and 206 pounds, young Jim Jeffries was ready to give the performance of his life when the two men clashed at Coney Island on June 9, 1899. Though Bob landed hard, on occasion, he could not endure the younger man's punches. Felled by Jeff's ramrod straight left in the second round, he managed to last to the eleventh.

Later Fights

Some thought now that Bob was finished. But in 1900, at 37, he was game to go again. By now Jeffries had defended his title against Tom Sharkey in a ferocious battle, and had signed to defend it against Corbett. Bob launched his comeback in Philadelphia on March 27 at the First Regiment Armory against a heavyweight named Jim Daly. He wasted no time, putting Daly on the canvas before the opening round was thirty seconds old. Down twice more, Daly retired at round's end in his corner.

Next in line was Ed Dunkhorst, a huge fighter dubbed the Human Freight Car for his bulk, which would have made him a big heavyweight even by today's standards. The bout took place at the Hercules Athletic Club in Williamsburg, New York. At 170, Bob conceded more than sixty pounds to Ed and four inches in height. It is said that this fight was the one for which Fitzsimmons coined his phrase, so famous in later years, "The bigger they are, the harder they fall."[65] The comment seemed apt, as he put on a clinic through most of the first round, landing nearly at will.

In reaction, Dunkhorst adopted the crouching stance of Jeffries, with whom he had worked in camp before some of Jeff's fights. Then, near the end of the round, he connected hard. Coming out for the second with confidence, he rocked the older fighter with a left hand on the nose. That was the end of his success. Blows to the body made him gasp, and as they broke from a clinch, Fitzsimmons landed a hook that yanked the big man's head and made him slump to the floor. As he lay, jerking involuntarily, the referee tolled.

Soon after, it was announced that the November 1896 Horton Law, which had protected boxing shows from police interference, would be repealed. The availability of boxing to the public, starting August 30, would be scaled back. Thus the fight community was now anxious to see what it could in the time that remained. On May 11, 1900, Jeffries, on the receiving end of a boxing lesson, suddenly laid Corbett out cold in the 23rd round at Coney Island. On June 26, at the same venue, towering Gus Ruhlin, one of the hardest punchers in the game, dished out a beating to Sharkey, stopping him in fifteen.

Gus, who had gone 20 rounds to a draw with a young Jeff two years earlier, had worked with Corbett for Jim's fight with Jeff, and Corbett, in turn, had helped Gus to train for Sharkey. Corbett continued to dislike Fitzsimmons, and he hoped to see Bob's comeback effort derailed. He persuaded Ruhlin's manager Billy Madden to match his man with Fitz — the best way, he said, to get Gus another go with the champion.

Fitz and Gus met at Madison Square Garden on August 10 in front of 12,000 spectators in a bout scheduled for 25 rounds. With two inches and 25 pounds to his advantage, plus a fearsome right hand, Ruhlin was a man to be reckoned with. In the opening round, he cut Fitz over the left eye and had him bleeding from the mouth. Encouraged, he began to trade in earnest in the second. But inside a minute, Gus was in trouble. A right hand staggered him, and he was on his knees before the bell sounded.

The former champion, wrote W.W. Naughton in covering this bout, was "a hard-fisted fellow, as cold as a fish ... with an eye that notes every move on the Queensberry chessboard."[66] In the fourth round, his right hand opened a gash over Ruhlin's eye, and body shots in the fifth had Gus hanging on. In the sixth, a left uppercut sent him down dead to the world.

Now there was the prospect of another go with Sharkey, against whom Fitzsimmons had wanted to even the score for the past four years. While Tom had lost some fire since his fight with Jeffries at Coney Island, he still believed that he could whip Bob, and said that he could have done it last time without the help of Wyatt Earp's decision.

By now the sailor owned a saloon on East 14th Street in New York. Shortly before Bob fought Ruhlin, the former champion he had heard that Tom was talking things up, in regard to their last fight. In early August, he strolled into the joint and said, "What about it, Tom? You and me can earn some nice spending money if we meet before they close the hatch down on boxing. And you owe me a fight, anyway."[67] Sharkey was not one to back away, and the two agreed to a return bout at the Seaside Club at Coney Island. While the matchup lacked the luster it might have had awhile back, it figured to produce a battle.

As it turned out, the event, held on August 24, drew a crowd of only 5,000. Before going on, the fighters were told that money, as a result, would be a problem. Fitz was unhappy, and the fans, already getting soaked from a thunderstorm that now poured through the ceiling, had to wait out a delay. When Bob finally joined the sailor in the ring, there were boos and catcalls.

Fitz smiled at Sharkey, however, when they met the referee at ring center, and pointed to the tattoo on the Irishman's wide chest.

"Tonight I am going to sink that ship, so watch out."

"You ain't got guns enough," answered Tom, turning to his corner.

The next exchange was fists and leather. Sharkey tried for Fitzsimmons's body with sweeping right hands, and took a shot to the heart in return. Then the sailor landed a roundhouse left that shook his rival to the soles. Another left put Bob on the floor. It looked for a second like an early knockout, but the blacksmith made it to his feet as the bell sounded.

Queried by his cornermen, he grinned and promised now to sink the ship. Sharkey, figuring that the fight was his, came out with guns blazing. Fitzsimmons, still looking a little rocky, managed to snare him in a clinch. Then, pushing Tom away, Fitz scored a fearsome right over the heart. Now it was Tom who grabbed hold.

After referee Charlie White pulled them apart, it was a shoot-out, each man looking to end it. Fitzsimmons found paydirt with a right hand on the chin. Another shot had the sailor reeling to the ropes, and one more dropped him. When he rose, he was as good as dead. Several punches put his arms at his sides, mouth gaping. A hook on the chin felled him on hands and knees, head down and blood spilling from his mouth in a violent conclusion.

Basking in cheers, Bob walked to the side of the ring and looked down at Jeffries, seated at ringside. He implored the champion to give him another fight, and to shake on the deal right there. While Jeff was reluctant, the presence of onlookers left him no escape. He accepted the challenger's gloved hand to thunderous approval.

Once sure that Sharkey was all right, Fitzsimmons made a joyful statement to the reporters, saying that he was in the shape of his life and ready to win back the title. He spent the remainder of the night at the Alhambra, a club in the Bergen Beach area of Brooklyn, regaling the crowd with a display of his excellent tenor voice and promising to become champion again.[68]

It seemed now that Bob should be next in line, but it would not happen just yet. On the last night of action protected by the Horton Law, Corbett stopped Kid McCoy in five rounds, and there was talk that he and Fitz ought to be matched again. By now, though, for all the drumming he'd done for a second go with Fitzsimmons, Corbett hoped to get now another chance at Jeffries. Yet Jeff, engaged in a theatrical tour under the direction of Brady, was in no hurry to fight either man just yet.

For awhile Bob did little in the ring. In June of 1901 he engaged in a wrestling match with Ruhlin, which turned into a virtual no-holds-barred with punches included. Ruhlin, his nose streaming blood from a head-butt, finally was able to use his bulk to gain a pin victory in a first "fall" that lasted some eleven minutes. Following a fifteen-minute rest, they went at it again, with Gus getting the win.

Rose wanted Bob to settle down, but his yen would not subside. In

December of that year, he was persuaded to box a five-round exhibition with Sharkey before a private audience at the Theatrical Business Men's Club in New York. The two men did business in serious fashion, but ended on good enough terms to head off to Sharkey's saloon afterward, and to remain fast friends from that day. A few months later, Fitzsimmons made news when he faced seven heavyweights during an "all comers" exhibition in Chicago. Then the papers began calling on Jeffries to give him a return. The two fighters signed to go 25 rounds at the San Francisco Athletic Club for 70 percent of the gate, to be divided 60–40, winner and loser.

While Jeff prevailed, it was victory hard-won. In recalling the fight several years later, he marveled at how Fitz was able to trade punches with him despite their difference in weight. In the third round, he recalled, after they had each landed terrific blows, they continued to stand their ground in a furious exchange. It was "all body hitting," Jeff's favorite game, yet the older man did not flinch. It was, by Jeffries's estimate, the toughest encounter he ever had in a prize ring. The fight ended in the eighth with Jeff cut to pieces and Fitzsimmons, hands damaged by the impact of his own punches (delivered, some said, with doctored handwraps), succumbing to a hook to the liver.

Bob suffered a deeper loss when Rose passed from typhoid pneumonia in April of 1903. After receiving a letter of condolence from the heavyweight champion, he joined Jeffries's camp and was instrumental in getting him into shape for his bout with Corbett in San Francisco later that year.

On his way across country to join Jeff, another thing happened to Fitz: While attending her performance in Chicago, he was transfixed by stunning young singer-actress Julia May Gifford. The two were introduced after one of the shows and in days following fell madly for each other. They were married in July.

Bob's fighting career, as it turned out, still was not done. In the same month that he lost Rose, Jack Root had defeated Kid McCoy for a new "light heavyweight" title created to fill the gap between middleweights and men the size of Jeffries. On July 4, Root lost to George Gardner, who had wanted to fight Fitzsimmons some years earlier for the middleweight honors. In the former champion, now 40 and seeming like used goods, Gardner saw an easy mark for his first defense.

Fitz was game. He agreed to a couple of exhibition matches in Philadelphia to get ready. But again, misfortune would visit, as one opponent, a fighter named Coughlin (his first name also Con, like Riordan) fell in the first round and went into a coma, nearly dying the next day. Bob decided nonetheless to carry on with the second bout, two weeks later. This time he met a curious little fighter named Joe Grim, a welterweight, whose durability at age 22 was already legend. It was one of the few times in his life that Bob entered the ring enjoying a weight advantage. The bout was what it figured to be, with Fitzsimmons landing hard and Grim earning his reputation, hitting the canvas, by one account, some 17 times before the six rounds were over. At the close, Fitz hugged Joe and proclaimed him to be a marvel.

On November 25, he met Gardner in San Francisco in a bout scheduled for 20 rounds. Following a tack used by Jeffries in their first bout, he gained the upper hand at the weigh-in, where he provided a casual show of strength to the man he was facing. As Gardner was slipping out of his trousers, Fitz delivered a good-natured whack across the shoulders that nearly felled him.

"*Hi, George,*" he sang out, "I hope you're feeling like a good fight tonight." His confidence was still brimming when he entered the ring, and George was looking wary. Scoring well from the start with his left hand, he continued to dish out a lesson as the rounds passed. In the fourth, Gardner was shaken with a right, and a couple of lefts put him down. Before the round was over, he was down again. Floored once more in the fifth, Gardner was adrift on a canvas sea. While he managed to get in some licks in the succeeding rounds, he was down yet again in succeeding rounds and thoroughly whipped at the end of 20. Thus Fitzsimmons was an unprecedented three-division world champion.

* * *

Much has been made by historians of the great weight difference between Bob and his opponents. The official difference is this case was slight, with Gardner at 170 enjoying only two pounds' advantage. But regarding Bob's actual weight in the ring, on this and other occasions, the story may need revision. In the present day, it is common for fighters to hit a downward "spike" for an early weigh-in, then use the coming 24 hours to gain back pounds and enter the ring well over the official limit. Possibly, Fitzsimmons did the same thing.

In his autobiography, Jim Jeffries makes an interesting comment, based upon a time when he and Fitz worked together in training. Near the end of Jeffries's career, after his exhibition bout with Jack Munroe, Jeff and Fitz went to a Turkish bath in Salt Lake City after one of their shows, they each weighed on the scales. Jeff was 235, Fitz 202.[69] The men had not been inactive for a long period, since they had either fought or been at work together most of the past year. They went into the steam room for fifteen minutes and came out to cool off. Over the next few hours, they repeated the procedure five or six times. Afterward they slept into the forenoon, and on rising, Jeff wondered how much they might have lost. Jeff had lost 18 pounds, Fitz 24.

While Bob was now only 178, it was clear from subsequent horseplay that he still had his strength. Now what if he had hit a required weight for some of his fights, in this fashion, and then had come into the ring with the advantage of the extra pounds, besides? The episode made Jeff suspect that Bob had been appreciably heavier, at times, than spectators imagined. But pounds aside, he said, Bob was a wonder: "He hit as if he weighed three hundred."

Even so, Fitzsimmons's best years were now behind him, and he would have little success in the new mix. In July of 1904 he boxed a six-round no-decision bout with Philadelphia Jack O'Brien in Philly, an encounter that each man figured in his own favor. O'Brien said that he let the bout go its scheduled distance only because he wanted the experience, while according to Fitzsimmons, "I ... had O'Brien on the floor, whipped and practically out when the police jumped in to save him...."[70] In December of the following year, he and O'Brien met in San Francisco with the title on the line. At the end of 13 rounds, Fitz sat beaten and exhausted. He fell off the stool in a faint and was quickly revived by his seconds. Referee Ed Graney, seeing his plight, came to the corner.

"Eddie," gasped the old warrior, "I'm all done up. I can't go on." He nodded off again, then was brought around with whiskey and sat heartbroken, face down, as O'Brien was proclaimed the new light-heavyweight champion.

Final Years

Fitzsimmons faced another loss when Julia ended their difficult marriage, citing his growing alcohol use and accusing him of cruelty. While she would retain a soft spot in her heart for him, the marriage was dissolved. Now Bob's days as a major player in the fight game were also at an end — two years later, in 1907, he would fall in two rounds to coming champion Jack Johnson. He would manage one win in the coming year before being stopped by Bill Lang in Sydney in 1909. His final bouts on record were two no-decision six-round bouts in 1914, when he was nearing 51 years of age.

In March of the next year, Fitzsimmons would marry again, to Temo Ziller, a staunch religious convert, and in time Fitz himself developed evangelical aspirations. According to Temo, years later, Bob was planning to attend the renowned Moody Bible Institute in Chicago when he was felled for the final count by lobar pneumonia on October 22, 1917.

* * *

"No monuments," observes Billy Rocap, "are necessary to perpetuate the memory of Bob Fitzsimmons. He was the greatest fighter for his pounds and inches that ever lived, and coupled with it, he was a real man."[71] This view is seconded by observers past and present. He was the hardest hitter for his weight, said Mike Donovan, who ever entered the ring. If Bob was not a stylist, he was resourceful, and thoroughly ring-savvy. In the estimate of Robert Davis, he was "a perfect judge of distance and a master of timing. Any fighter who would mix it with Fitz did so at his own peril."[72] When the distance closed, he became somehow even harder to hit, and was such a master of short punching that at times "the impact of the wallop was heard before the spectator saw the blow start."

Ironically, one of the finest compliments ever paid to him came from his nemesis Corbett, who admitted, some twenty years after Carson City, that Bob was a true immortal. While the two men could not be said to achieve friendship in the span of mortal life, Gentleman Jim had mellowed enough to say, on Bob's passing in 1917, "Bob Fitzsimmons will live in memory, so long as pugilism lasts. For his weight and inches, he was the greatest fighter that ever drew on a glove; a ring marvel whose like may never be seen again."[73]

As to Fitzsimmons's standing among the greats, note will be made in the end portion of this book. For now, let us leave this warrior at the scene of his celebration at the Alhambra, noted earlier, after he had disposed of Sharkey. Tripping the light fantastic until 3 A.M., he also raised his voice in an improvisation, rewording Sir W.S. Gilbert's tune "Titwillow" in his silly and amiable manner:

By the shores of dear Bergen
Lives honest old Fitz,
With his wallop, his wallop, his wallop.
He met Gustave Ruhlin
And knocked him cold
With his wallop, his wallop, his wallop.
Then he took on Tom Sharkey
And gave him a cramp
And he'll make Big Jim Jeffries
Look just like a tramp
And win back his title
Of heavyweight champ,
With his wallop, his wallop, his wallop.[74]

IV

A Demon from the Barbados: Joe Walcott

That Walcott is a fistic marvel, there is no question.
New York News column, April 1895

"A sort of sawed-off Hercules," marveled *The Ring* founder and biographer Nat Fleischer, "an abnormally powerful puncher, his conical skull possessed the hardness of *lignum vitae*. Men who fought him were handicapped sorely."[1]

He was a curiosity, this bronze slugger from the Caribbean, standing but 5'1½" and weighing in the range of today's welterweights. Possessed of great reach and extraordinary power, Joe Walcott punched men thirty pounds heavier into oblivion.

Like Sam Langford after him, he could use his short stature to his advantage, catching blows on his cranium and often wrecking the hands of his opponent. "Mah folkses in de Barbados," he would say after one of his biggest victories, "dey wanted me to make a scholard ob me, an' I went to school for two, t'ree weeks, but somehow mah head was too thick to let the letters in."[2] Maybe, he added, "dat's why dese scrappers break dere mitts on mah cocoanut." More men, figured Nat, probably ruined their hands on Walcott than on any other fighter of the day.

Erratic, prone to off nights, Walcott would sometimes finish second to men less memorable. But Joe on a good night, by the estimate of some, was like no one else in the game. Born March 13, 1873, in the colony of British Guiana, he craved adventure at a young age, and while in his teens went off as a cabin boy on a ship sailing for Boston. Soon after, he made the acquaintance of a fry cook on a boat that ran to Rockland, Maine, and worked as his helper for two years. Later he was slinging hash and waiting tables in a Boston eatery, where a customer took a liking to him and hired him as an elevator boy at the American House Hotel.

While at sea, Walcott had been in some scrapes on board, where his aptitude for violence was fast discovered. Now he began spending his evenings around Jack Sheehan's gym, where for 25 cents a week he learned to box and wrestle. After a month, he entered a New England amateur grappling tournament and swept the lightweight and middleweight titles. Boxing he found even more to his liking. Soon he was an amateur champion in that game, as well, at 130 pounds.

When no one at that weight would go near him, he entered competition in the higher divisions, and so his reputation as a giant killer began. In time Joe won a regional middleweight title, after which he accepted a challenge to meet Pat Reilly, who had won a title at heavyweight. A right hand sent Reilly down and out in the opening round.

At seventeen, Walcott began to punch for pay. He won several fights in 1890 and '91, the most notable a four-round decision over the seasoned George Meakin. On the same card, he went another three, dropping a nod to Teddy Kelly. (By the best current estimate, it was the only loss in Walcott's first 31 fights.) That evening's endeavor, which paid him the grand sum of $2.50, entered him into worthy ranks. In October of 1892, Joe again fought a double-header in Philadelphia, this time winning both ends.

It so happened at this time that the great bantamweight champion George Dixon was in the area, appearing that week on stage with a burlesque show at a place where he was taking on all comers.[3] Shortly after Walcott had scored one night a double victory, Dixon introduced him to his manager Tom O'Rourke and asked that Walcott join the troupe.

O'Rourke wanted Walcott to have a tryout in which he would take on anyone from the audience for four rounds, with a $50 prize going to those who lasted the distance. Joe said yes, but it soon became apparent that men around Boston knew the danger in that proposition. As challengers faded away, Walcott proposed to Tom that they offer $25 to anyone who could last fifteen minutes with him on the wrestling mat. When he whipped three takers, all heavyweights, O'Rourke knew that he had a warrior. Joe accompanied them on the remainder of the tour, boxing and wrestling roughly twelve bouts a week, and making his new manager happy with the deal.

Rise to Fame

In 1892, Walcott fought fifteen times without a loss. The following year, he dropped a decision to Mike Harris, a rangy, well-schooled fighter out of New York, his only loss in some twelve outings. The year after, he beat Harris convincingly by a knockout in the sixth round. On August 22, 1893, Joe electrified New York fans when he knocked out Jack Hall, Australian lightweight champion, in the first. On April 19, 1894, he met Tommy Tracey, Australian welter champ, in Boston, in a bout fiercely waged until Walcott ended it in the 16th round. Afterward he flattened Dick O'Brien, an unbeaten welter hitherto counted as being the best in New England.

On October 15, Walcott faced outstanding lightweight Austin Gibbons in a fight that was gauged even money. It was a typical Walcott fight, Joe seeking to bore inside while his opponent tried to keep it at long range. When Joe started to connect, the result was decisive. Gibbons was done in four.

Maybe the best man that Walcott fought at this stage of his career was Tommy West, a tough, stocky hitter who engaged him several times at the close of the century. On the first occasion, in Boston, January 11, 1894, Walcott won the fight in three rounds. When they met again, in New York, in December of 1896, West was a full-fledged middleweight, and it ended in a draw.

Meanwhile, on March 1, 1895, Walcott had his first go with a memorable fighter named Mysterious Billy Smith, with whom he would share the stage five more times before it was done. Blessed with speed and staying power to no end, Smith was also a plainly dirty fighter who would use any tactic in a bout if he could get away with it. In turn, he had two redeeming qualities: He expected the same from his opponent, and he feared no man alive. He was one of the few welters in the world with no hesitation about getting into the ring with Walcott.

Joe and Billy clashed for the first time on April 3, 1895, in the Boston Music Hall, in a bout to establish the rightful challenger to welterweight champion Tommy Ryan. It figured to be one of the best fights of the year at any weight, and the result left no one disappointed. "From the call of time," said Nat Fleischer, "there were never more than five seconds between the leads and as the work was all of the fast, rugged type, the spectators were given frequent opportunities to vent their pent up enthusiasm in a manner that defies description."[4]

While the betting favored Joe at 7–5, most of the crowd was for the white fighter, and they made it loud and clear. Each man was in peak condition, and what Walcott gave up in height, he got back in strength and durability. In the early going, he got home with right hands to Smith's midsection that would have sawed a lesser fighter in half. Yet Smith came back undaunted, and the tide swung back and forth. In the ninth, an odd trickle of blood came down Walcott's face when the referee parted them from a clinch. He would insist later that the wound resulted from a bite!

Years afterward, in fact, Smith would remark, "I didn't like Walcott's wooly head in my face and I did give him a bite on his roof."[5] According to some accounts, the audience was so hostile to Walcott that Joe weathered fouls time and again without a complaint. In the fifth round, says one, Smith bit Joe on the shoulder and then complained, though unsuccessfully, to the referee that he himself had been bitten.[6]

No stranger to roughhouse tactics, Walcott could mix on that level when occasion demanded — one of his favorites, as noted earlier, was to grind his laces into a man's ear when in close. Probably that maneuver figured into this contest, for in the eleventh round, the Barbados fighter landed a left hand on Smith's swollen ear that split it open. Yet when Joe tired in the twelfth, Smith again went on the attack. In the final minute of the 15th round, each man gave all he had left, and the crowd went wild. Boos shook the arena when the referee held up the hand of each man in sign of a draw. Most in the fiercely pro–Smith crowd wanted him to get the nod, but fairness dictated otherwise.

A month afterward Walcott went against Mick Dunn, a strapping Australian middleweight, at Coney Island. O'Rourke, who had let Joe take on anyone in the barnstorming period, came under some criticism for this move, since Dunn represented the best in his division. As it turned out, the concern was misplaced. According to commentary, "Walcott's delivery was terrific. It carried the force of a pile-driver. Dunn was dazed on more than one occasion when one of those sledge-hammer blows staggered him. Whenever Mick tried to take the offense, he was driven back and compelled to retreat under the bombardment...."[7]

While Dunn had a smart jab, he was hurt every time that Walcott landed. Near the end of the eighth round, Joe landed a left to the body and the hands of the Australian went down. A right to the jaw sent him out. By now the media were trumpeting Walcott as a phenomenon. But he faced a different challenge on December 2, when O'Rourke pitted him against George "Kid" Lavigne. This time, for one of the few times in his life, Walcott faced a smaller opponent. The catch was, he had to pare down to minimize the difference.

The Empire Club at Maspeth was packed on that occasion, as each man had an energetic following. On seeing Tommy Ryan in Lavigne's corner, O'Rourke issued a challenge for Tommy to defend his middleweight crown against Joe, and though Ryan announced his acceptance, the fight never did materialize.

Of Walcott and Lavigne, note has already been made. It was a bout that had hardened spectators wincing before it was done, and it remains a classic of the early gloved era. Three months later, when Walcott and Tommy West met for a third time in March of 1897, it was another war. On this occasion West proved an opponent of the first order, meeting Walcott head-on from the opening round. After being rocked to the ropes by a right hand in that frame, Joe had West backing up in the exchanges. Then West rebounded, and it was a battle into the late rounds, which found Walcott groggy, his left eye closed and his nose streaming blood. At the end of 20, Tommy was the winner. When they met for a fourth time the following year, in a no-contest bout of six rounds, West showed none of the old determination, and local newspapers affirmed that Walcott had the upper hand.

Joe and Mysterious Billy went at it again on April 14, 1898, at the Park City Theatre in Bridgeport, giving the fans another show for their money. This time it was 25 rounds, with editor Sam Austin of the *Police Gazette* as the third man. But unlike the first fight, which had been savage, this one had an air of science, and Smith fought, for once, by the rules all the way.

In this one it was Smith early, and Walcott evening matters with strong punches to the body in the middle rounds. Then, in the tenth, a searing right had Walcott holding on. In the thirteenth, Billy's right hand again had him dazed. From that point until the 19th, it was anybody's fight, but in that round, Walcott wobbled his man with a right to the jaw. In the following round, Smith came back, and the rest was ebb and flow. A right hand sent Walcott into the ropes at the final bell. Again it was a draw, and this time the crowd approved.

On December 6, they met a third time, at the Lenox Athletic Club, with a capacity crowd on hand. Odds of 10–7 favoring Joe found few takers. On this occasion Smith fought what might have been the fight of his life, setting the pace from the opening bell with a left to Walcott's face. In the eighth, a right hand to Walcott's mouth brought blood in a wicked stream.

Two hectic rounds followed, Smith getting home hard from the outside and Walcott returning it in close. Smith bolted out in the eleventh and rough tactics were traded without apology until Billy landed a right hand and Walcott was down. When Joe got up, another right put him in the same place. Up at seven, he heard the bell come as a welcome relief.

Still bleeding from the mouth at the start of the twelfth, Walcott tried gamely to end it, but Billy had as much "give" as granite, and he rallied late in the round. Over the next two rounds, Smith beat Walcott around the ring. After getting a warning from the referee for roughhousing, he redoubled his effort. In the 15th, a right hand swelled Walcott's slashed mouth to grotesque size, yet he fought back without flinching. They mixed it with unwavering spirit to the final round, when Smith again had the edge, and there was no argument when referee Charlie White raised his hand.

On April 25, 1899, in New York, Walcott met highly ranked middleweight Dan Creedon. When Walcott's right hand found the Australian's jaw in the first round it was over. When Creedon asked for another chance, he got it, and the two squared off on June 23 at the Broadway with Joe getting the verdict after 20 rounds. Five months later, they went six in Chicago, again with Walcott the winner. Only four days after, they fought in Utica, and again Creedon waged a worthy battle, yet once more, at the end of 20, Joe's hand went up.

Joe Choynski

A couple of years before his 1946 passing, Jack Johnson paid a visit to New York's Madison Square Garden and found Nat Fleischer in his office at work on a story about great fighters he had known. A gab session commenced, and Jack regaled his friend with opinions of his own about fighters and promoters worth note.

Who among the older men, asked Nat, could *punch*? Like a bolt from the sky, Joe Choynski came to Jack's mind. Though a supermiddleweight on today's fighting scale, this Polish Jew with his conspicuous mop of flaxen hair was a terror to men of every size during the decade of the '90s.

"Blond Joe socked me with a left-hander that staggered me," recalled Johnson of their 1901 meeting, "and then he let fly a left hook that caught me on the point of the chin and the floor came right up and kissed me. I came to my senses just as the referee was finishing the count.... I didn't get up like a lot of our present day fighters do, to make the public believe that they want to fight some more. I'd had enough and was willing to admit it."[8] Any man in his place, said Jack, would have fared the same. As it turned out, he and Choynski were arrested afterward for their activity and were carted off to the nearest jail. While they did time, young Jack got valuable tutoring from the veteran and was a far savvier fighter when he again breathed free air.

When writers make note of Walcott, they often count his greatest performance to be against Joe. As noted earlier, Choynski fought a hellacious draw with Bob Fitzsimmons when Bob was the middleweight champion. A ring immortal, he was known also for his early rivalry with Jim Corbett and his 20-round draw with a young Jim Jeffries in 1898. When the match was made with him and Walcott, there was criticism of the parties involved, on the grounds that Choynski, a world-class fighter some ten inches taller and 30 pounds heavier, would have an absurd advantage.

They entered the ring on February 23, 1900, at the Broadway A.C., with the Californian favored at 5–1. At the bell, looking ridiculously small, Walcott sprang from his corner, getting home with a right to the midsection and a left upstairs. Choynski fell hard. He took a count of nine before rising and hit the canvas two more times before the round was out. While the Polish fighter could hit, pound for pound, as well as any man around, he was not used to punching down, and he had trouble now. In the second, when he staggered Joe with a right, it was his only success.

In the third and fourth, Walcott plunged ahead, giving the California fighter all he could handle. On it went for two more frames. "The Californian," noted one report, "was groggy when he came up for the seventh round, and after he received a right on the wind and two lefts on the face, he staggered in an evidently helpless manner."[9] When Walcott sent both hands to his jaw, Choynski went down thoroughly whipped. The result left spectators dumbfounded, and only after Walcott went across the ring to shake Joe's hand did they give out with the customary yells.

Indeed it was shocking—Choynski himself for several years had enjoyed the reputation of a giant killer against full-fledged heavyweights. A few years later, he would knock out coming champion Jack Johnson with the punch that Johnson would describe to Fleischer. Then again, as to Joe's collapse against Walcott, there may have been extenuating circumstance. Seven days before, he had defeated Peter Maher in a six-round bout. On leaving the building, he had slipped on an icy sidewalk and fractured a rib against a lamppost. He then had sought to withdraw from a scheduled bout with Kid McCoy at the Broadway, but was told that he needed to come to New York before it could be canceled. By the time Joe arrived, McCoy himself had bowed out, and the club had obtained Walcott as a substitute. When they offered him 75 percent of the gate, win or lose, he decided to take the offer. (Choynski, as Fleischer notes, asked that all bets be canceled before he entered the ring. While the club managers made a promise, they later tipped off their gambling contacts, and the insiders cleaned up nicely on the long odds favoring the bigger man.)

On May 4, 1900, Walcott met Mysterious Billy for the fourth time, this one taking place at the Broadway A.C. In this fight Smith showed that he was game to the core, standing up to the best that Walcott threw and rallying back even after he had been banged from pillar to post. From the tenth round on, Smith was holding one hand to his side to protect a broken rib.

(The pain was so great that his corner, at one point, asked the club doctor to inject Billy with cocaine to keep him in the bout.) Feeling maybe a twinge of pity for the man who had fought him tooth and nail this many times, Walcott actually eased up on his attack. But in the late rounds, no quarter was given either way, and Joe himself was bleeding hard from nose and mouth. In the 24th, Walcott smashed open Billy's swelled left ear, and continued to hammer him to the end. At the bout's close, "both men shook hands very good naturedly," Smith's body splotched with his own blood and his face ravaged. There was no contesting the referee's verdict in Joe's favor.[10]

More Big Fights — and the Title

As noted at the beginning of this chapter, Walcott was an uneven performer, invincible one night and thoroughly beatable the next. On August 27, 1900, he met Tommy West in a fight in Madison Square Garden that would always have a dubious air. In this fight, Walcott, entering the ring a sound favorite, had things his way from the start, knocking West around and bloodying him plenty. Then, at the bell for the twelfth round, he refused to leave his corner.

"What's the matter?" asked O'Rourke, suddenly horrified.

"I'se broke mah arm, Mistah Tom," wailed the fighter. "'Deed I has, sir! It ain't no use of me tryin' to go on!"[11]

While those present figured that he could beat West, at this point, even with one arm, he quit then and there, and the referee had no choice but to award it to Tommy. Believing that the Barbados fighter had bowed out deliberately, he made no pretense otherwise. Now the arena was alive with rage, and with yells of "Then call off *the bets*, too!" But after a fast exchange between managers, referee, and attending fight promoters, it was announced that no one present had the authority to make such a ruling.

In the dressing room, club physician T.F. DeNaouley examined Walcott's arm. Feeling the joints up and down, he announced to the fighter, "Walcott, there's absolutely nothing the matter with your arm." But Joe was resolute, saying that the appendage was "hurted," and he would admit to nothing else.

Though some saw it as cowardice, another explanation is more likely — during this period, as Fleischer notes, boxing was more corrupt than at any time since the transition to gloves. There were occasions when fighters and managers had to do exactly what they were told by underworld figures if they wanted to remain active. When he asked O'Rourke about this fight later, Nat remarked, he was told that "Walcott didn't dare win the fight." The arm, said Tom, wasn't hurt, but if he had kept fighting, "the winner would have gone to the morgue a little later on, and I'd probably have been [lying] nice, peaceful, and natural on the next slab!"[12] Thus Walcott's performance, or lack of it, may stand actually as a reminder of the dark influence of gamblers and their ilk that was prevalent at the time.

One can only estimate the impact of such circumstances upon the record of a fighter a century after the fact. By the reckoning of Fleischer, in any case, Joe's seven fights in 1901 were against men who each would "rule the roost" if fighting in the modern day (meaning then the late 1930s). The first of these was with Kid Carter at Hartford on January 17. On this occasion Walcott again met an opponent who showed him no fear. It was a rough fight, ebb and flow, until Joe was disqualified in the 19th for repeated head butting.

When they met again on October 15, at Mechanic's Pavilion in San Francisco, Carter provided an encore by stopping the Barbados fighter with a right hand to the pit of the stomach that sent Walcott to his knees for the count. (They would clash twice more in 1903 with Joe winning each time in 15 frames.)

But the rest of 1901 saw Joe at his best, and the year would end with the most joyous win of his career. On March 21 he stopped contender Charley McKeever in the sixth round with a blow to the solar plexus that practically cut McKeever in two; he also prevailed over 15 rounds with a miner named Jack Bonner in a bloody war at Bridgeport.

"There was not," observed one source present, "a dull moment in the entire fight. Walcott cut out the pace in every round, his superabundance of confidence ... manifested by his frequent laughs and sallies when he would accuse Bonner of holding."[13] Joe followed up with a great performance against George Gardner at San Francisco on September 27. Gardner, who would reign briefly as light-heavyweight champion a few years later, was touted at the time as a coming middleweight ruler. At the end of 20, he was sorely beaten.

Walcott's most savage fight that year was on November 28 in Baltimore with Young Peter Jackson. A fierce episode, going 20 rounds, it was another of those rock-on-rock contests, plentiful in the day, pitting one much-avoided black hitter against another. When Joe got home in the early rounds, he did damage, and Peter, solid as ebony, rebounded. In the sixth round, hard punches with both hands brought blood streaming from Walcott's gashed mouth.

At this point, Joe came back hammer and tongs: "He hit him so hard above the heart that Peter was groggy when the bell sounded. The gong saved Jackson, who was still weak when he came out for the next session. A right to the mouth cut Peter's lips and the blood flowed freely. Then a left closed Peter's right eye. Joe followed his advantage and crashed a right to the ear that almost took that organ off. It swelled, and the next punch caused the claret to come forth in a steady stream."[14]

By the fifteenth, the beating had become so bad that police intervened. Yet Peter, with astounding gameness, insisted that the fight continue. For five more rounds he hung in, and it went to a decision in Walcott's favor.

On December 18, Joe closed out 1901 with a performance to remember when he finally got his shot at the welterweight title. Matched against champion Rube Ferns at Fort Erie, Ontario, he left no doubt as to who was best in that division. By now he had been fighting more than nine years, and finally getting his chance, he wasted no time when the bell rang.

Ferns played his best hand, working a jab from the outside, but in no time the shorter man's strength came to the fore. By the end of one round, Rube was in trouble. In the third, Joe tore into his man and sent him to the ropes. A right hand had the champion dazed late in the round. In the fifth, another right sent him down. Ferns, a warrior to the end, hauled himself up with the aid of the ropes, at which point, "Walcott went at him like a whirlwind and sent both hands all over him, and as Rube staggered about the ring, Referee McBride stepped between them ... declaring Walcott the winner."[15]

It was an unusual situation. Normally contenders trail a champion like starved dogs after red meat. Now, against Joe, hardly anyone dared to offer a challenge! In 1902, all but one of his foes were bigger men. Fred Russell stood better than six feet and weighed well over 200 pounds. Yet Walcott took it to him and managed a six-round draw. That year he fought a draw and a no-decision in return bouts with Jackson, and went six rounds in a no-decision with Philadelphia Jack O'Brien. In England, he fought Tommy West in a 15-rounder, winning a decision. Then, in October, he was forced to quit in a bout with Frank Childs, who gave young heavyweight Jack Johnson some tough bouts in the same period. Though Joe held his own with Childs for two rounds, he quit in his corner before round three, claiming an arm injury. (While it was rumored that Walcott had quit because of the difficulty of the fight, his inactivity for five months afterward might lend credence to the claim.)

In 1903, Walcott fought 16 times, losing but once in a 15-rounder to heavyweight Sandy Ferguson, no soft touch even for men his own size. Joe's outstanding fight was a 15-round battle near the end of the year with a black hitter named Larry Temple, who gave him a fierce time from the opening bell.

By now Walcott had separated from O'Rourke, and Tom, as it turned out, was working this night in Larry's corner. During the bout, O'Rourke began needling Joe, adding insult to the injury that Joe was getting from Larry. But as rounds passed, Walcott went into overdrive, pounding Temple and paying back his former manager with words of his own before being proclaimed the winner.

On April 29 of the following year, Walcott lost on a foul in 20 rounds in San Francisco to Aaron Brown, whose fighting name was Dixie Kid. While there was much commotion as to the rightness of that verdict, the referee's decision was upheld, and the Kid was the new champion. Still, Walcott continued to enjoy practically universal recognition as the premier fighter in the division.[16] Before 1904 was out, he would fight spirited battles, each ending in a draw, with Temple, Joe Gans, and up-and-coming Sam Langford. Walcott, Sam would later say, hit as hard as any man alive, and had a head and fists of iron. (These latter two fights will be noted in chapters ahead.)

Later Fights

Walcott had money now, and he indulged himself in every impulse, sporting diamond jewelry and a wad of green wherever he went. But this habit, as it turned out, would factor into his downfall. For now a friend suggested that Joe get a gun in order to ward off troublemakers. When Walcott picked up a handgun, it became another shining bauble.

One night, bragging of the piece's destructive power to his friend Nelson Hall at a Boston dance club, he accidentally discharged it. Two bullets ripped through Joe's right hand and into Nelson's chest, dropping him dead where he fell. In the aftermath, though he was exonerated of blame, Walcott was beside himself. In addition, the hand was so much damaged that it was feared he would lose several fingers, or even the hand itself. Though a skilled surgeon was able to save the fingers, injury to tendon and muscle tissue made it hard for Joe to make a tight fist, and it reduced his use of the hand thereafter.

Several months later, he returned to action, never with the same success as before. After registering a loss, win, and draw in three fights, Walcott faced up-and-coming welterweight Billy "Honey" Mellody on October 16, 1906, at Chelsea. Each man looked strong at 145, and Walcott came near a

Joe Gans, right, squares off with the great Barbados Joe Walcott before their September 30, 1904, battle. It was a contest lasting 20 rounds, with Gans holding his own against a man who fought at around 140 pounds and was avoided even by heavyweights.

quick win when he dropped Honey for a count of nine in the opening round. Yet Mellody survived and he became stronger. Despite 2–1 odds, going in, that he could not last eight rounds, he turned up the heat in the latter half of the fight and got the nod after fifteen.

Billy's manager Johnny Mooney announced that his man was the new welterweight champion, and New England writers supported him in the claim, bypassing Dixie Kid in their consideration. The next month, Walcott faced Mellody in a return, this time with a contracted weight of 142, in order to speak to claims that the last bout was fought over the limit. The outcome was similar, Walcott having it his way through the first five rounds. Then Mellody came on again, dropping Joe to his knees with a right hand in the sixth. From there it was all Billy, and when Walcott broke his right hand in the ninth, it was all over but the formality. In the twelfth, Walcott was done.

By now Mellody had overwhelming support in his claim to the title, as Dixie Kid restricted his efforts mostly to low-profile names around Philadelphia. Walcott was finished as a contender. Knowing no business but fighting, he lingered for a few more years, getting knocked out by Larry Temple in ten rounds in 1908. Following that he had ten more fights, ending his career in 1911.

When his ring days were over, Joe made his way as a firefighter on a steam freighter, and later as a porter at the Majestic Theatre in New York. He worked also as a handyman around Madison Square Garden. In 1932 he was committed to the Bellevue Hospital in New York after being taken comatose one day from his Harlem flat. On being treated for arteriosclerosis, he was released.

An Amazing Discovery

Early in August of 1935, New York City mayor Jimmy Walker learned that Walcott was destitute. He wanted the fighter found and brought to his office. Not long afterward two police officers located Walcott in the Bowery. When they tried to approach, he struck an instinctive pose. "Come a step more," he said, drawing back his right fist, "and I'll smack both yo' heads off."

The men got it across to him that this was a social call, and that the mayor wanted to see him. Learning that "Ol' James" was behind this visit, Walcott instantly brightened. Walker called Garden president Bill Carey and persuaded him to put Joe on the payroll. As "head porter" Walcott pulled down $35 a week.

The position required little of Joe but posing, on occasion, broom in hand, for photographers, and the Ranger hockey team dressing room gave him a place to sleep. After about a month, however, he disappeared. Rumors that he was in Philadelphia, or in Cincinnati, did not pan out. But years later, a devout fan named Bill Cereghin in Defiance, Ohio, when learning of the situation, became determined to find out what had happened. He did every scrap of research on the fighter possible, cranking out letters in the process to anyone who might have a connection.

By the late '40s, Cereghin had centered upon Massillon, Ohio, as an area of promise. Visits to the surrounding towns, studies of burial records, and conversations with local undertakers at last yielded one lead. There was a party who recalled a man fitting Walcott's description who worked in the town of Dalton (population about 600) around 1935. On his summer vacation in 1955, Cereghin drove to the village. Entering the only cemetery around, he searched for a headstone with the fighter's name. Then, walking disappointed back to his car, Bill spotted one rough old sort digging a grave in a corner of the yard. On hearing Walcott's description, and knowing of his boxing career, the digger led Cereghin to the place where the fighter had been buried. He referred him to an authority in Dalton who knew, as it turned out, the whole story. Walcott, Cereghin was told, had met his end some 20 years earlier, being killed instantly when he was hit by a musician driving a Model A Ford. For lack of information, Joe had been buried as "John Doe, Negro, 1935."

* * *

"Joe Walcott," said Jack Johnson to Nat Fleischer in that office conversation noted earlier, "was the greatest fighter that ever laced on a glove and you can lay all you have on that statement." Nat, he maintained, might live to be a hundred without seeing Joe's like again.

So had ended, 20 years before Cereghin's discovery, the life of a man whom other experts, including Tad Dorgan, Tom O'Rourke, Dan Morgan, and Jimmy Johnston had likewise called "the greatest pound for pound fighter who ever lived." Cereghin managed also to make the acquaintance of a bartender who had been perhaps the last person to talk to Walcott before his death.

"I knew him very well," the man recalled, "He acted like a pug, always bouncing around the place like he had taken one too many in the head. He liked to tell about his old fights and the good times he used to have."[17]

V

The Old Master:
Joe Gans

Gans has learned two things in the boxing game that have been accomplished but by few.... He is never out of position, and he has mastered the art of hitting with both hands at any angle ... each "clout" carries with it every ounce of his body.
The Baltimore American, August 29, 1906

When the great lightweight and junior welterweight champion Tony Canzoneri was asked, in his later years, to provide a list of the ten best lightweights of all time, he said that he would confine his choices to men whom he had seen firsthand, with one exception — Joe Gans. Such was the reverence for Gans, among those who had seen or had fought him, that Canzoneri would not hold the Baltimore legend to that requirement. In making this decision, he leaned to the advice of a sly old pug who had seen Gans plenty.

"Abe Attell," said Canzoneri, "whose opinion I respect, saw Joe box several times, and ... boxed with Gans himself, [and] said to me, 'Tony, if you don't say that Joe Gans was the greatest lightweight who ever lived, you're going to look like a damned fool.'"[1] Apparently Tony thought well of this opinion, for he ranked Gans the greatest of all in the division. (Rounding out Canzoneri's list behind Gans in order were Sammy Mandell, Benny Leonard, Freddy Welsh, Barney Ross, Billy Petrolle, Sid Terris, Henry Armstrong, Ruby Goldstein, and Joe Mandot.)

Born in Baltimore on November 25, 1874, Gans began fighting as a professional in 1891. He would end his career in 1909, dying of consumption (the going name for tuberculosis) the following year at the age of 35. In that time he is credited with having fought upward of 150 battles, and estimate has it that he could have engaged in a few more.

A Learner

Who was this slender, quiet figure who continues even now to elicit fierce admiration? Gans, as more than one writer has remarked, was a man of both talent and sensitivity. Kind of heart, reserved in manner, he won respect in a time when black fighters received it seldom, and often got it in backhanded fashion when they got it at all. (To cite one index involving Gans himself, featherweight champion Young Corbett, recalling Joe's personal kindness, once bestowed on him the honor of being "the whitest black man that ever lived."[2]) He was generous with his help when approached by young fighters in the gym, and he was possessed of a deep sense of fair play.

While it might be stretching things to call him a saint, Gans was like few in the game. Quiet, sometimes brooding, he

Joe Gans, right, and the formidable Young Peter Jackson, circa 1902. Jackson, namesake of a great black Australian heavyweight, engaged Joe Walcott, Sam Langford, and Philadelphia Jack O'Brien in furious contests during his career. Gans continues even today to top some lists as the greatest lightweight of all time.

was in some way otherworldly. At least one scribe has ventured to describe him in spiritual terms: "In appearance and demeanor," writes Ted Carroll, "there was a sort of *pathos* about Gans which had a mystic quality."[3] Moreover, "There was never the slightest suggestion of savagery in his boxing. The brooding, doleful expression never left his face. He could seem indolent, at times, in the ring, yet at the slightest opening, his punches were delivered with deadly, dispassionate precision."

In various ways, Gans was seen as an exception. Robert Edgren, notes Carroll, a contemporary white author not known for generosity toward black athletes, described Gans as being a sportsman and a gentleman. He was also a ring genius. There are languages, observes Norman Mailer, "other

than words, languages of symbol and languages of nature. There are languages of the body. And prize-fighting is one of them."[4] As to style, Joe was
a blend of artistry and power, a forerunner, of sorts, of coming dance mas-
ters like Ray Robinson and Muhammad Ali. "To this day," state his most
recent biographers, "he represents the gold standard when it comes to
pugilistic form."[5] Yet his movement was not so much a bounce as a glide,
a natural flow of ease and grace that stood him well in a long contest.

He was also a student. There are fighters, as there are practitioners in
every field, who are open to truth where they find it and who never rest
content with what knowledge they have. In his youth, Gans sought out
fighters who were local, studying them for anything, good or bad, that
would add to his game. In time, when Bob Fitzsimmons appeared at a Baltimore theater, Joe's eyes never left him. For several weeks, he trailed Bob
from town to town, gleaning insight from Fitz's "all comers" routine. Thus
he saw firsthand the value of body punching, and the left hook with which
Bob would eventually win the heavyweight title. He beheld also the great
fighter's "six inch punch," a straight right hand that sounded the knell when
it reached an opponent's chin. When he was able, Gans took comparable
notes on Jim Corbett, Kid McCoy, and George Dixon. Day by day he prac-
ticed leverage and timing until he was a puncher to reckon with.

A Rough Education

But for his nimble fingers, wrote Nat Fleischer, there was nothing in
the early days to distinguish this brown-skinned oyster-shucking youth
from his neighborhood peers. But one night a local theater manager, a man
named Kernan, included a boxing show in his fare. Gans was persuaded to
take part in a "battle royal" that put several fighters in the ring at once and
declared the last man standing to be the winner: "Joe couldn't box then,
but he could step around lively. He discovered that he possessed a good
punch with either hand. In other words, he was a "natural" fighter. What
other pugs acquire, by dint of long and painful experience, came to him as
a matter of course."[6] This event, which was a favorite among patrons, could
become a rough exercise indeed, as competing young African Americans
were sometimes blindfolded at the start to further enliven the spectacle. By
some measure of luck and agility, Gans survived the show and caught the
eye of some observers. He also gained confidence when a couple of foes bit
the dust by way of his right hand.

After a few amateur wins, he was approached by Al Herford, owner of
a restaurant in downtown Baltimore. Herford, a boxing fan and a keen

judge of talent, had chanced to see Joe, at the age of eleven, dust off a kid from the neighborhood in a street fight. He had not forgotten that display, and now he invited Joe to come under his wing. Gans's response, characteristic of his makeup, was to downplay his assets. Though he had done all right so far, he feared that Herford might lose his investment. "That's my funeral, not yours," replied Al, and thus he and Joe joined forces.

In three years, Gans was a full-fledged lightweight, plying his trade in the fighting hotbed that was Baltimore. He attracted wide attention in 1895 when he stopped Walter Edgerton, the ever-game "Kentucky Rosebud" who had given George Dixon hard fights not long before. After a ten-round draw with Young Griffo, he was at work without a letup, meeting the best in his division.

In March of 1896, it appeared, Joe would get a shot at lightweight champion Frank Erne when Erne's opponent Dal Hawkins dropped out of their scheduled fight. But when Joe's wife passed away, leaving him with two small children, the situation changed and the fight did not materialize. In October, he dropped a disputed decision to the hard-hitting Hawkins, and he lost again, in the following year, to Bobby Dobbs.

In Dobbs, Gans met a ringman whose name has since been all but lost to the fight public. Yet Bobby was among the best of his time, another of those black wayfarers who took what employment he could find, and who entered the ring, by some estimates, as many as a thousand times before his career was over. On this occasion, only six days after a 15-round draw with Griffo, Joe went 20 hard ones with the veteran at Brooklyn's Greenpoint Sporting Club. Dobbs's superior strength, an advantage that older fighters often enjoy over less experienced foes, showed itself in the final rounds.[7] Dobbs's career, as best it can be determined, lasted until 1914, when at 44 he was stopped by a fighter named Lew Williams at Savannah, Georgia. After the World War, he taught boxing in training camps around the country, and developed numerous fighters in gymnasiums in New York and Philadelphia.

As for Joe, every fight, win or not, was a step forward. Some years ago, handlers of lightweight champion Roberto Duran, one of the greatest fighters of recent decades, took note of how he not only could hit, but could place his shots where they did the most. It was an art that Gans, too, perfected. Typical of the going commentary is the statement of columnist Ben Benjamin: "There never was a fighter who could block with such skill and precision as Gans. He is a marvel at stopping, using either hand with equal facility. He rarely wastes a blow, his judgment on distance being almost perfect."[8] In months ahead, he won over critics from San Francisco to New

York, gaining celebrity when he fought front-line contender Billy Ernst in August of 1898 at Coney Island. In the opening seconds, Billy, outweighing his young foe by a pound and a half at 133, caught him with hard shots, but soon Joe regrouped and landed punches that shook his man to the heels. Ernst went down and out in the eleventh.

So did Joe now arrive in a division thick with talent. Three months later, he won a 25-rounder over Kid McPartland, and by 1899, he was seeking a world title bout with Kid Lavigne. He was close to getting his wish when he met cagy veteran George "Elbows" McFadden for 25 rounds at the Broadway Athletic Club on April 14. In this fight, Gans suffered one of the few losses in the mature phase of his career, and before a recurring weight grind and chronic lung trouble would take their toll.

Odds of 4 to 1 on Joe seemed right, and all the more so when McFadden tipped the beam at only 127 to 133 for the fighter who was already being called the Master. From the opening minute, Gans seemed to have things under control. By the end of the second round, McFadden had been shaken by his right hand. According to one source, "The two men had not been sparring more than a minute when Gans' superior knowledge was apparent. He was cool, calculating, [and] shifty, and blocked with consummate ease the few blows that McFadden aimed at his head."[9]

Figuring that there was no winning a boxing match, George began to slug. By the sixth, he was getting through, and the crowd was cheering his gameness. After 13, Joe's lips were gashed and he was bleeding badly from the nose. McFadden, sensing that the fight was his, scored heavily with punches to the body and an occasional left-hand haymaker upstairs. In the 23rd, a killing left to the body and a right to the jaw sent Gans tottering and down, face forward, blood running from his mouth. He was dragged to his corner without a count.

It was one of the most thrilling bouts ever seen in the city, and the two were matched for 25 more on July 28, 1899, at the Broadway. Here, as he would often, Gans demonstrated his capacity to learn. At the end, he had scored several knockdowns, and though it was ruled a draw, most thought that he had gotten the better of it. Gans, said a *Police Gazette* columnist afterward, was clearly entitled to the win, and the referee, in rendering an even verdict, "displayed deficiency of judgment which cannot be accounted for."[10] Elsewhere it was said that he had hit his man "when and where he pleased," scoring knockdowns in the 9th, 22nd, and 24th rounds without taking a fall himself. As noted above, he won the third meeting without an argument, and when they met yet again on June 27, 1902, the fight was all Gans—by one account it was not so much a fight as an "assault" with

McFadden's corner stopping the contest in the third round.[11] When they met yet one more time that October, only McFadden's courage kept him in it to the end.

Gans closed out 1899 with two more victories and a six-round draw with Kid McPartland. But another misfortune was in store for the Baltimore fighter on March 23, 1900, when he met Frank Erne at the Broadway. For eleven rounds, Joe had the upper hand. Then, in the twelfth, Erne landed a left downstairs and a right on the chops. As Gans sought a clinch, they collided, and Erne's head nailed him over the left eye, opening a gash that shot blood down the side of his face.[12] When referee Charlie White stepped between them to check the injury, Gans said without hesitation, "I quit." Were the fight today, the bout would be stopped and the scorecards consulted. But this was a different time. White motioned for the men to continue.

Gans refused. While it was a sensible decision, neither referee nor scribes would give him credit. It was said that he had "quit," and suspicions were raised as to his mettle. Furious at this, and at the rumor that he had folded merely to collaborate in a betting scheme, he begged for a chance with Erne in the ring again. They would meet in 1902, in a fight billed for the lightweight championship of the world, with a weight limit of 136 pounds. But other bouts would come first. In April (remarkably, this was only ten days after the Erne bout), he entered the ring again and knocked out tough competitor Chicago Jack Daly.

On May 25, 1900, he had another go with Dal Hawkins. The last time out, Hawkins had reached him plenty with his left hand, and for this fight Gans spent time in the gym drilling himself on that one point. He entered the ring at the Broadway ready to avenge the loss of three and a half years earlier. It was a brief bout, yet one that had the crowd on its feet and yelling from the opening minute when Gans, despite his caution, again caught Hawkins's left hook, falling flat and nearly suffering a knockout.

Thinking his man ripe, Hawkins cut loose. In a furious exchange, a Gans right hand had him down and nearly out. When Dal got his bearings, he struck back, and the two fighters went to their corners with the crowd raising the roof. In the second, Hawkins took a right hand on the ear that made him wobble. Seizing the chance, Gans landed a hook and a scorching right that caught Dal on the chin, sending him to the canvas for the toll of ten, a sweet sound to the winner, still stunned by punches he had taken.

The one real scandal of Gans's career would come that December when he met featherweight champion Terry McGovern. It was an odd pairing, and despite McGovern's stirring success (see the chapter ahead) at 126, it looked like a mismatch. But it figured to be a fight while it lasted.

Instead it was a quick sideshow, with Gans falling several times fast and early. The fans, who were not buying it, reacted with outrage. Joe would be asked about the fight many times in years ahead, and though his performance likely owed to Herford's gambling debts, he would never cease to regret what happened. Gans, according to Charles Samuels, confessed to newsmen about six months before his 1906 bout with Battling Nelson that he had taken a dive against McGovern, and had agreed to "carry" Britt prior to their fight. In saying this he implicated Al Herford and both Jimmy and Willus Britt. When all three men denounced him as a liar, "The Old Master swore with tears in his eyes that he would never fake another fight as long as he lived."[13]

In 1901 Joe went undefeated in 14 fights, including two knockout wins over Bobby Dobbs. He stayed on the winning track into spring of the following year, and met Erne again on May 12.

The Rematch

Years afterward, Nat Fleischer would recall how welterweight champion Jimmy McLarnin had once visited the *Ring* offices and spied a copy of Fleischer's primer *How to Box*. To his surprise, Jimmy lifted it from the shelf and began poring through it. When Nat made light of its value to a man of his caliber, the fighter replied that such a work might always have in it one insight new to even a seasoned professional.

Gans, as noted earlier, was such a learner — a pioneer technician who helped to move boxing out of its Dark Age. Fleischer, in describing Joe's preparation for the return bout with Erne, relates an instructive story. Gans, he said, had noticed in their first go that Erne had habit of feinting, every so often, and drawing back about twelve inches before throwing a punch. Now, working with Harry Lenny at the gym for the coming bout, Gans proposed that they work together to find a way to deal with it.

"Mr. Lenny, you have a left hand like Mr. Erne. Will you keep on trying it with me? I want to sort of study out something."

Lenny agreed, and they spent a week, Lenny working the left hand one way and another, and Joe devising a counter. When they were done, Gans continued on his own, in front of a mirror, playing first his role and then Erne's. One day he bid Lenny to try the left hand with his best effort. When Lenny did as asked, Gans countered with a perfect right to the jaw.

"That's good enough," announced Gans, pulling off the gloves. "I've got Mr. Erne's number now. That lead will beat him."

Sure enough, the first time that Erne made his erratic move, Joe hooked a right hand to a spot a few inches back of his chin, and the fight was over. In less than a round, Gans had annexed the lightweight crown with a clean knockout. It was, at the time, the fastest conclusion to a lightweight championship battle ever recorded.[14]

* * *

No man, asserts Fleischer, ever bested a tougher field than did Gans in working his way to the top. In the process, he demonstrated the ability to dish out punishment and to take it, when need be, with cast-iron resolve. The dynamite-punching Dal Hawkins had him on the floor in each of their contests before being knocked out. McFadden had been a challenge from hell, until Gans figured out an answer. After his loss to McGovern in March of 1900, Joe went unbeaten for three years, proving himself a boxer and a puncher without peer in the division. Following his win over Erne, he defended the lightweight title several times, scoring knockouts of both McFadden and Kid McPartland.

A rare loss came when he faced the young pride of Boston, Sam Langford, in a bout that saw him concede both size and youth to a fast-growing phenomenon who would one day trade leather with heavyweight immortals Jack Johnson and Joe Jeannette. After winning the opening rounds, jarring Langford on occasion with a right hand, he began to give ground in the exchanges and ended up dropping a fifteen-round decision.

By now the high-ranking Jimmy Britt had challenged Gans to a fight at 133, and when Joe turned it down, Jimmy became heir to the title in the eyes of some in the boxing circle. It was apparent now, in fact, that Gans would fare nicely at welterweight. Thus he ventured into that class and took on the cream of its talent — Jack Blackburn, Joe Walcott, Mike Twin Sullivan, Willie Lewis, and others, facing some contenders two and three times.

These contests could be withering. On September 30, 1904, he met Walcott for a battle in which he scaled 137 and the Barbados fighter 141. The two men went the distance in a 20-round spectacle. Much of the way Gans scored with his jab from the outside, but when the shorter man closed the distance there came a slam-bang trade. In the 16th round an overhand right had Joe in peril. So it went into the twentieth, Walcott banging the body and Gans using his left for all he was worth. The result was a draw.[15]

Jimmy Britt

Many accounts of Gans's career make reference to his likely involvement with gamblers, and his agreement, now and again, to throw a fight, or to modify its natural outcome. If so, there was surely extenuating circumstance: In a number of cases, recalled lightweight champion (1912–1914) Willie Ritchie, Gans had to do as he was told, if he wanted to fight again, by various controlling interests: "They were crooks, they framed fights, and being Negro the poor guy had to follow orders, otherwise he'd have starved to death."[16]

His first fight with Jimmy Britt is one example. While Gans could now hold his own with any man on Earth at 150, there was still money to be made at 133. Free spender as he was, it was powerful incentive, but the effort would eventually be his undoing. He agreed to meet Britt.

It was a strange deal, struck with a dubious element, with Gans being promised beforehand by his own manager that if he let Jimmy make a decent showing, the California fighter would soon "foul out" to give Joe the victory. Yet from the opening bell, it was a bruising go, with Britt committing fouls that started in the second round with a wicked left below the belt.[17] There was no disqualification, and in the fourth round Gans, probably wondering what game was afoot, went to the canvas from a right to the body. He rose and fell again, and this time Britt struck him while down. When Gans got up and complained to referee Ed Graney, Britt rushed past Graney on the attack. Gans went to his knees once more, and incredibly Britt hit him again in the face, prompting Graney to wave a finger and say that one more such move would end the fight.

One more? Joe's seconds were on the ring platform, demanding that he be awarded the fight. When Graney refused, they stayed there, and a riot was in the offing. In the fifth, a right to the head dropped Gans to his knees. Then, instead of leaving well enough alone, Britt stood over his foe and belted him right and left, and Gans voiced another complaint. Britt threw more punches, and Graney at last kept his promise, awarding the bout to the fallen fighter.

Incredibly, Jimmy tried to go after Gans once more, and failing that, he turned and cut loose on Graney! Ed, who could handle himself pretty well, punched back, and the two men wound up on the floor, scuffling amidst pandemonium as police sought to pry them apart.

It has been said that no good deed goes unpunished, and this might be an example. Whether or not it was a good deed, it certainly did serve the interest of Herford and of Britt, and it was likely the one feasible choice Gans had at the time. Had he gone straight after Britt, he probably would have taken care of him in sure fashion. But he might never have fought at the championship level again.

In fact, if one wants an index of the haphazard nature of the game, in those days, there is a story told by longtime observer George Pardy wherein Britt was once locked in a tough 20-rounder with Charley Seiger. As Charley came on in the final round, with Britt tiring, the lights in the arena suddenly went out. When they came back on, Seiger was lying on the ring floor, out cold, by courtesy of a blackjack applied to his head by someone from the other side — at which point, says Pardy, the referee declared Britt the winner![18]

And now, for Joe's cooperation in his fight with Jimmy, a price came due. Media coverage of the fight, and editorial comment in the months following, was heavily on the side of the fair-haired San Franciscan, making it out that he had overpowered Gans and had lost only on a technicality. The result was a virtual new line of the lightweight championship, relegating the greatest fighter in the world to the division's back burner.

By the end of 1904, Joe was in financial trouble, heading back to the East Coast in what might have been the loneliest time of his life. His wife was now suing him for divorce, and he and Herford were headed toward a split. In September of the next year, he fought a 15-round draw with ranking welterweight Mike Twin Sullivan. In January of 1906, when he and Sullivan met again, Joe cranked up the volume. In the 15th round, by one ringside account, "A dusky right arm swung over with electric quickness" to the back of Sullivan's ear and a volley of punches sent him down for the count.[19] In March they met a third time, Gans winning by a knockout in ten.

The Durable Dane

On June 29, Gans went six hard rounds to a no-decision with Jack Blackburn, getting bloodied by Blackburn's wicked left jab before it was done. The following month, he went 20 rounds to a decision win in his fourth encounter with another black fighter named Dave Holly in Seattle.

Holly, bull-strong and ready, was routinely avoided by front-runners in the division. Afterward, playing to the scribes, he insisted that he had been robbed. A local account, it might be noted, did indicate otherwise, maintaining that Gans had dominated the fight, especially in the late rounds. According to the *Seattle Times*, "When referee James W. Morrison waved the men back to their corners after the last gong sounded and tapped Gans on the shoulder to indicate [that] he had won, Holly stood exhausted ... his face covered with blood, [surrounded by] his seconds, who were bringing him back to earth."[20]

Still, there did exist doubt now as to what Gans had left. His last four fights had gone the distance, and some wondered if he could yet deliver. But one big fight was in demand. The win over Britt two years ago, believed

Joe, had entitled him to the lightweight crown, if there had ever been any doubt. But the claim was disputed by another fighter, one Oscar Matthew "Battling" Nelson.

Born in Copenhagen on the Danish Independence Day of June 5 in 1882, Nelson was nonetheless, by his own reckoning, "an American in every sense of the word." He came of age in the Scandinavian community of Hegewisch, Illinois, where at 13, he was employed as an ice supplier — cutting, packing, and hauling, and netting the sum of 90 cents for his first six grueling days of work. By his own reckoning Nelson was no "parlor" fighter — he believed that a real fight meant a fight all day long, if necessary, and until one man was on the canvas. Unequaled perhaps in ring history for sheer staying power, the Durable Dane insisted that he was the rightful champion following his 1905 defeat of Britt, albeit after Jimmy's fight with Gans.

In Nelson, Gans was meeting a wild man, one who thrived on exchanges whatever they cost. A natural lightweight, Bat took on opponents of every size and had been in the game since entering into carnival competition in his puberty. In beating Jimmy, he had reversed a points loss in the prior year against a man whom he resented for his more polished demeanor and his dress — aside from his own title aspirations, said Nelson, "My desire to lick Sir James Edward Britt was because he wore a high hat and a Prince Albert coat." Britt, he admitted, was a formidable foe, with a left hand, a hook-uppercut to the body, that was one of the best punches that had ever been used in the ring.[21]

It thus figured to be a donnybrook, and it was. The fight brought forth a literary rapture from the great novelist Jack London, who covered the bout for the *San Francisco Examiner*. The outcome, said Jack, was largely foretold in the first round, when Britt threw half a dozen blows that caught Bat coming straight ahead. Bat kept coming, and when he landed on Jimmy, the effect was dramatic. "Nelson," summarized the author, "is a fighting animal. Britt is an intelligent animal with fighting proclivities."[22] Britt, a scientific fighter, was up against an *abysmal brute* in Nelson — a man possessed fundamentally of "the basic life that resides deeper than the brain and the intellect in living things. It is itself the very staff of life — movement; and it is saturated with a blind and illimitable desire to exist. This desire it expresses by movement."[23] This quality, London maintained, we see at times, as in the rage of a Berserker or in a fit of fierce anger. We see it in a horse that is tied by a rope too short; in a bull that catches sight of the red flag; in a cat as it breaks free of restraint with "long, ripping slashes" of its hind legs. While this quality, he added, is lower in the greater scheme than intelligence, in a direct contest it will prevail. Britt was too complex, too sensitive, to withstand the assault that was mounted against him. Even as he rose to the occasion with rallies of his own, he was beaten down by Nelson. He fell in the 18th round.

Epic in the Desert: The Fight of His Life

Nelson was a rough-hewn little piece of work, and he made a stark contrast in several ways with Gans. Short on social graces, he now reminded at least one sportswriter, according to Charles Samuels, "of a gray wolf by the way he showed his teeth in the ring, and by his manner of crouching, protectively, over his food as he ate."[24]

It was also a matchup in which the race element figured strongly, and Oscar himself, strongly race-minded, figured to bring his attitude to the ring when he and Gans met.[25] It would be the first major show of promoter Tex Rickard, who would become in years ahead the preeminent boxing promoter in the world.

The total fighters' purse was $34,000, of which Gans would get $11,000 with the rest going to the Dane. The injustice could only add to bad blood already present, which stemmed from the time that Gans had seconded a fighter named Kid Sullivan in his bout with Nelson a year earlier. Gans, alleged Nelson's manager Billy Nolan, had smeared ammonia on Sullivan's gloves during that fight, which had nearly blinded his man during the bout.[26]

In confidence neither man lacked. "I will fight Nelson on any terms he may demand," announced Joe in late July of that year.[27] He offered to fight "winner take all" or on a 60–40 basis, and to make a weight of 133 pounds, which was the preference of Nelson's camp. He also offered to post $5,000 forfeit money if he failed to meet any conditions agreed upon. And he agreed to any number of rounds that Nelson's people wanted, knowing that they would probably opt for a long-range affair.

Nelson admitted that he might have it tough for ten rounds, but he knew that his chances would increase as it went. The referee finally decided upon was George Siler, a man whom Gans did not fully trust owing to his friendship with the Battler. They signed for a 45-round "fight to the finish" at Goldfield, Nevada, on September 3, 1906.

The bout got notice in columns around the country, with opinion fairly divided on the outcome. The *Baltimore American*, Gans's hometown publication, figured that it could be the highest purse in fight history, pitting the day's two most celebrated fighters in an open-air sun-broiled marathon. In Gans, the bout had what might be "the most scientific pugilist in the world today," and in Nelson, "the toughest and gamest lightweight pugilist that ever donned the padded mitts."[28] Gans, went this opinion, was the best at his weight, while Bat could beat anyone at that weight but him. There lingered, too, some question as to what the veteran had left.

As it approached, each man sounded ready. "I know that I have the science over him," stated Gans, "and there is a punch in me that will put him or any other man in our class to sleep."[29] His biggest fear, he said, was that Nelson would run from him. Whereupon Nelson replied that he would run *at* Gans, and not away. The betting, which favored Joe, did not concern him. "It is the fight and not the betting that settles the results," he explained, "and you will find me there at the finish with the title of world's lightweight champion."[30] Asked about his tactics, the Dane gave a blunt answer: "There's only one way I know how to fight, and that is to fight from the drop of the hat. I have not got any tactics. I'm going in and mix it up until he or I are out of the game."[31]

There arose concern in that camp when training reports indicated that Gans was more comfortable with the 133-pound limit than expected. One observer, eyeing him carefully during workouts, noted that he was breathing "almost as easily when he gets through as when he begins."[32] Each man, ten days before the fight, was at the limit. Gans, moreover, was showing recuperative power and vital signs nothing short of remarkable.[33]

Yet most historians agree that for Joe, making the required 133 ringside weight was a hardship. With ceaseless work on the road and in the gym, he did it, but he may have done lasting damage to himself in the process. But the task was not quite finished — missing no chance for an advantage, Nelson's manager Billy Nolan insisted now, on the day of the bout, that Gans make the weight not stripped, as he had done, but clad in fighting togs!

The demand was perverse, but Gans did it, and he entered the ring prepared for war. By 9:00 that morning, $70,000 had been taken in, with "still a long line of miners waiting to purchase $5 seats." The betting had settled at 10–7 Gans, though there was not a lot of action.

It was a makeshift production: Goldfield lacked an arena, and a great haul of green lumber had been brought to the site in order to remedy the situation. Baking in the sun, the wood bled out its resin, practically gluing spectators to their seats once they had planted themselves. But when the fight started, all else was forgotten.

And a fight it was, an epic of the early twentieth century prize ring. From the opening, Nelson pressed the action, as Gans met the assault with textbook jabs to the face. Though Nelson got through a couple of times, he was bleeding at round's end.

The second and third rounds were more of the same, with Nelson on the receiving end of a lesson meted out by a fistic scholar. It was not until the fourth that he might have had the better of it, backing the champion into the ropes and landing his best shots of the fight. He went to his corner with the cheers of the crowd ringing in his ears.

Still, it was Gans's fight for now. Nelson came on again in the fifth, taking Joe's best and winging his own, spitting blood on his way back to the corner. Yet by the end of six, it was hard to think that he could endure much longer. After eight, he flopped groggy onto his stool.

Eyewitness accounts of Nelson abound in testament to his ability to digest leather and come back fighting. Bat, according to Charles Samuels, was a freak of nature, with a heart rate that prompted one examining physician to compare him to "the colder-blooded animals which survived the days of antiquity and the cold of the Ice Age."[34]

He also had a cranium like a bowling ball that he used without qualm when the going got rough. According to Dr. Walter Peet, who carried out the exam, Nelson was built to function with a low supply of oxygen, which helped to account for his staying power. He would later remark also that Bat's cranium had extraordinary mass, and barring a great miscalculation on his part, "Battling Nelson carries in his head the thickest skull bones of any human being since Neanderthal man."

In the ninth, even while getting the worse of it, Bat drew blood from Joe's mouth; in the tenth, he brought the blood streaming. In the eleventh, Siler warned him for butting, yet the Dane, seeing that here was his best chance, kept inside as much as possible.

Through all of it, Gans remained true to his craft, and on occasion he even managed courtesy — in the twelfth, when Nelson slipped to the floor, he extended a hand and helped the Danish fighter to his feet. Before the round was over, Nelson's head connected with Joe's mandible again. In the 13th, there was increased clinching, as the Nevada sun continued to extract its price on each athlete.

When Nelson got home, he pounded his man to the body with a vengeance. Four times between rounds, Gans vomited over the ropes in his corner. It went like this into the fifteenth, until each man slowed, and wrestling became the main fare.

Now and again, Gans would land a fierce right hand, only to have Bat shake it off. In the fifteenth, Nelson was warned again for use of his head and elbows. After Gans put him on the canvas with a straight right, the crowd, which had naturally favored the white fighter, was cheering Joe at the bell! In the sixteenth, a writhing struggle landed them both on the ring apron. While Bat had the better of it in the next frame, he was warned again, this time for low blows. More warnings came in succeeding rounds for his use of his head, and Siler resorted, at one point, to yanking him back by his hair.

Astoundingly, his left eye swollen and his right discolored, Nelson came up fresh in the 21st and showed that he could still land. In the 23rd came more wrestling. Warned yet again for his tactics, Bat made a rally late in the round that raised yells from his supporters. The next several rounds were marked, now and again, by hot exchanges, and it was still hard to call a winner.

In the 28th and 29th, Gans landed shots that Nelson took with a casual shake of his head. When Bat resorted to a sneak punch at round's end, someone started up "three cheers" for Joe, and the crowd responded. Now the men were holding each other for up to a minute at a time. At the end of 33, each man was exhausted, and Gans had limped a few times, making ringsiders think that he had hurt his leg (in fact, it would be learned, it was the result of a broken right hand).

So it went into round 35, the golden orb setting in the distance. Throughout these rounds more warnings were issued to Nelson, but it made little difference. As to scoring, it was a virtual deadlock, neither man able to sustain an attack and each now saving ammo like a determined grenadier. Each man landed his last meaningful punches in the 41st, and then came the finish. In the 42nd round, Nelson got yet another warning for punching low, whereupon he drew back and unloaded a shot to the abdomen that sent Gans to the canvas, prompting Siler to wave a halt and announce an end to the fight.

"Gans wins on a foul!" he yelled, to resounding approval.

Final Months

Nelson himself would concede nothing, in regard to the blow that ended the fight. In his climb as a fighter he had developed a particular delivery of the left hand, inspired by watching the veteran Joe Choynski in action. Every so often, it seemed, Choynski managed to deliver a blow with the heel of his hand to an opponent's liver, after which, said Bat, "Joe would whang him on the jaw and the fight would be over."

Nelson developed what he termed a "half scissors hook" that he aimed at the same area. The blow, by his own account, "is dealt with the side of the left hand." Rather like Fitzsimmons, he sought to concentrate the impact of his blow into a smaller area: "Instead of hitting with the knuckles of the fist I take a swing of not more than six inches and plunge the side of my hand with thumb and forefinger on top of my opponent's liver." To find this pressure point, he would say, "Get a friend to tap you about three inches below the armpit and a little forward. To be explicit, the spot is on the two lower ribs about two inches above the lower right hand pocket of your vest. A slight tap on that spot will send a pain shooting all the way to the spine."[35] Gans, he would say later, had been all but finished at the end of the preceding round, heaving violently and ripe for the kill. At the gong for the 42nd, said Bat, "I sailed over to Gans' corner and met him within a yard of his chair.... I had backed about half way across the ring when I delivered the final punch, a hard left half-scissors hook to the liver, that traveled less than a foot."[36] This punch, he insisted, was delivered in the manner described above, "directly on his liver, on the right side of his body," just over the second rib.

Be this as it may, mass opinion had it otherwise. Reviewers trumpeted their admiration of the Baltimore fighter afterward. "So fast was Gans," read an account the next day, "that two-thirds of the time Nelson did not know where his opponent was, and when he raised his head to look, Joe pounced on it with both gloves."[37] Yet it was victory at a terrible price. Seeds of tuberculosis, already present in Gans's system, began to sprout.

Joe himself could see the writing on the wall, and made up his mind to get what wage he could while he could still command it, if only for the sake of a wife (he had by now remarried) and two children in Baltimore. On New Year's Day, 1907, he engaged in a bout at Tonopah, Nevada, with tough Chicago lightweight Kid Herman. It was a battle staged in a snowy setting, with a northwest wind that burned like dry ice through any who braved it. In this fight the great veteran demonstrated that his skill and strength were not yet gone, nailing the highly touted Chicago Hebrew with shots that snapped back his head from the start. In the eighth round, a finishing right hand came "in the matchless manner which places Gans in a class by himself."[38]

On September 9, Joe again fought Jimmy Britt. The bout was similar to their first in its start, Britt nailing Gans hard with a right hand late in the opening round. But this time truth prevailed: Joe came out for the second ready set the record straight. By the end of three, Britt's face was a testament to Joe's left-hand accuracy. In the fourth, Gans landed his jab several times, then threw a winging left that caught Britt hard on the elbow. Though the injury was not obvious, it was soon telling. Jimmy took a right to the nose that started blood running, and another right on the jaw. In the fifth, he was on the ropes and rocked hard before motioning to his seconds that he could not continue. With tears streaming down his cheeks, he said that the arm was broken.[39]

Ring patrons wanted to see another go with Nelson. Though Gans at this point was plainly ill — at times, he shivered, and he was beginning now to show discoloration — the bout was made. On July 4, 1908, the two men entered the ring in Colma, California.

Maybe it was the best fight that Nelson ever fought. While it was a hard go for several rounds, when Gans could still muster an attack, Bat was unrelenting. After five, the champion began to yield.

Yet even if Gans had little left, at this point, he still could hit. "He hit me one punch in the ribs," Nelson would remark later, "and I thought he carried a knife. I was in agony, but he had nothing left." In the ninth, when Joe looked for a moment like the Gans of old,[40] it was his last rally. A right to the heart put him against the ropes in the twelfth, and a right and left sent him to his knees. Up at nine, he lasted the round. Down again from a left to the body in the 16th, he beat the count, but in the next round he went to the floor to stay.

While it was a sad passing, much praise was given to Bat by those who witnessed the fight. "Of Nelson," wrote columnist R.A. Smyth, "it must be written that he is the most wonderful athlete of his inches in all the world. He hardly drew a long breath during the fight. Added to the fact that he seems to be absolutely tireless is the ... quality of being insensible to pain. He took blows from Gans which seemed to have enough power to fell an ox."[41]

Believing that he could draw one more payday with Nelson, Gans requested a third bout. On September 9, 1908, at Colma, he again put up a fight, bloodying the Dane early before falling in the 21st round. It was, reckoned Nelson, that "half-scissors" shot to the body that won it for him — as it had won, so he insisted, both of the others.

This time there was no room for argument. "I hit him with blows with which I have knocked out many heavier men than he," said Gans some days later, "but they had no effect other than to snap his head back." Nelson, he admitted, "is as tough as nails, as game as they make them, and the most determined, desperate, persistent fighter I ever saw in action." And even while no man alive, in his shoes, could have borne the Danish fighter good will by this time, he called Bat "the best lightweight over a distance that I ever saw."[42]

Gans's last fight was a ten-round no-decision bout with Jabez White of England on March 12 of the following year. Though his days as a champion were over, he managed to persuade ringside folk that he had gotten the better of this one.[43] Immediately after, Joe announced his retirement. He traveled to Prescott, Arizona, the following year, hoping that the climate might provide some relief from the disease that was now ravaging his system. At last, near death, he asked to be taken back to Baltimore to see his family.

Against all expectation, in one last show of his profound inner strength, Joe hung on long enough to say his farewells.

The Old Master

Decades years later, Harry Lenny, far up in years yet still lucid, described his experience with Gans, whom he regarded as one of the finest human beings he had met, and the best of all the lightweight champions who had ever lived. "There was never anybody," said Lenny, "like Gans. There probably never will be." Never, he insisted, did anyone equal him

Battling Nelson, standing, in his September 9, 1908, fight with Joe Gans. It was the last of their three bouts, ending in the 21st round with Nelson retaining the lightweight title. A ring phenomenon, the Durable Dane ranked no. 5 on Nat Fleischer's list all-time among the lightweights.

in pure skill or in dedication to strategic fine points.

"Joe," he recalled, "never wasted a punch.... He had the spots picked out, mentally marked in big red circles on his opponent's body; the temple, the point of the chin, the bridge of the nose, the liver, the spleen, the solar plexus. He'd pick out one or two of these points and maneuver his opponent until he left a clear opening. It was a thing of beauty to watch Joe in the ring."[44] Gans, he added, never missed a chance to see a prospective opponent in the ring. As his closest friend and confidant, Lenny had often accompanied him on scouting missions.

"We would sit in the gallery," said Harry. "Sometimes we would watch only one round and then leave. Other times we might sit through two, three, four, even five rounds, before leaving. Gans would glue his eyes on the man in the ring and make mental notes." Joe, at some point, would lean to Harry and remark on how one guy tipped his head when throwing a left, or on some other slight quirk or defect worth note. And when he put on his hat, it was time to leave. He had what he needed.

Harry had another intriguing recollection: Gans had "the kindest pair of eyes I ever saw in a human being." He was generous in the extreme, as more than one of his associates would attest. Young Corbett remembered, shortly before Joe fought Nelson the first time, how he had to argue Gans into accepting three hundred dollars for training him for a fight of his own. Charlie Simms, who had worked with Gans in camp, recalled many years afterward that the great fighter was "very generous and understanding, a quiet, humble man ... the finest fellow I ever met."[45] Gans had taken on Simms as a sparring partner, at one time, at the suggestion of Tex Rickard. He was supposed to pay Charlie a hundred dollars a week for his services, but always gave him more. "One day, [Joe] asked me how much money I had and I pulled out $12. Know what he did? He gave me three hundred dollar bills."[46]

It was the report of Gans's marathon sparring sessions with him, according to Simms, that had prompted the last-minute demand from Nelson's side in their first fight, that Gans make the weight suited up. The day of the fight, swore Charlie, it was 115 in the shade. In that heat, he added proudly, "I was the only guy in Joe's corner the entire 42 rounds."

* * *

So does this modest kid from the wet market streets of Baltimore continue to excite admiration even today. A singular specimen of talent and character, he was the prototype on which highly profiled men like Jack Johnson modeled their ring styles. Were he around today, he would win, in the estimate of biographers Colleen Aycock and Mark Scott, five or six titles in the region of the feather to welterweight divisions. An apt conclusion of his story is found in Johnny Brannigan's article, cited earlier in this chapter. It was Joe's knockout of Dal Hawkins, reports Brannigan, that prompted massive ring announcer Billy Jordan to hoist the victor's arm and bestowed on him an enduring title when he trumpeted the words, "Winner and still champion — The Old Master, Joe Gans!" No man in the annals of the ring, insists Johnny, "was ever more appropriately named." Ask the veterans, he adds, what the man was like in the midst of battle: "They tell, with shining eyes, how he stood in the middle of the ring, his hands open, plucking punches out of the air like peaches from a tree, stopping them effortlessly and throwing them back ... making [fighters] wish they had taken up some other line of work. And they tell of how Joe could stand, without moving his feet, and remain untouched by the human hand...."[47]

VI

The Brooklyn Terror:
Terry McGovern

He is an aggressive fighter, from the tap of the gong to the finish, and has made a small fortune since he started ... to wipe up the "squared circle" with all the bantam and feather-weights [who] have heretofore adorned it.

January 14, 1900, Portland Oregonian

The fight game, as should now be apparent, had no lack of heroes at the turn of the century. But for a few short years, at the close of the 1890s and after, scarcely a man alive inspired a thrill like a 5' 4" stick of dynamite from Brooklyn named John Terrence McGovern. Known to all as Terry, dubbed also the Brooklyn Terror, he exploded onto the scene in his late teens and was all but done by the age of 22.

Born in Johnstown, Pennsylvania, on March 9, 1880, McGovern came with his parents at six months of age to the city with which he would always be associated. He was spawned from rugged stock on at least one side, with a mother who stood 5'11" and could reputedly enter into a tavern fray herself when the occasion called. According to Charles Samuels, one city official, following a run-in with Terry, made the error of going to her flat to complain and was summarily tossed down the stairs for his effort.[1] (This woman, he notes, would eventually bear 13 children by three husbands, and would end up sporting all three wedding bands "on the same fat finger.") Shortly after her son won the featherweight title, she was quoted as saying, at age 56 and weighing some 300 pounds, "Champ or no champ, I can lick him right now with me left hand."

Young when his father died, Terry came of age in a neighborhood where an Irish working class thrived and fights were plentiful. By one account, his own reputation for toughness began at age eleven when he threw a truant officer into the rank waters of the nearby Gowanus Canal. His wages as a truck driver for the Litchfield Lumber Company, though they were meager, helped hold the family together.

Baseball was the rage in Brooklyn in that day, and McGovern lived for it.[2] Perhaps a key moment in determining his destiny came when his team took on the gang run by a man named Charley Mallay. Charley's bunch dominated town competition, and was used to having its way when a dispute arose on the field. In the eighth inning of the game, with the score knotted at 5–5, one of McGovern's teammates hit a drive to left and reached second as the fielder's tag was applied to his leg. Taking exception to the umpire's call of safe, Mallay charged out to deliver an opinion. As men from each side entered into the mix, he swung at Terry.

Proud and volatile, McGovern swung back. The scrap was broken up, and it was agreed that the two men could settle the issue at an old lumber-yard five blocks away. One player, who had at home a ragged pair of gloves, high-tailed it there to get them as an eager mob took up residence in the yard. Once fitted, shirts hoisted, Terry and his rival made ready for war. Outweighing McGovern by some 25 pounds, Mallay had the early advantage, even while getting his own right eye closed in the process. On it went, until the mitts were in shreds and the action went in stubborn spasms, each man using the other to avoid collapse.

When it was declared over, McGovern and Charley shook hands, in the manner of the day, and remained friends thereafter. But during the fight, something else had happened. Terry's boss Charley Mayhood had seen enough to know that his young Turk was destined for more than work in a lumber outfit.

Mayhood was acquainted with Harry Fisher, one of the East Side's aspiring welterweights. The three men formed a partnership, and soon Terry was entered into a 105-pound championship for amateurs. He won it in spectacular fashion, whacking out a handful of young competitors over the course of three nights. When he had rung up about 30 wins, McGovern turned pro. His debut, at a local club on April 3, 1897, saw him foul out in the fourth round against a local named Johnny Snee,[3] but from that point on, he burned a hole in the competition.

A Searing Comet

New York was a tough circuit, and fighters, if they made ends meet, climbed the ring steps often. By September, Terry had won six fights, five going a ten-round distance. On September 18, he appeared at the Green-wood A.C. as a headliner, stopping Jack Leon in the seventh round. Two weeks after, he faced lanky young up-and-comer Johnny Reagan.

While each man scaled 112, Reagan's range and savvy caused trouble for Terry until he was able to close the distance. When McGovern over-whelmed him in the sixth frame, police intervened. Several more wins encouraged Mayhood to match him in contests upward of 20 rounds. In 1898 Terry went full speed ahead, and by the time he closed the year with six straight knockouts, word was pulsing through Gotham like an electric current that a new terror had been loosed on the division.

Among his victims that year were men like Harry Forbes and Austin Rice, each highly respected in the business. The October 1 bout with Forbes, set for 20, saw Terry on the receiving end most of the way. With the bell to start the 15th, it appeared that Terry would get his first points loss. Yet Harry, not satisfied with that, met his young foe in a free-swinging trade. The two men had at it, when suddenly McGovern did something he never did, backing off, hands down, as if fazed. When Forbes rushed, Terry let go a right hand that caught Harry on the chin and sent him down and out. Thus Terry had outfoxed one of the craftiest men in his class, and the house thundered its approval. For this victory he got $200, with $100 going to the game loser.

On December 31 at Brooklyn's Pelican Club came the bout with Rice, a fighter dubbed Iron Man with good reason — in with some of the best of the day, he had never been stopped, and he had compiled quite a resume in the process. For ten of the scheduled 25 rounds, Rice lived up to his name. But there was no containing Terry. Staggered by a right hand in the eleventh, he had Rice hanging on at round's end. From that point, Austin took a pounding. His corner tossed the sponge three rounds later.

In style, Terry was one of the new guard, a raging hitter who fought like a demon, yet prided himself on blows that traveled no more than eight inches. And he loved to mix it as few fighters ever have. "In a fight," he would explain to young learners after his glory days had ended, "I generally attack my opponent from the waist up.... I begin hammering at him just above the belt, and work upward toward the face until I find his weakest spot, and then I bang away...."[4] As to roundhouse swings, "I don't care much for them. In all my fifty-five battles I never used a single swing nor saw the especial need of one."

The Austin fight was typical, a melee in which Terry took punches in order to land them. Maybe this willingness to trade, head to head, was the reason that he did not last long at the top, peaking at twenty and going downhill after. But for now he was unstoppable.

At the time, as Nat Fleischer notes, Terry was one of many Irishmen plying their trade in the ring. So much, in fact, did his kinsmen predominate that fighters of Jewish, Italian, or German extraction often took Irish names when they went into the business.[5] One man proud of his own heritage, however, was Sicilian veteran Casper Leon, idol of Italian fans throughout the eastern states. Clever and hard-hitting, he had managed several draws with the great Jimmy Barry after being stopped by Barry some years earlier. Casper and Terry met at the Greenwood Club on January 30, 1899.

The bout was described by *New York Journal* writer Paul Armstrong as being the bitterest scrap between little men that he had ever witnessed. It was a fight that occasioned plenty of action in the seats, as well, as ethnic fans of each persuasion got involved during the heat of battle. The fight itself was no letdown, as Leon showed that he could still wing it with the best. But relentless shots to head and body at last had the Sicilian fighter seeking the clinches. When Leon answered for the 12th, the writing was on the wall. Body blows had him in trouble, and two hooks on the whiskers finished the job.

Champion of the World

In McGovern the game had a phenomenon — a miniature Sullivan who traded with mad joy from the opening bell. So dynamic was he that the astute Mike Donovan, some ten years later, would rank him alone, in that virtue, with the first modern heavyweight champion. "Of all the fighters in recent times," he observed, "the only one who compares, in my opinion, with John L. Sullivan as a natural fighting genius who battled from the love of combat, using only instinctive methods to destroy his enemy, was little Terry McGovern."[6]

Terry roared like a train through the ranks in the months that followed. Growing stronger, more ring-wise, ever more dominant, he could now set a pace that no man in his division could equal. Time and again he faced the cream of the New York crop, and when he flattened contender Johnny Ritchie in three rounds at Tuckahoe, he had seven straight wins on the year. Soon after, he signed to fight world champion Thomas Pedlar Palmer.

A few years earlier, in November of 1895, Palmer had won the bantamweight championship of England, gaining a disqualification victory over countryman Billy Plimmer in 14 rounds at the National Sporting Club of London. The following January, he had surprised the fight world by holding his own in a six-round draw in New York with featherweight champion

George Dixon, even while conceding to George several pounds in weight. Since then, Dixon's manager Tom O'Rourke had sought to rematch the two, but Palmer's people were reluctant.

At about this time, Sam Harris contacted Palmer's manager, a Mr. Peggy Bettinson, and proposed a bout between Pedlar and Terry. Figuring the Brooklyn boy, for now, to be an easier foe than Dixon, Bettinson accepted. He had seen Dixon whip Britain's Nunc Wallace at the National Club, and realized that despite Pedlar's earlier showing against George, no man would have an easy time with the one they called Little Chocolate. McGovern he knew only from hearsay and by what he estimated to be Yankee exaggeration. Palmer and McGovern signed for 20 rounds and the title on September 11 at Tuckahoe. It was a *coup* for Harris, who knew that Terry was a world-beater, and that a victory over an invading Brit by his man

The quintessential young Turk — Brooklyn's Irish Terry McGovern, shown here as he looked around 1899. McGovern was a miniature fighting machine and captured both the bantamweight and featherweight titles with sensational knockout wins. For a brief time he was perhaps the greatest fighter, pound for pound, in the world.

would capture nationwide fancy. The timing, too, was good, since McGovern was finding it hard to make the 118 limit and wanted the fight now rather than later.

Palmer and his men arrived in New York and established training quarters at Mamaroneck, while Terry set up at McElroy's roadhouse on Jerome Street, near the site (some 24 years later) of Yankee Stadium. The estimable George Siler was chosen to referee. The fight was set for an open-air arena framed by a rough plank stockade, with rain forcing a postponement until the following day. On September 12, 1899, more than 10,000 came to town for the action. Pressmen played up this battle to the hilt, and a profit resulted despite a loss of $21,000 coming from the change of date. Trains came from New York City loaded with patrons, and even tall trees near the enclosure had their takers, as young boys climbed up for a view. In the upper window of a house near the arena sat Terry's wife Grace, holding their two-month-old baby girl and enjoying a nice vantage of her own.[7]

Tension was thick and opinion was divided: While McGovern was a slight favorite, the going wisdom was that Palmer, a seasoned ring general, would prevail if it went the distance. Prior to the fight, fans gave a rousing welcome to celebrities like Jim Corbett, Bob Fitzsimmons, Tom Sharkey, and Jack McAuliffe. The strongest cheer by far was enjoyed by John L. Sullivan, rotund and heavily mustached, a bellowing son of Eire if ever one lived.

Then came the principals: Palmer entered the ring followed by his seconds, after which came Terry, accompanied by Harris, Mayhood, and Al Mc-Murray, to strains of "The Star-Spangled Banner."

A great young fighter, when he is on the way up, is a stranger to his own vulnerability. When he is honed to the shape of his life, he senses that he can whip the world, and he is not far wrong. On this night McGovern bobbed through the ropes radiating a savage confidence that proved well-founded. At the opening bell, Pedlar led with a jab that fell short. As McGovern stepped back, he tried another and then slipped, grabbing the challenger's legs as he fell. After Palmer righted himself, Terry was on him like a crazed badger. At the end bell, there was a moment's pause before it was determined that the club timekeeper had dropped the hammer too soon. When Siler sent them back to it, Terry nailed the champion with a hook that sent him down.

Dazed, legs trembling, Palmer was up at six, veering to the ropes. Terry went first to the body, then shook his man loose from a clinch and caught him with a hook to the ribs. A right to the jaw put Pedlar down and out.

Stunned for a moment, the crowd now erupted. Fittingly, the great John L. hauled his 270 pounds into the ring to congratulate the new titleholder. Terry then offered his hand to the dethroned Englishman, who accepted it while still unsure of his bearings. The official time was 2:32 of the first round.

In three weeks McGovern was in action again, scoring a fast knockout over Fred Snyder in Philadelphia. In response to demand further west, Harris signed with Lou Houseman, who operated the Tattersall Arena in Chicago, to let Terry fight two men in one night. These two were no soft touches, one being Turkey Point Billy Smith, who had gone 14 rounds with Harry Forbes earlier that year, and the other Patsy Haley, who had given McGovern himself a hard go seven months back. But when the duo held out for high money, Houseman nixed it. Instead he took the offer of Chicago featherweight Billy Rotchford to meet the champion on the October 9 date by himself. Rotchford was a tough comer who had lost on a foul to Palmer five months before McGovern won the crown, and local fans were anxious to see him try the new division ruler.

Rotchford fared no better than had Palmer, falling five times in the opening round before cornerman Joe Choynski threw the sponge. On November 18, Smith and Haley went through with the original plan. Haley entered first, meeting a storm of leather that laid him flat.

Smith, nimbler afoot and possessed of stiff goods in each hand, figured that he could go the four if he was careful. And careful he was, running and grabbing, to McGovern's open distain, through the whole first round. In Terry's mind, to hold without punching was not just bad form, it was a veritable breach of ethics, and he sought to impart that notion to referees before some of his biggest battles. Cornering Billy in the second, he got in a few whacks that had his man falling all over the ring. Warned in the next round by ref George Siler that he needed to fight or quit, Billy managed a couple of swings before a left hook landed him hard on the canvas. Up groggy at nine, he caught a volley that brooked no dispute.

Chicago fans were thrilled, and Harris agreed to two more weeks that had Terry sparring in matinees and evening shows with a camp mate or a volunteering local. The rub was that stage owners did not like calling such features "exhibitions," and wanted instead to bill them as fights with the champion "meeting all comers." Sam was apprehensive, but Terry insisted that he could handle it without getting banged up or hurting his hands in the bargain. Harris said OK and put up $25 to anyone who could last four rounds. No one collected, as McGovern flattened nine contestants in the fourteen days. (Only later did Joe Humphries, who had handled the staging of the bouts, learn that McGovern had slipped a five-spot as consolation into the hand of each man afterward.)

The "two in one night" stunt attracted promoters in Ohio, and Harris and McGovern repeated it at an arena in Cincinnati. After Terry dropped each opponent in quick fashion, he and Sam headed back to New York. By this time Harry Forbes, who had given Terry that tough go for 15 rounds the previous year, was drumming for a rematch. Terry was all for it, and he and Forbes closed out 1899 by meeting on December 22. This time he sized up Harry fast, destroying him in round two.

Little Chocolate

"Dave, that young colored boy has the makings of a great fighter." These words were recalled many years later by the man who spoke them — the earlier noted Tom O'Rourke, a café and billiard hall owner who was also a fight manager and a world-class authority on the sport that was his first love. O'Rourke was trading ideas with the manager of the arena in which they sat, the Boston Athenaeum. They were watching 15-year-old George Dixon go at it with a gamester named Paddy Kelly. The kid, though barely a hundred pounds, fought with the instinct of a tiger.

So taken with George was O'Rourke that he sought out the neighborhood where he resided. After hours of wandering he was ready to call it a day, when standing on a curb he spotted a buxom woman of good size leaning out a window across the street.

One more time Tom made his inquiry: "Do you happen to know a colored boy by the name of Dixon around here who is a boxer?"

"What you want with my *Gawge*?" she answered. "He's my husban'."[8]

Wide-eyed, O'Rourke made her acquaintance and explained that he and the young man of that house might make some money if they joined efforts. The alliance was made, and Dixon proved himself to be a tireless student, never, but for Sundays, missing a chance to refine his craft.

Born July 29, 1870, in Halifax, Nova Scotia, George was of mixed blood, descended in part from black emigrants loyal to King George III who had left the colonies during the American Revolution. Arriving thus in the world several years after the American slave emancipation, Little Chocolate, as he would be known in ring circles, had his first professional fight in 1886 and fought his last one twenty years later.

In that time, he would ply his trade with astounding frequency, once facing 22 opponents, afternoon and evening, in one week at Miner's Theatre in New York City. O'Rourke once estimated that he might have entered the ring some 800 times in his professional span. Scaling between 108 and 116 for most of it, Dixon often faced men ten pounds heavier. By the time he was done, he would be the first man of native African ancestry to own a world title and would carve his niche as one of the greatest fighters in history.

Unfortunately, George met with less success outside the ring. Prone to squander his earnings when he got them, hopelessly fond of wine, women, and the track, he was dead at 38. Yet in his time, he combined skill, savvy, and coolness under fire as few have. He also benefitted untold numbers by his charity to those in need and his large gifts to black causes in the States and abroad.

At the time he met O'Rourke, Dixon was apprenticed to a photographer named Elmer Chickering, whose place was frequented by name boxers of the period. When the men came to Chickering to have shots taken, George made their acquaintance, and the experience fueled his ambition. Soon after he began an amateur career came the meeting with O'Rourke, a former champion oarsman and a decent fighter himself in his day. Scaling at the time but half an inch over five feet and weighing 93 pounds, George caught the eye of fans around Boston. He ran up a fast string of wins before getting a pair of draws on his record, each of which was deemed an act of robbery by those present. On May 10, 1888, he fought a nine-round draw with Tommy Kelly, the renowned Harlem Spider, in a bout that was billed for Kelly's 105-pound "paperweight" title.

When the Harlem fighter retired two years later, Dixon became unofficial ruler of the division. On February 7, 1890, George took on established star Cal McCarthy at Boston's Union Athletic Club. Like a number of Dixon's big fights, it was waged with skin-tight two-ounce gloves and set for the long distance. Long it was indeed, neither man willing to say *give* despite the pace and the punishment. Four hours later, after 70 rounds, the fighters were offered a draw and accepted. The bout put 19-year-old George in the limelight as a world-class fighter.

In the spring of 1890, O'Rourke decided to go after British champion Nunc Wallace. George and Nunc met at the Pelican Club on June 27, each man tipping the scales a little under the going bantam limit of 114. Dixon won over the English critics with a resounding 18th round knockout.

In his claim to be the preeminent fighter in that division, Dixon had three rivals: Johnny Murphy of Rhode Island, the recognized American champion McCarthy, and Australian champion Abe Willis. On October 23, he bested Murphy in Providence over 40 grueling rounds. On March 31 of the following year, he fought McCarthy again, in Troy, New York. This time it would have been over early, when Dixon felled his opponent in the third round with a volley to the head, had not McCarthy's seconds been allowed to drag him to the corner without a count. The bout finally did end at the close of the 22nd, by which time Dixon had all but killed his man and sent him down several times. Saved by the bell, McCarthy was taken to his corner, where manager Billy Madden declared that it was over.

Dixon was now considered to be the world ruler by American fans, but there was still Willis, called the champion by his fans at home. All doubt was erased when George faced Abe on July 28 at the California Athletic Club in San Francisco. Now 21, standing five feet, three and a half inches and weighing 114, Dixon was a ring virtuoso and a miniature slugger who could hold his own with any man near his size. To the thrill of the 8,000 in attendance, he went after Willis in the opening round, rocking him several times, after which the two engaged in a 30-second mix that had them ecstatic. In the fifth, Willis went down from a right on the jaw. Floored by a left, he needed several minutes to be revived.

For this bout Dixon won a 75 percent share of a $5,000 purse and the undisputed right to the title. In fact, O'Rourke maintained, the win over McCarthy had already earned George both the bantam and the feather-weight honors. He held also that the rightful limit of the latter class was 118 pounds. Shortly after, *Police Gazette* founder Richard K. Fox agreed to rec-ognize George as world featherweight champion.

Never was it more true of a champion to say that he met all comers. On September 25, 1893, Dixon knocked out Solly Smith in seven rounds in a torrid fight at the Coney Island Athletic Club. Thereafter he took on the cream of the lower weights for several years: Young Griffo, Johnny Griffin, Frank Erne—each among the most formidable of the era. Griffin he deci-sioned twice, over 25 and 20 rounds. With Griffo, the Australian wizard, he fought three fierce draws, and he split a pair of decisions with Erne and fought a draw on another occasion. In 1897 he lost a decision to Smith, and with it the title. He asked to fight Solly again within two weeks, but the new champion went the route of vaudeville and was on the stage for six months.

As Fleischer notes, George's acquaintance with Griffo provides a glimpse of Dixon's good nature outside the ring. After their second bout, a 25-rounder in January of 1895, the two met in a saloon, where Griffo typ-ically went to unwind. Griffo put the bite on George for $150, which Dixon, true to his style, handed him. Awhile later, at another watering hole, Griffo—already fifty dollars poorer—ran into his benefactor and began to growl about "the rotten deals" that he'd gotten in his fights with George.

Trying to provoke Dixon, who was still sober, only got him laughed at, whereupon he finally slammed down his remaining money on the bar and challenged George to another go, with the promise that this time he'd win by a knockout. Dixon only laughed, saying that he was not in the habit of displaying his wares, for nothing, in a tavern. When a burly Irish cop sent Griffo packing with the application of his nightstick to the Australian's behind, Dixon drew a laugh by remarking to his friends, "What you think of that? Only this afternoon I gave up one hundred and fifty bucks to Mistah Griffo.... *An' heah he comes around, wantin' to fight me with mah own money!*"[9]

In September of the following year, Smith lost his title to Dave Sullivan when he retired in the fifth round with a fractured arm. O'Rourke offered Sullivan a bout, and Dixon, riding a streak of wins, got his shot at the cham-pion on November 11 at the Lenox A.C. Weighing 119 to Sullivan's 122,[10] Dixon was the Irishman's superior at every turn, snapping back his head in fierce one-two fashion. In the tenth, when Dixon dropped his foe with a right to the jaw, Dave's brother Spike, working the corner, made a remark to the other second, and the two men jumped into the ring. George was the winner and new champion.

Thus began another Dixon reign. Once more, he was a fighting champion, closing out the year with a 25-round decision over Oscar Gardner and going undefeated in ten fights the year following. In the opinion of some, he was the preeminent fighter in the world. On January 9 of 1900, however, things would change.

A Contest of Little Supermen

Now McGovern stood head-above what his division had to offer. Harry Forbes, though he had been around the track plenty, was still as good as they came. (In fact, he would go on to win the bantamweight title after Terry let go of it.) Harris announced that Terry was going after the featherweight crown at 126.

Years, inches of reach, punch-counts and punch-land percentages — boxing commentators, of late, seeking to give the game a cognitive cast, offer up a burgeoning litany of numbers. In truth, there is little substance in these data, age being an example: It is not so much how *old* a man is, as what miles he has behind him, and the roughness of that terrain! By now Dixon had been a professional for fourteen years, and his ring miles had been long and brutal. Still, O'Rourke believed that his man could whip McGovern, and agreed to a bout of 25 rounds at the Broadway A.C. in New York. Interest ran high, with McGovern enthusiasts offering two-to-one on their man to win. While not much action transpired on this point, some money was laid down by George's people on whether the fight would last ten rounds.

McGovern was ready. If he'd had his way, it might have been fought in a 10 × 10 cell with iron bars and no referee. In days preceding the bout, he repeated his claim that full clinching — holding on without attempting a punch — was a violation of the Queensberry rules, which forbid "hugging or wrestling." Contests of late, he remarked, "last too long." If referees would enforce the rules, "fights would be shorter and more decisive."[11]

Knowing Terry's sentiment, a vibrant crowd jammed the club that night, and it got what it wanted. For three rounds, Dixon had his old skill, stabbing the challenger with a left hand in educated fashion. But in close, it was McGovern with short slams to the body. In the fourth came a premonition, as those shots had George slowing. Now and again, McGovern was also finding the range with an overhand right to the head. Soon it was only a question of how long Dixon would last. When he sank to the canvas in the eighth, O'Rourke threw the sponge.

McGovern, the scribes now conceded, was not only a slugger, but a ringman of the first order. By the estimate of the *Police Gazette*, "They'll wait a long while and look a great way to find a man to beat 'Terry' McGovern."[12] Furthermore, according to this source, the fight "was clean, remarkably free from the brutish characteristics which are inseparable from prize fights. No fouls were committed, no enmity displayed, a courteous gentlemanly regard for each other was shown by the principals throughout the battle...."

And for McGovern the praises kept coming: "Ring Career Ended," cried a headline the next morning, declaring that Dixon was finished.[13] "McGovern a Marvel," announced another, calling the new champion a "wonderful little fighting machine" and praising him as a ring general.[14] The new champion, affirmed one columnist, "is a thinker and tactician, and body blows are his *forte*, as was demonstrated in the fifth [round] with Dixon, when he punished the latter terribly about the ribs, heart, kidneys and stomach, not neglecting ... to nearly smash the plucky negro's nose. He is tireless, swift, and crafty ... employing short-arm jolts in a 'mix-up' in preference to spectacular swings and other gyrations intended for the delectation of the gallery."[15]

Defending the Crown

When heavyweight champion Jack Dempsey passed his crown to Gene Tunney (see also the concluding portion of this book) in 1926, he said to the new crown-bearer, "Your real troubles are only beginning."[16] Such a claim is appropriate to some fighters, who win titles only to feel the weight of the world now on their shoulders. Yet those who knew Terry found that even as champion he was still, at times, a happy-go-lucky kid.

On one occasion, the fighter was starring in one of Harris's theater productions in a melodrama that ran in houses all over the country. Sam had arranged for him to hold a talk with some reporters on one day, but Terry skipped out, fleeing happily to the streets as he had in his school days. Roaming the town, he eventually came to the place where his own name was in lights, and spied a cluster of unkempt kids shooting craps in a back alley.

Instantly Terry was in his element, shouting "come seven" with the rest. Soon there came a hefty Irishman, a theater employee who was policing the area, and who had developed a running feud with the boys. A running contest indeed it was, when the gang went on the lam. Terry, perhaps harking back to earlier days, took off as well. Heading in the wrong direction, he was suddenly trapped in a dead end. Managing to duck once past the cop, he went into the theater's back entrance, leading his pursuer on a merry chase around the stage scenery. When the bigger man, making a dodge of his own, managed to nab Terry at last, he was in no mood for an explanation.

Shaking free, McGovern threw a right hand that dropped him flat. Then, pausing for a second to make sure that he was coming around, Terry took off for the hotel.

Later that night, when waiting in the wings for his cue, the champion spotted the man, still in uniform and sporting a bruise from the blow that he had received. Affecting innocence, he approached.

"Been havin' a scrap?" he asked, touching that badge of battle in admiration. Unrecognized by his victim, the champion was regaled with a veritable Irish saga of how the man had thrashed two oversized gang members, one of them escaping and another going to the hospital! The bruise on his own face, explained the fellow, was a reminder of his victory.

"Good work," said Terry, good-naturedly pressing a fiver into his hand, "You're the real stuff." Then, answering his call, he headed onto the stage and a thunderous ovation, with no one knowing what had just happened.

In June 23, 1900, he won a six-round decision over Dixon, and on July 16 he fought one of his greatest battles, a non-title clash with lightweight champion Frank Erne. While it was not a straight across-the-weight matchup — Harris insisted that Erne make a weight of 128, about five below Frank's preference — it was a spectacle. On this night, before a sellout crowd at Madison Square Garden, McGovern showed that he was likely, pound for pound, the greatest fighter on the planet.

Feeling that his best chance would come early, Erne went at it hard from the opening bell. But McGovern had the same idea. Swinging for the head, he crowded Erne in the opening minute, refusing to back off come hell or high water. A left to the chin had Terry down, but he was up and charging again. Reverting to his stick-and-move style, Erne settled into his rhythm in the next frame, landing stiff raps on McGovern's nose and chin. But by the end of three, his own nose was broken and he was bleeding from the mouth. Blows to head and body brought the sponge flying.

Erne, once revived, offered no excuses. McGovern, he stated frankly, was a great fighter, the best that the world had ever seen, and he had been fairly whipped. The Brooklyn Terror said that he was satisfied with the featherweight title for the moment, but offered to fight Gans, McFadden, or any other lightweight willing don the gloves at 128.

As noted in the last chapter, Terry did meet Gans in September of 1900, and scored a knockout in the second round, though the fight failed to convince those who saw it. The bout took place at Tattersalls Arena in Chicago on December 13, with the pre-fight stipulation that McGovern, who at 124 conceded more than ten pounds to the Baltimore fighter, would be awarded a victory if he went the distance. It does not appear that Terry himself was aware of any duplicity in the arrangement, and he waged his usual war from the opening bell. Gans went down in the second round without mounting an attack.

Footage of this fight is interesting regardless of the skepticism that attends the outcome. McGovern, ever on the attack, looks rather like a small Roberto Duran, with a murderous shot in either hand. Still, as noted earlier, the result was too one-sided to convince the spectators. "There were 17,000 fans present," remarks Fleischer, "when Gans did his act and did it so badly that a child wouldn't have been convinced that he was fighting on the level."[17] Referee George Siler, according to Nat, never did provide an adequate reason for failing to announce fakery in the outcome, and thereby to call off the bets. As a result, boxing in the Windy City was dealt a severe blow. As for Gans, "he kept out of sight of the thousands of members of his race who had lost their money on him and didn't linger along around Chicago."

The spring of 1901 saw another contest of great little men when Terry crossed gloves on May 29 with Mexican sensation Aurelio Herrera. Few in the present age remember Herrera, but in his day he was one of the most feared men in the business. No less a warrior than Battling Nelson, a few years later, would call him "the greatest whirlwind fighter that ever lived," marveling at a shot from the Mexican that had floored him during their 20-rounder. Aurelio's right hand, short and straight, with all his weight on it, was called by some the hardest blow, for the weight, in the game. A legend on the Pacific Coast, Aurelio would be remembered by experts for decades after he was gone.

The men clashed at Mechanic's Pavilion in San Francisco, and it turned out to be a brush with disaster for the Irishman. Herrera, a slow starter, did little for the first couple of rounds. In the third, McGovern caught him hard to the body and appeared to have things going his way as shouts now rose for him to "finish the greaser!"

Seeing the way paved, Terry went out strong in the fourth, backing the Mexican fighter from one side of the ring to the other. Then, as he readied a finisher, Herrera caught him coming with that killer right hand. McGovern reeled, momentarily out on his feet. Herrera's corner yelled for him to seize the chance. But the fighter, amazed to see the champion still up, hesitated, and Terry, fighting on instinct, began to come back. At round's end he stunned Aurelio with a wild swing to the head.

Given a full minute, Terry could recover from anything. He came out for the fifth with fire, hammering the challenger with a left to the body and another to the chin. Aurelio dropped. He rose at nine and went to the ropes, where he sank once more. When he got up, he took a left on the chin and had to be carried to his corner. In the aftermath, there was rumble in the papers that McGovern had allowed his opponent to last to the fifth only to accommodate gamblers who were leaning that way. In truth, Terry would say, he had been shaken to his soles by that right hand. Hitting Aurelio on the chin he compared to hitting a Marvin safe. He had fought one of the best men of the day, and had been lucky to escape with his crown intact.

Sudden Disaster

By now Terry was riding an amazing streak — his only loss on record, after his debut, was a disputed disqualification against Tim Callahan in July of 1898 — and seemed invincible. (Not long after that fight, McGovern and Callahan fought a 20-round draw, and Terry knocked him out in ten rounds that autumn.) But it all came crashing down on the afternoon of November 28, 1901, when he met a fighter out of Denver named Billy Rothwell, better known as Young Corbett.

They met in the Hartford (Connecticut) Coliseum on Thanksgiving Day. Erratic in performance, Corbett had suffered four losses, and had fought seven draws, against men less able than Terry, and he was not long on discipline. For this one, however, he checked his appetite. In camp, he would pound out ten or twelve miles on the road and box endlessly — working spar mates, by his own estimate afterward, some 20 or 25 rounds in a day.

He also had the tongue of a viper, and a knack for hitting an opponent's nerves with it. This time was no exception. When the high-strung champion was in his dressing room, getting a pre-fight rub, Corbett strolled by, calling through the door with words that required Terry to be restrained by his own handlers.

Still bristling when he climbed the ring steps, McGovern was ripe for trouble. (According to Fleischer, Corbett provoked him further by fiddling with his belt for as much as a full minute before he would consent to having the bell rung, driving McGovern further over the edge.) By now, Terry was used to having the edge on a man from the start, but this time he met a fighter ready to take charge. In the first frame, each man was rocked, and near the close, when Terry got home a right hand that bloodied Corbett's nose, he was shaken in turn by a right-hand counter.

In the second, with McGovern still brimming, Corbett was coolly focused. Then, at the apt moment, he caught Terry coming with a left jab and a right hand with everything on it. McGovern went down flat on his back. Clambering up with the aid of the ropes, he tried gamely to mix it again. Stunned by another right, he muscled Billy into a corner, punching doggedly in a last-ditch effort. As Terry threw a hook, Corbett landed a hellacious right that dropped him on his shoulder blades, his head whacking the floor, out cold.

In less than five minutes, a new champion had been crowned. McGovern was helped to his corner and revived with ammonia. Once realizing the situation, he sat and sobbed with head in hands.

End of the Line

It is likely that McGovern was on the decline even when he fought Young Corbett, and he had few moments of glory afterward. Still, interest in a rematch was strong, and there were many in Terry's crowd who thought that the loss was a fluke. Corbett, however, was now in the driver's seat. He was in no hurry.

On February 22, 1902, McGovern scored a 15th-round KO of lightweight contender Dave Sullivan in a cliffhanger fought in Louisville. After a six-round no-decision bout with an old rival named Joe Bernstein in February of the following year, he knocked out journeyman Billy Maynard in Philadelphia. Now came a second shot at Corbett. They met on March 31 at Mechanic's Pavilion in San Francisco, fighting for a $10,000 purse, 65–35 agreed upon for winner and loser.

While this bout went longer than their first, it was soon clear that McGovern could not mount his old attack. The crowd, largely for Terry, cheered his efforts, but Corbett again had the answer. In the first round, it looked for a moment like another quick finish, when he leveled the former champion with a right hand, a blow from which Terry probably never did recover. Corbett, again, carried out a verbal attack, baiting Terry in the clinches and getting his goat when the former champion flailed in the exchanges. In the eleventh, Corbett finished him.

Now Harris urged his man to quit the game. He had seen what becomes of men who stay under the lights too long, and he could not bear to see it happen to one whom he loved and respected. Indeed, by this time Terry was showing signs of an early *dementia* that was now beginning to erupt here and there in public outbursts. Less than six months later, however, he was at it again, boxing four more times before the year was out. McGovern appeared in the ring a few more times in 1904, a year that brought the deaths of his two infant daughters Lilly and Annie. The loss sent him into a depression from which he never did fully escape.

Harris again succeeded in getting him away from the ring for awhile, but in October 1905, he was lured back against the renowned Harlem Tommy Murphy, who figured to dispose of him with little trouble. Yet fans were amazed, on this occasion, to see Terry fight like the man of several years earlier, stunning Murphy and dropping him four times in the opening round before it was stopped.

Maybe Harlem Tommy suffered an off-night. Maybe Terry somehow regained, for one night, a strain of his young brilliance. Either way, for better or worse, the Terror was a drawing card once more. He was matched with the raging lightweight Bat Nelson in Philadelphia on March 14, 1906, for a no-decision six-rounder.

Nelson, as it may be recalled, was on an upswing at this time, vying for a shot at the world title in his division. In November of 1904, he had gained much notice when he met Young Corbett at Woodward's Pavilion in San Francisco. Corbett was figured as a 2–1 favorite, too wily for the young Dane. But on this evening Nelson scored an upset. From the start, he seemed impervious to anything that the veteran could manage, shaking off a flash knockdown in the third round and coming back to punish his opponent on the inside.

"Whoever told you that you could fight?" muttered Corbett when they were on the inside. "You're a joke." But when Corbett landed his Sunday right hand, Bat was unfazed. Billy did finally succeed in getting under Nelson's thick hide when he asked, at one point, "Say, kid, what's the name of that town that you came from?"

This time, the jibes did not have the effect that Corbett wanted. In recalling his key bout with Californian Jimmy Britt, Bat remembered a moment when the cry of "Knock him out, Jimmy!" came from a crowd of some 10,000 Colma fans. They were, down to a man, it seemed, Britt's friends. "I was out there all alone," said Bat, "but I knew that far away in little Hegewisch I had a mother who is my friend." Thus he was spurred to a great performance. Remembering, perhaps, that one fan who was always in his corner, and proud of his Swede-Dane farming roots, he dug down now and laid it on Corbett in grim fashion. By the ninth round, the Irishman was a punching bag. His corner tossed the sponge at 1:50 of the tenth.[18]

In the following February, Nelson scored a resounding encore, flattening Corbett, this time, in nine rounds. Now, against Terry, he had all the advantages. Bat, as said in a previous chapter, was something of a throwback, actually recalling, said some, an earlier phase of the human story. Certainly his style was prehistoric — his skull made a handy weapon, when he could manage it, and on this occasion, against Terry, he managed it plenty. At the end of six rounds, McGovern was a sorry sight, thanks in part to the work of Bat's "third fist."

While no one expected this meeting to look like a tea party, the Dane was asked afterward why he had employed such a tactic against a smaller man past his peak. "Butt him?" asked Nelson, raising high both scarred eyebrows. "I didn't butt him. I was only rubbin' my hair in his eyes. Feel that hair of mine. It is spiky, ain't it, just like wire? I rubbed it in Terry's eyes so much that near the end he couldn't see good enough to hit me."[19] Staying to the last bell, Terry won cheers for his courage.

On May 28, he met Jimmy Britt at Madison Square Garden. It was a relatively tame affair, Britt keeping his distance and the bout going ten rounds to a no-decision. On October 17, McGovern met Young Corbett one last time in a six-rounder in Philadelphia. By now Corbett, who tended to gain pounds easily, had slowed a mite, and he had suffered knockout losses to Aurelio Herrera and Nelson.

Despite his own advanced physical age, Terry seemed to have some of his old fire. Prior to the bout, he held that Corbett should refrain from his tactic of insult, a request that made Corbett laugh, though he did promise, and he kept his word. From the opening bell, however, the bout itself was fought in full spirit, each man gunning for a knockout. It went the full six, each man cut and bleeding at the end, at which time they buried the hatchet and shook hands. While the bout was officially a no-decision, columnists said that McGovern had managed a slight edge. The report pleased Terry to no end, for at last he had gained some measure of satisfaction against the man who had taken his title.

Terry's final two bouts, fought in 1908, were of no consequence, each going six rounds without a verdict. Not long after, his mind began to fade. In coming years, he suffered breakdowns and was confined more than once to a sanatorium. By the efforts of friends, funds were amassed to buy him a home and establish a trust fund in his name. In early 1918, while refereeing a bout between soldiers at Camp Upton, he fainted and was taken shortly afterward to his home in Brooklyn.

He died of pneumonia in late February, less than three weeks shy of his 38th birthday. The funeral was a grand occasion that brought a procession of 40 carriages, four of which were needed for a fantastic flower display. On hand were many of the fight game's most famous. As they lowered Terry into the ground next to Lilly and Annie, it was said, Young Corbett had tears running down his face.

VII

The Boston Tar Baby:
Sam Langford

Man, how that baby could hit.
Joe Jeannette, remembering Sam Langford

In every era of the game is a basic rift, a division of sense and outlook that separates fans of the present-day fighter from those who look to the past. As the decades roll by, however, time outstrips memory, and few fans today, even if they lean to the old days, are "up" on the men of a hundred years ago. Yet a peculiar reverence still attaches to this ebony blockhouse of a man who began his career as a lightweight and plagued the higher divisions for more than two decades. At best he stood 5'7" and weighed under the light-heavyweight limit. But before it was over, he would terrorize the biggest men in the game.

"There are still some old timers left," observed fight historian Stanley Weston in 1956, "who saw Sam Langford fight and they stick stubbornly to their belief that he was the greatest pound for pound fighter that ever lived."[1]

Surely if there are any around at *this* writing who made the acquaintance of Sam when he was active, they were very young at the time and they met the fighter when he was quite long in the tooth. But the high estimate continues—as recently as August 2003, a survey named Langford as the greatest fighter of the past century.[2] Another called him the second greatest puncher per weight of all time.[3] Extant footage of his 1909 bout with Iron Hague shows that Sam was a cagey fighter who could bang with both hands. And across the board, the testimony of his contemporaries vouches for it: When Sam landed, men hit the floor like wet rags.

A Hungry Kid

He was, by reliable accounts, a kindly sort, possessed of that deep goodness of soul that is sometimes forged out of early life hardship. He thought — and punched — with the geometric beauty of a straight line, and he wasted little time on theoretical assessment of his own talent. It was a mere turn of his backside, Sam ventured, that supplied most of his power. As to strategy, "Whatever that other man wants to do, don't let him do it."[4]

Born in Weymouth, Nova Scotia, on March 4, 1886, Sam was the son of a deep-water sailor on a windjammer, a man of granite constitution who brooked no nonsense. Pop Robert Langford feared God and loved discipline, and he labored long hours to keep body and soul together on a hard stretch of land that lay near the ocean. When Sam's mother Charlotte died, there was little to keep the youngster at home. Years later, he would say that he had run away from a home "no biggah'n a dawg kennel" that he shared with six brothers and seven sisters, "because mah pappy always done licked me."[5]

He left, by some accounts, as early as age 11, and would see much of the world — scrubbing horses, fixing houses, painting fences, and catching his sleep in barns and sawdust heaps — by 15. Riding often on the freight car, he picked up the essentials of life in that element, after which the ring might have seemed tame by comparison.

Details of Langford's start in the fight game vary some with the source. "My fighting," he himself recalled at age 22, "came about almost by accident."[6] By his own account, he was a tramp when still a boy — "not much more than a pickaninny" when he took to the road. At 16, he offered his services to a promoter of an amateur fight card in return for a nickel. "I was mighty hungry, I tell you, and was willing to do anything for a meal, so I ups and tells him if he'll give me five cents for something to eat, I'll box for him. I had had many street fights, like all kids living on their merits have, but I never had a glove on in my life."[7]

"Well," continued Sam, "he gives me the nickel, and I goes right out and fills up on doughnuts." Bolstered by a full craw, he promptly flattened his opponent. The extra reward of a dollar from the boss was enough to sell the young wanderer on a career.

The record shows that Sam fought nearly 300 battles over his career, a modest estimate since tallies were not closely kept in the late 19th and early 20th centuries. As often noted, he never held a world title. He lived in a day where that honor was harder to come by than today, where new weight classes thrive and burgeoning title organizations multiply belts beyond meaning. He lived also in a time when black fighters often were effectively barred from contention for what titles there were.

In the words of his foremost literary champion, "the injustices that Sam suffered in his chosen field of endeavor were even more so when one considers his greatness," and the respect he had among those who knew him best.[8] Many who saw him said that he had no peer. Some thought that he could rule the heavyweight division if given the chance. Yet he was shunned as an opponent by Jack Johnson, after Jack himself had become the first black heavyweight king. Often, too, he had to fight "to order," agreeing ahead of time to let his opponent go the distance if he wanted work. While nearly always Sam's foes were taller, his lack of height was offset dramatically by bone and muscle, and by a reach more fitted to a man six feet in height. It was offset as well by Sam's ring savvy and by his ability to stretch a man cold with either hand.

Sam and Joe

Many years later, in 1956, 82-year-old Joe Woodman was sitting in a front row seat at Stillman's gym when someone spied the front page of the daily *New York Journal*. A line read, "Famed fighter Langford dead." The messenger held the page out for Joe to see. The old man took it and saw the story. He handed it back without a word. Then, as distant visions crossed his mind, his eyes welled. Minutes later he was walking up Eighth Avenue.

Now every boxing writer in town wanted a word with him. He did his best to oblige, sharing the story as he recalled it. He told them of the first time that he saw this scrawny ragged kid who had come down from the Canadian north, with burlap on his feet and a yellow mutt under his arm. "He hadn't had anything to eat for a couple of days," said the old man, "and I took him into my gym and fed him and let him sleep under the ring."[9]

In November of 1901, Woodman was running a small drug store in Boston and staging fights at the Lenox Athletic Club. It was here at this store, he now recalled, that he had encountered young Sam, about 120 pounds, cold and hungry like the little dog that was his companion. The first thing that Woodman noted was Sam's wide-toothed grin, a portent, as it would be, of Langford's ability to smile in later years amidst adversity.

The youngster was willing to do anything for a meal, and Joe pulled a quarter from his pocket to remedy the situation. When he returned from an errand at the club, Joe found Langford and his four-legged companion putting down sandwiches, and was informed by his handyman that Sam had paid in full by his labor. Woodman took Sam to the club, where he figured that the boy could do enough chores to earn his keep under that roof. There Sam learned to be a janitor, and to administer rubdowns to the athletes and to serve, in a pinch, as a sparring partner.

Once getting practice in the Queensberry rules, Sam proved his merit. Soon Woodman entered the young wanderer into an amateur tournament in Boston. After Langford had picked up his fighting togs and paid four bits as an entry fee, Joe thought little more about it. Yet several days later, Sam appeared, all smiles, with a gold watch as the badge of his success. Over the course of two nights he had won five times, knocking out three opponents.

As Sam rang up more wins, Woodman saw that he had all the makings of a great fighter. April 11, 1902, saw Langford's first effort as a professional, which he won handily, and by 1903, he was in the thick of the competition, fighting three and four times in a month. Before the year was out, Woodman matched him in a non-title bout, scheduled for 15 rounds, with the great Joe Gans.

Joe, it may be recalled, was the lightweight champion at this time, though Langford exceeded the division weight limit, scaling 139 to 131½ for the Baltimore fighter. The fight, held on December 8 at the Criterion Club in Boston, turned out to be a surprise. Sam had been in the pro ranks now for barely two years, while Joe, as noted in a previous chapter, had been a world-class figure since the mid–90s. The youngster, thought most, was in for a bruising, and in the early rounds it appeared so. But as the action heated up, Sam discovered that Gans was not invincible. In the fifth, he stepped up the pace and had the great Baltimore fighter relying on every trick to survive. At the end of fifteen, the referee raised Langford's hand.

Two weeks after, Sam went 12 rounds to a draw with highly regarded welterweight Jack Blackburn, one of the best in his division, a man who would become known years later as mentor of the young Joe Louis. In July of 1904, he met cagy veteran George "Elbows" McFadden, who had mixed fiercely with men like Gans and Kid Lavigne. In the opening round, a left hook dropped McFadden to his knees, and the bell came to his rescue. In the next round he took the count.

On September 5, in New Hampshire, Sam faced a man to whom he bore conspicuous resemblance, the Barbados demon Joe Walcott. By some accounts, it was just before this fight that Sam got the nickname that would remain with him throughout his career. It happened when writer-cartoonist Tad Dorgan was talking to some local women of color outside a mill in Manchester.

Dorgan, knowing that the veteran Walcott was the favorite, asked them who they thought would win. "Our baby," was the unhesitating answer. Dorgan took this to mean Joe, but he was greeted with laughter. "Don't you know," they said, "that Sam Langford is *our baby*?" Somehow the words remained in Dorgan's mind, and he hit on "Tar Baby" as a moniker for the fighter.

Billed for 15 rounds and the welterweight title, it was an intriguing matchup. By now Walcott had a reputation like no other man at his weight. There was also bad blood leading up, since Sam had given Joe's brother Belfield a going-over some time back. Joe was known to dish out hard repayment to men who had beaten his sibling, and besides this, he resented Langford's intrusion on his Boston following. Sam and Joe were slated to meet in the resort area of Lake Massabesic near Manchester, New Hampshire. Owing to fan interest, the site was soon crowded well beyond its usual September residence, with scribes predicting that Sam would get what-for from Walcott.

While Sam did not scare easy, he knew Walcott's reputation. The tone of this fight was set when Joe confronted the younger man before the opening bell, calling him a "black monkey" who would take to the trees outside the arena and swing by his tail when Joe was done with him! It was an ironic insult, since Walcott himself must surely have heard this kind of thing a time or two over the span of his ring years. But Sam would hand back a worthy retort over the next hour.

Sam, by the estimate of one scribe, "could roll more dynamite" into a short punch than any man who ever laced a glove.[10] It came in handy against Walcott, who was hard to hit squarely because of his tendency to crouch low and catch blows on his shoulders and head. Time and again, in close, the veteran fighter got rocked by Sam's uppercut. As Joe took the fight to his young opponent in the latter half of the fight, Sam showed that he could stand the heat. In the 13th, Walcott landed his best punches when he nailed Sam with rights to the head and hurt him with one under the heart. In the next round, Sam brought blood from Walcott's mouth, and late in the round a furious exchange drew the crowd's roar.

At the last bell, Walcott refused to shake hands, which prompted a razz from the customers. While it was ruled a draw, *New York Illustrated News* editor Arthur Lumley was moved to write, "My personal opinion is that Langford was entitled to the verdict.... He looks like a sure thing to win either the welterweight or middleweight championship, though he may outgrow both divisions before he reaches his peak!"

By now Sam had a girlfriend, young Martha Burrell, who loved her man even if she detested the sport that provided his living. Before long they would be married with a baby girl, though wife and child would have a strained relationship with the fighter in years ahead. In time, Langford would purchase a large farm outside of Boston and valuable property in town, all of it in her name. But love of travel and the high life would eventually cost him much where wife and daughter were concerned.

A large part of Sam's recreation involved gambling. While making the rounds in his adolescence, he had become friends with a senior fellow named Doc Blodgett, who kept a stable of more than 60 racehorses. Sam could not get enough of the animals, and might have sought a career on the oval track if he had been scaled a little smaller. In coming years, when his purses increased, Sam renewed that acquaintance. In time, he would drop fabulous money on the action in Australia and on roulette wheels in Paris. When on the trains, he became absorbed head over heels in dice games.

Fighters then, and black fighters especially, as it has been noted, had to fight often in those days, and with white boxers frequently skittish about crossing the color line, black competitors got to know each other well. During these years Sam mixed repeatedly with brick-hard journeymen like Dave Holly and Larry Temple, each of whom shared his predicament. The result was an education in ring warfare — in the shifts, the feints, and the subtle bend of the wrist, on impact, that supplied extra power in a punch.

Over time, Sam mastered the techniques and the opponents. When he met Holly for a fourth time in Salem on February 13, 1905, he had clearly the better of it, though by a pre-fight stipulation the fight was called even when both men finished on their feet. He went at it also with Young Peter Jackson, deemed by the great light-heavyweight Philadelphia Jack O'Brien to be one of the toughest men that ever lived. Langford and Jackson crossed swords repeatedly, with Sam winning three and losing one, and a draw being rendered in another. In the sixth and final bout, on November 12, 1907, in Los Angeles, Sam had Peter's number and won a resounding decision over 20 rounds.

Near the end of 1905, Sam had his first encounter with a man whom he would meet many times in years ahead, the great Joe Jeannette, another of the stellar black fighters of the day, and one who in time would be compared on near-even terms with Jack Johnson. Jeannette receives little press these days, but not for lack of merit. Dubbed "The Master Strategist" by his followers, he stood 5'10½" and weighed in the region of 185. Born on August 26, 1879, in North Bergen, New Jersey, he turned professional in November of 1904, at the mature age of 25, and reportedly on a personal dare.

After going six rounds to a no-decision in his debut, Joe decided to try again. In the following year he was fighting in earnest. Tough, clever, and courageous, he learned the trade in go-rounds with men like Langford, Jack Johnson, and Sam McVey. (In April of 1909 he engaged McVey, a 5'10" sepia Hercules, in a battle in Paris that reportedly saw Joe and Sam each on the deck a few times before Sam called it quits after 49 rounds.) A true gentleman, Joe had the respect of fellow ringmen and public alike. Faithful to his family, honest and unassuming, he would continue to make his life in boxing by opening a school in Jersey City after his fighting days were done.

Langford's weight fluctuated in the early years with the size of his opponent. At times he was expected to weigh under 140, while on occasion the other man was big enough that it didn't matter. When Joe met Langford, he was a full-fledged heavyweight, with Sam in the mid–150s. Joe by this time had already seen combat with Jack Johnson in Philadelphia, a couple of the bouts going the distance to a no-decision. He had also won from the Galveston fighter once on a foul in two rounds, when in the midst of a heated exchange Jack hit him a blatant shot below the belt.

Knowing what they were up against, Woodman told Sam to play it safe. In the first three rounds, Jeannette set the pace, but in the fourth and fifth, Sam began to score to the body. In the next two rounds he entered into more exchanges, and in the eighth, he staggered Joe with a right hand on the jaw.

While Jeannette rallied to gain a TKO in that round, the two fighters would develop a lengthy rivalry. When they met again, on April 5 of the following year, Sam took charge early and had Jeannette dazed in the late going. In the fifteenth and final round, the bell saved Joe from collapse.

By now heavyweight champion Jim Jeffries had retired, and Jack Johnson was looming as the best big man in the game. There were few who wanted to test him, but Woodman decided to venture it. Jack and Langford met at Chelsea, only three weeks after Sam's fight with Jeannette.

The Galveston Giant

Jack Johnson, recalls scribe Damon Runyan in his preface note to Jack's autobiography, "could take fellows larger than himself and set them around the ring like nine pins at his own peculiar pleasure, chatting jovially with the crowd as he did so. He had a knack of catching punches as an outfielder catches a baseball."[11] No greater defensive fighter, holds Runyan, ever lived. Indeed the notion of defense probably came into Johnson's mentality at a young age, for like many of this era, his beginnings were meager, and his dark skin did not endear him to the wider Texan society of his day. Born

March 31, 1878, John Arthur Johnson had from his youth a yen for adventure, which first made itself obvious when he was (by his own recollection) twelve years of age and residing in Galveston.

"One of my earliest ambitions was a strange one," notes Jack, and one that bore no relation to the greater course of his life. He was seized with the desire to see Steve Brodie, an enterprising bookmaker who had gained some measure of fame by leaping (so he claimed, at least) on July 23, 1886, from the Brooklyn Bridge into the East River. Like Sam, Jack was a precocious adventurer, experienced, early on, at hitching a ride on the boxcar. Eventually choosing a freight that might take him in that direction, he settled in for the ride, but soon found that the train was going nowhere of importance, and that club-wielding railroad men had no sympathy with his effort. He fared little better with a revised plan, as a stowaway on a boat that ended up not in New York, but in Key West. Trying again, he found himself aboard ship at work as a potato peeler in the service of a cook who dished out occasional abuse to the youngster in the process of the voyage. On one occasion, when the older man had whipped him especially hard, Jack tried to leap overboard, but was stopped by passengers who took up a collection that would get him to his destination.

To his first desire, notes Jack, was now added another — "to find the cook who had abused me and wreak vengeance upon him." For some twenty years, he adds, "I went about with that plan in mind," always keeping an eye out for his nemesis. In time, and after much disappointment, and a few false claims to Brodie's identity made by self-amused pranksters, he actually did make Steve's acquaintance and the two became long-time friends.

Maybe this early quest does reveal something in Jack's nature — an innate drive, even to the point of wild stubborn oddity, to fly in the face of alleged good sense and majority opinion, and to see an ambition through to the end. Jack was now, by his account, a little past his thirteenth year, back in Galveston doing a man's work in the company of some of the roughest types imaginable. Run-ins were frequent, and they could be costly. Yet he ran this gauntlet, and in time he had a reputation as a fighter. In the process he took up boxing, not with the intention of a career, but for the sake of survival.

A decisive moment came when an older and larger fellow assaulted him in the street, and Jack, surveying the possibilities, tried to back down. At this point, said Jack, his sister Lucy figured into his destiny. Outraged at the offense, she pushed him angrily back into the fray, and to Jack's own surprise, after several minutes of bare-fisted give and take, he triumphed. Not long following, a dispute over 25 cents in a dice game got him into a contest with another roughneck of the same type, and Jack's reputation was on the rise.

Some time later, working in Dallas as a carriage painter, Jack came into the orbit of Walter Lewis, a highly touted amateur who furthered his education with the gloves. Soon he was home again, and entering into regular ring battles. When police raided a Sunday morning dice game, Jack and a Galveston tough named Dave Pierson were hauled into custody. Taking exception to Pierson's description of him as a stool pigeon, Jack called him a liar. Pierson was determined to get his revenge, and Jack's friends advised him to leave town. But Jack was his own man, and would not take the easy way out. In time a confrontation came, and there followed a barefisted battle as grim, by Johnson's recollection, as any he would ever have. When the older man was whipped, 16-year-old Jack was known throughout the city. For several days afterward, the question was asked, "Did you hear what Li'l Arthur did?" The name would last throughout his career.

After winning 25 dollars for lasting four brutal rounds with a savvy veteran named Bob Thompson, Jack against cast himself to fate and hopped a freight that landed him eventually (and after several near-brushes with starvation) in Springfield, Illinois. In knocking out four men to win a battle royal, he caught the eye of Johnnie Connors, who brought him to Chicago, and Jack became a full-fledged fighter. It was no easy climb, but within a few years he had become the premier contender in the division, taking on fellow black heavyweights like Hank Griffin, Denver Ed Martin, and Sam McVey. Facile of wit, fast of hand, he soon had the best moves of any big man in the game. In 1908, he would get his long-awaited shot at the title.

Sam's Quest

Langford, too, was making his strides, but now, against Johnson on this April night in Chelsea, by his own admission, he got a whipping. By the eighth, Johnson had dished out enough punishment to stop two men, and in that frame he floored Sam for a count of nine. At the end of 15, there was no doubt as to the winner. (Later, when Jack was heavyweight champion, Woodman would spread the notion that the big man had been fortunate to get the win, and that Sam had floored *him* for a nine count during the action. It was not until many years later than Woodman admitted his mischief.)

As Sam grew in stature and ring wisdom, however, a rematch became plausible. It was a fight for which he campaigned, but never with success.

True, Sam would admit, the loss to Johnson was "the only real beating I ever took." But he noted also that he had been no more than a welterweight at the time, and added, when asked about his current chances, "now that I'm 15 pounds heavier I think I could do better with him."[12]

With Jack and Sam, boxing had a presage of the personal rivalry decades later of heavyweight champions Muhammad Ali and Joe Frazier. Johnson, like Ali brimming with sass, delighted in playing to onlookers at the expense of whoever could supply his "straight" half. In the squat, plain, dark-skinned Langford, he saw (much as Ali would see in Frazier) a backward type who did not belong in his company.

Johnson, in fact, was one of the few men whom Langford ever bore real animosity. "I never hit a man outside the ring in my life, save [in] street kid fights," he would one day remember. But once, he added, "I felt like smacking Jack Johnson. He was a high-hat darky what used long words to fool me. That didn't get him no place."[13] Johnson, insisting that a challenger of his own hue would not draw a sufficient gate against him, avoided Langford like veritable Black Death after he won the title.

Sam was back at it six weeks later, losing in five rounds to Young Peter Jackson, though later he would have his revenge. In January of 1907, he and Woodman had a falling out, and Sam set off on his own. Now few men in the game at any weight wanted a part of him, but his luck took an upturn when he visited the office of Sam Austin, a New York sporting editor who had seen him against Johnson. Langford made no bones about it, saying that he was game to take on the best that Austin could find. Learning of the split between Sam and Woodman, Austin suggested that they try the waters in England. He warned Langford that it could mean fighting men about whom they knew nothing.

"Sure, I'll go to England," said Sam. "I'll go anywhere, fight anybody, don't matter who it is." Austin wrote to a matchmaker at the London Sporting Club. He offered the fighter against anyone in the country. Two weeks later he received a cable saying, "Will give Langford $1,500 to fight Tiger Smith twenty rounds, April 22." Austin accepted. Langford was jubilant.

To the day he died, Sam had a child's appetite for merriment, and he loved a celebration. At times it could cause a quite a situation. On this occasion, before his departure he spent hours at the bar with a bevy of well-wishers, downing champagne and finally promising everyone a free trip on the mainliner if they came along! On arriving, he went up the gangplank and gestured to Austin, as if to say that the situation was now in his hands. To Austin's alarm, a horde of would-be travelers came at him, and only the action of police kept them from making it up the plank after the "all visitors

The incomparable Sam Langford as he looked in his prime. Dodged even by Jack Johnson, who ironically drew the color line, after winning the heavyweight title, against his fellow African Americans, Langford fought bigger men throughout most of his career. He ranks on ring historian Clay Moyle's list as the greatest fighter in history (c. 1908).

ashore" whistle had blown. When Austin headed for Langford's cabin, he found Sam, head at the porthole, blowing razzberries at the disgruntled mob.

Against Smith, Sam conceded as usual both range and weight. The British, quite high on their own man, saw Tiger as a world-beater. In the first round, nothing dampened their hopes, as Sam bided his time, gauging his man for the delivery. He also was helping to get some money moving, as his own backers were now finding wagers with members of the Smith crowd. In the second, Sam again held off. As Smith forced the action in the third, the crowd went wild.

"How's the betting going?" he asked one of his men during the rest. Assured that all was well in that department, Sam was satisfied. "Fine business," he replied, "Now I's going to get going."

Smith, warming with confidence, was now ripe for a surprise. Out for the fourth with guns blazing, he got it. When Sam exploded a left hook upstairs the British fighter went down like he'd been hit with a crowbar. He lay on the canvas, blood running from a gash over the right eye, thoroughly done.

Other fights had been sketched for Langford in England, Scotland, and Ireland. But in June, when lone taker Jeff Thorne fell in two minutes of the first round, Sam's visit to the Isles was done. Later that summer, he was in Boston, where he reunited with Woodman.

At least a dozen times during these years, Langford fought a good-sized white heavyweight named Jim Barry. Hard-drinking and pugnacious, Barry was a willing mixer always in demand. While he could not be called likeable, Langford respected him for his willingness to fight, and for his refusal to ask, as many men did, to be "carried" the distance. Before it was over, Jim and Sam would meet in New York, Boston, Philadelphia, Los Angeles, Sydney, and Melbourne. While Barry never did get the better of Sam, he gave it his all, and when he met an untimely end years later from a gunshot in a saloon row, the news caused Sam genuine sorrow.

More wins followed before the year was out, and Sam rang up six knockouts in 1908. One opponent for whom he had little affection was Hoboken fireman Andrew Haymes. Known to all as Fireman Jim Flynn, Haymes was a willing mauler who disliked black fighters generally and who could bend a rule book, or tear it in half, when things were not going his way. On one occasion, when unable to contend with the savvy of Jack Johnson, he ended up using his head on Jack like a wild mountain ram. Some years later, he would gain a measure of fame by knocking out an adolescent Jack Dempsey when the young Manassa fighter was on the way up. Woodman figured that this was a chance to make an indirect comparison of Sam with Johnson, using a common opponent as the measuring stick. Sam dropped Flynn in the first round.

* * *

In February of 1906, Tommy Burns, all of 5' 7½" and 172 pounds, won a 20-round decision over Marvin Hart to gain the honors as heavyweight champion of the world. He proceeded to run up a remarkable number of wins in defense of that title, but one contender was left out in the cold. The years of 1907 and 1908, recalls Jack Johnson, "were arduous ones. I struggled diligently in backing up my contentions and I fought in many hard ring events. I took on every potential contender between myself and the champion. I virtually had to mow my way to Burns. I made offer after offer. I proposed all sorts of inducements and made every possible concession."[14]

On December 26, after much fighting, travel, and campaigning, Jack had his long-awaited bout with Tommy Burns at Rushcutters Bay in Australia. Jack, stropped to a razor-fine 192, would remark later that he had trained for that fight like no other in his life. By the time that training wrapped up, he said, he could not succeed in tiring himself with any amount of effort (on one day, he claimed, he succeeded in running down a jackrabbit) by the day that the fight arrived.

It was a sad outcome for Burns, who conceded his challenger nearly five inches in height and at least 25 pounds in natural body weight. Floored in the first round, Tommy could not match Jack for strength, handspeed, or durability. Nor did he have the ring skill that the bigger man now possessed. It was a fight soon marked by much taunting, Johnson ridiculing the champion's pathetic efforts and Burns calling Jack a "yellow cur." It was not an exchange that Burns figured to win on any level, and the bout ended in the fourteenth round when police would not abide the spectacle another minute.

So did an African American ascend to the most coveted throne in the sporting world. A mortified Jack London, seated near the ring, wrote that the bout was like unto "a fight between a colossus and a pigmy ... a grown man cuffing a naughty child," wherein not a single second had belonged to the white man.[15] London's cry ended with an exhortation to former champion Jeffries to come out of retirement to rescue the honor of his own race.

As for Sam, when Johnson now backed out of an earlier tentative agreement to fight him at the National Sporting Club in London, Woodman used it as fuel to convince the British press that Jack was running scared. While Sam would call out the bigger man plenty, when they crossed paths, he never did succeed in getting Li'l Arthur into the ring again.

Langford was soon matched to fight William Iron Hague, who had laid claim to the British heavyweight title after beating Gunner Moir. Thus accompanied by Woodman, he set sail anew for England. Great Britain then, as in later years, was having trouble fielding a credible heavyweight, and longed to see another comer like their own Charley Mitchell, one of the world's best in the late 19th century. Hague, a sturdy 5'10" and 190, could hit a ton with his right hand. He had mopped the ring with several of England's best, and he had beaten Frank Craig, the Harlem Coffee Cooler, one of the better black heavyweights from the States. He and Sam met on May 24, 1909.

A familiar scene — Langford standing over a fallen foe! The bout with Iron Hague, London, 1909.

When he forced the action in the first three minutes, Hague's admirers raised the roof. In the second round, he caught Langford with a right hand, and Sam, off-balance, went down. Back in the corner, Woodman asked Sam if he was in trouble. Sam admitted that Iron was a puncher, but he promised to take care of business. When Hague came out for the third, Sam had at him, and in the fourth, a right on the chin dropped Hague dead to the world. Once more, Sam had put a major dent in British competition — so much so that no one there, at this point, wanted any part of him. Thus he and Woodman sailed for home.

Later Years

Sam, said Joe Jeannette years later, hit like no one else, with the possible exception of Joe Louis, who outweighed the Tar Baby by 30 pounds. "Langford," he insisted, "was the greatest fighter who ever lived. Sam would have been champion any time Johnson had given him a fight. And Johnson knew it better than anybody."[16]

Big or small, Sam continued to fight any man who was available. In the remainder of 1909, he knocked out Klondike, a towering Chicago black heavyweight who had stopped Jack Johnson when Jack was a fledgling novice. He also had furious encounters with a slick middleweight contender, a black–Amerind contender, noted earlier, called Dixie Kid.

Lithe and cute, the Kid was a master of unorthodox moves, such as leaning into the ropes and springing off with a sneak right hand. From the start, the two men played bull and matador, Dixie slipping and sliding, left hand down, inviting an attack so as to sling that counter. Sam, seeing that he could not win a game of tactics, went at his man hard, hammering him where he could. In the fifth round a hook to the ribs folded the Kid like cardboard, and another hook ended it.

Crushed by the loss, Dixie wanted another go, and they met soon afterward in Memphis. This time Sam sailed into him with a vengeance, stopping him in three. (While this fight was thought to mark the Kid's downfall, it is interesting to note that he still had enough left to stop rising Georges Carpentier a year later. Carpentier would fight Jack Dempsey for the heavyweight title several years afterward.) In 1910 Sam again met Jim Flynn, going ten rounds to a no-decision — a case of Sam once more laying off to wrangle a paycheck. On March 17, he faced Flynn a third time in a fight that was billed, to much interest, as a grudge bout.

A fellow named Billy McCarney, who was entering into the industry of motion pictures, had shot lengthy footage of the two men in training, and now he hoped to capture the fight in its entirety on film. As it turned out, however, McCarney had shot more film than he should have — when the time arrived, he was alarmingly short on celluloid.

McCarney, as the story goes, entered Sam's dressing room in a state of desperation, telling him that if the fight went more than eight rounds, he was ruined.

"Billy," said Sam, "there ain't nothin' to worry about."

"What makes you so sure?" asked Billy. "Flynn's no pushover."

Raising his right arm and closing his fist, Sam answered, "This baby will push *anybody* over."

When Sam knocked out Jim in the eighth round, it was said that McCarney all but smothered him with embraces and kissed the glove that had dropped his opponent.[17]

By now Woodman was pushing for a match between Sam and middleweight champion Stanley Ketchel. The two finally met in a Philadelphia ring on April 27 in a six-round bout with no decision. It was mostly a low-key affair, probably geared to set up a more serious encounter, and opinion was divided as to who had the better of it. Unfortunately, there never was a return, as Ketchel met with disaster a few months later at a ranch in Conway, Missouri (see the chapter ahead), where he had gone to regain his health after a stretch of hard living.

In 1910 Jeffries, now hounded for two years from one end of American society to the other, finally made his effort on July 4 in Reno. At 35, dropping some 90 pounds to regain an outward semblance of his old form, he failed miserably, and the search for a White Hope continued. Of Johnson's talent there was no dispute. Jack, Nat Fleischer would remark, "was one of the brainiest fighters I have ever known."[18] He knew the game both in the ring and judging from a distance, and fought with a brilliant economy of motion. In coming years, he would enthrall Nat with accounts of his exploits in the ring, as when he commented on the Reno fight:

> "Well, it's like this, Nat," he said, standing up and throwing himself into fighting pose to demonstrate. "I think it was the blow that closed Jeff's left eye that started him on his downfall.
> "You see, I led and drew him out like *this*. He thought I would come back with my right hand, but I crossed over and shot a strong uppercut to his chin with my left — like *this*. I think that's good ring strategy, although I say it myself, and it certainly won the fight for me and lost it for Jeff."[19]

* * *

Jack London, seated nearby and again reeling in anguish, would admit that there was nothing "beary or primitive" about the Galveston fighter: "His mind," said Jack, "works like chain lightning and his body obeys with equal swiftness."[20] But now Johnson was fighting the dregs of what the division had to offer. In 1911 he repeated an earlier win over Jim Flynn, and continued to refuse — ironically enough — to offer a shot to Langford, or to any fighter of his own race! To confidant Dan McKetrick he once remarked, "I won't fight any of these colored boys now, Dan. I am champion of the world. I have had a hard time to get a chance and I really think I am the only colored fellow who was ever given a chance to win the title. I gave Langford, Jeannette, and those boys a chance before I was champ."[21] When pressed to defend his policy, Jack would argue that another black fighter would not excite the same ticket sales as would a white challenger. The result, in any case, was a freezing out of any such fighter who might extend him a challenge.

Langford did get a worthwhile bout that year when Australian promoter Hugh McIntosh brought prospect Bill Lang to England as a star attraction. Lang, weighing in the mid–190s, stood fully six feet and looked the part of a coming champion. McIntosh put up the worthy sum of $17,500 for Sam and Bill to meet in London on February 21. English fans remembered how

Langford had disposed of other opponents in that town, and they turned out in high style.

Giving up more than five inches in height and some 28 pounds, Sam stormed like an ebony tank into Lang, who quickly sought to stave him off with a jab. Soon Langford's own left hand was bringing blood from the bigger man in profusion. In the sixth, Lang was dropped by a hook to the jaw. A right put him down again. When he got up, Sam swung for the fences and missed. Thus he slipped, and while on one knee, he took a glancing right to the top of his head. Though the punch did no damage, it was ruled a foul by referee Eugene Corri, and Langford got the win by disqualification.

Corri admitted later that he had seized the chance to stop the fight when he did, knowing that Lang would be wrecked if it went further. Langford had again thrilled the Brits, yet he was puzzled as to how the bout had lasted as long as it did, and why his punches had not had their killing force. The answer came later when he examined his gloves in his hotel room. McIntosh had ordered special gloves, white in color, for this fight, which Sam figured were for the benefit of cameras that might pick up better the sight of Lang's punches against his own dark skin. But when Sam cut the mitts open, he discovered the real reason. They had been stuffed with rabbit fur instead of hair, a switch that robbed his punches of much of their sting. Later, when displaying his find to the promoter, he drawled, "I nevah knew 'til I licked Lang how many ways there was to work the *rabbit* punch, Mistah McIntosh!" As a stammering McIntosh tried to play dumb, Sam smiled and walked away.

On August 15, 1911, Langford met another ring immortal, the veteran Philadelphia Jack O'Brien, who had fought Ketchel in an epic bout (see the chapter ahead) two years earlier. O'Brien, a master of footwork, lasted to the fifth round, when Sam got home a terrific right to the heart and Jack took the count.

Few men in the game have ever instilled fear like Sam. In time, heavyweight champion Jack Dempsey would admit that in his own early years, Langford was the one man he avoided. At times this fear could reach comic proportions, as when Sam met up with a good-sized black journeyman named John Lester Johnson. Strong and cagy, John Lester would later give young Jack Dempsey a fight to remember, breaking his ribs with a right hand in the process. But when he entered the ring against Sam, he started to backpedal from the opening bell. As Langford stepped up the attack, the bout turned into a literal race, with John Lester in the lead.

Winded from his exertion and in so-so shape from easy living, Langford decided to take prompt action. Pursuing his man again, he swung and hit the only thing that he could reach, delivering a right-hand haymaker "square on that spot of John Lester's anatomy that comes in closest proximity to his chair when he sits down to his pork chops."[22] Solidly stricken, Johnson went down and took the count. The audience, it is said, yelled "quitter" at the sight of Johnson on the floor, but in fact he was paralyzed from the legs down for some ten minutes by the force of the blow. While technically it was a foul, Johnson neglected to complain, since he wanted no part of a rematch.

* * *

Seeking a shot at either the heavyweight or the light-heavyweight title, Sam labored on through his best years, crossing gloves often with men like Sam McVey and Battling Jim Johnson. On one occasion, he approached Jack Johnson in a Philadelphia café and made his case for a chance at the big prize. Rebuffed, he demanded that they agree on terms, or else, said Sam, "I'se gonna take my coat off an' whale de tar right outen yo' here befo' all dese babies, and dey kin tell de rest ob de worl'." Johnson, it is alleged, invited Sam to sit down with him to talk business on this occasion, only to sneak out minutes later when Sam wasn't looking![23]

The shot never did come, yet through it all, the fighter managed to keep his sense of humor. On one occasion, during the reign of Jack Johnson, he climbed through the ring ropes at a show after several none-too-impressive "white hopes" had taken their bows as potential challengers for Johnson's heavyweight crown. Standing beside him was a fellow of even darker complexion than Sam himself. Sam said something to the announcer, who then laughed and said, "Sam Langford, ladies and gentlemen, has asked me to introduce to you Battling Charcoal, his own particular black hope."[24]

By Sam's account, the moment of his downfall came in 1917, in a bout with towering heavyweight contender Fred Fulton. "They bring this guy Fulton to fight me in Boston in '17," he recalled years later. But at two in the morning, "a man comes to my home in Cambridge ... and says I'm to carry Fulton the route of fifteen rounds or get no *jack*. I needed money, man. So I said OK.

"Then in the seventh round this big feller hauls off and smashes me one like a mallet —*whack* over the left eye. I've never been able to see with that eye since. That's what I get for making a gentleman's agreement. Fulton made his reputation on that fight with a technical kayo. I could have knocked him goofy in the first round."[25]

Years of taking shots on the skull and forehead, week in and week out, were finally taking their toll. In time, the other eye would dim, and Sam would be plying his trade when he could barely make his way to the ring.

Even then, he was formidable. In 1922, he stopped Tiger Flowers, who later became world middleweight champion. In the teens and early '20s he had numerous go-rounds with up-and-coming heavyweight young Harry Wills and at least two bouts with a towering young 6' 3" contender named George Godfrey. In their first meeting, in November of 1920, he flattened George in two rounds, after which an impressed Godfrey asked Sam to be his manager. Sam obliged, and proceeded to look after the young fighter's needs while teaching him how to get the most from his physical assets.

Then Sam's old nemesis Jack Johnson came into the picture. Seeing in George a future champion (the closest that George would ever get, as it turned out, was to become the chief sparring partner of champion Jack Dempsey), Johnson used his charm to pull him away from Langford. When Godfrey broke the news to Sam, the veteran fighter shrugged and (remembering times when he and Johnson had seemed close to nailing down a rematch) warned him that Jack was none too good with promises.

For months, Jack worked with Godfrey, learning in the process that keeping his hulking novice in food and drink was no small expense. In time, however, the investment looked ready to pay off. George was signed for another crack at Sam on August 17, 1921, in Covington, Kentucky. But when Godfrey came out of his corner, looking in style like a young Johnson, Sam laid it on him like a wild man, hammering George down inside a round. Later, as Godfrey climbed in the ranks, Langford's feat of twice knocking him out became a testament to Sam's ability.

As his vision waned, Langford did his best to conceal it. He also steered clear of New York, where he was apt to be examined by a physician prior to clearance. From October of 1922, most of his fights were in Mexico.

By now Sam had no one to handle him, and he had to fend for himself. In March of 1923, he fought journeyman Battling Jim Savage in Mexico City. The bout was first scheduled for 8:00 at night in a bullring, but shortly before the date, things changed when Sam was sweating off some pounds in a Turkish bath. As he was walking past Jim's trainer, Sam looked down. Seeing an object on the floor, he lifted a leg and stepped over it. In fact, it was only a flat rubber mat. Seeing how bad Sam's vision had become, the trainer ducked out of the room and had a quick word with Savage, his manager, and the promoter. In a short while, the fight was rescheduled for the daytime, with Sam's corner facing the sun.

At the bell, Savage came at him, pumping his jab aggressively and backing the smaller man to the ropes. Then, Sam did an odd thing — several times, during the mix, he reached out with his left and gingerly tapped his opponent on the shoulder. Thinking that Langford had nothing to offer,

Savage went for the kill. In fact, Sam was measuring him. As Battling Jim came forward, the squat sage delivered his Sunday best, felling him with a *thud*. Scarcely able to see where his man lay, Langford remained against the ropes as the referee tolled ten.

Since this fight was billed as a contest for the Mexican heavyweight championship, Sam had arguably won a title at last. His final victories of note were in Mexico City in 1923, in bouts with the Spanish (and, some said, Mexican) champion Andres Balsas. When he stopped Andres on April 8 in the sixth round, Sam reinforced his claim to the Mexican title.[26] (Asked years later how he could beat an opponent like Balsas when he could barely see the man, Sam is alleged to have replied, "I didn't need to see him, 'cause I could smell him, and I punched where it stunk.") He also managed a few more wins over his old rival Flynn, and was active into 1926, stopping a fighter billed as Young Jack Johnson in two rounds.

Discovery in Harlem

In time, an operation restored partial sight to Sam's right eye. He managed to make an appearance, now and again, at sporting events, and took a hand at running a saloon in Chicago. During the 1930s, he vanished from the public eye, and nothing more was heard. Yet there were many who remembered him and wondered if he were still around.

"About two weeks ago," announced columnist Al Laney one morning years later, "we began a search through Harlem for Sam Langford, the old Boston Tar Baby."[27] The effort had taken him up and down Lenox and Seventh Avenues into bars and grills, cigar stores, newsstands, and drugstores, all without success. One might have thought that a fighter of Sam's stature would be a hero to every youth in town. But such was not the case: "Zoot-suited youths accosted on street corners invariably looked blank and asked, 'Who he?' A dozen times we were told positively that Sam was dead."

Then, as if by a miracle, they heard that the old fighter was residing in a dingy hall bedroom on 139th Street. A woman led the searchers to the third floor and pointed them down a dark corridor. Entering the room, Laney encountered Langford sitting on the edge of his bed listening to the radio. Sam had little else to occupy him, since he was old, blind, and without a dollar.

He stood up and fumbled for a string that worked the pale bulb in the ceiling. "You come to see *me*?" he asked, wonder resonating in a melodious voice. He had been there alone for some time, and it took him awhile to understand that these visitors were in hope of an interview, which would appear in the paper. "What you want to write about old Sam for? He ain't no good any more. You ever see me fight?" Hoping to coax some words from this aged wonder, they said that they had.

At this time Sam was receiving a small payment each month from a foundation for the blind. His daily routine was to rise early, when two small boys led him to a restaurant for breakfast. He would sit or lie in the dark until late afternoon, when he went out to eat again. While the existence might seem dreary, noted Laney, Sam did not seem depressed. Nor was he the half-sentient creature that they had been led to expect. Though he was illiterate, and had not been to school a day in his life, he had an excellent memory, was a keen mimic, and showed himself now to be a remarkable storyteller.

All his stories were amusing. He could have told some of another sort, but when pressed, he would only drift back to those of a kind nature. He laughed continually, with a laugh so infectious that one forgot his situation. As Laney put it, "There is no drop of hate in his soul for anyone."

"Don't nobody need to feel sorry for old Sam," he said. "I had plenty good times. I been all over the world. I fought maybe three, four hundred fights and every one was a pleasure. If I had me a little change in my pocket I'd get along fine."[28]

Laney returned on Christmas Eve of that year, by which time his column and subsequent campaign had produced a $10,000 trust fund for the fighter. "Chief," said Sam on that occasion, "this gonna be the best Christmas I ever had. Maybe you could put it in the paper."

Many of these friends, observed Laney, had never seen Sam: "That is one of his remarkable qualities. You do not have to know him to be his friend and know the kind of man he is." On this occasion there was light in the room, and Sam had friends with him, not to mention gifts from all quarters. On this Christmas his old voice would ring the rafters.

"To hear Sam laugh and sing," said Laney, "is one of the most profound Christmas experiences a man can have." In his column for December 15, he wrote of Sam's gratitude to all who had helped him:

"You see that bottle, Chief?" he said last night.

"If you come back here on the Fourth of July it'll still be some in it. But tomorrow I'm gonna have myself a couple of good belts. Oil myself up some for a little geetar playin'. Boy! Listen to that thing talk. She shore talk sweet, don't she?

"You tell all my friends I'm the happiest man in New York City. I got a geetar and a bottle of gin and money in my pocket to buy Christmas dinner. No millionaire in the world got more than that, or anyhow they can't use any more. Tell my friends all about it and tell 'em I said God bless 'em."

VIII

The Michigan Assassin: Stanley Ketchel

It is disconcerting to be in the ring with a man who has two "best hands," who is as liable to start one as the other on a knockout errand.

W.W. Naughton, describing the power of Stanley Ketchel

There was never, thought Nat Fleischer, a truer fighter or a more colorful figure in all of the sweet science. Stanley Ketchel "was game as a bulldog and tough as a bronco. There was no stopping him."

The title "Assassin" fit him, for that he was—"a rushing, tearing demon of the ring, who made his opponent think that all the furies of Hades had been turned loose."[1] His strongest traits, adds this historian and personal confidant of Stan himself, were his generosity outside the ring and his relentlessness inside it; likewise, "his egotism and eternal confidence and faith in himself ... his utter fearlessness and superb courage."

Ketchel, called Steve by his friends, was born Stanislaus Kiecal[2] on September 14, 1886, in Grand Rapids, Michigan. Hailing from German and Polish ancestors, with blondish-brown hair and blue-grey eyes, he stood 5'9" and weighed at his best in the mid-to high 150s. In a torrid career that ended abruptly in a violent death, he went into the ring more than 60 times, suffering but four losses, two when still a novice. In that time he crossed gloves with men of every size, some of them ring immortals.

Whether it was his spectacular punching power, his hell-to-pay style, or his sudden end — in some mix these things emblazoned him forever in the minds of those who saw him. As to his story, one has to read much of what is written with reserve. Ketchel's life lent itself easily to legend, and he himself did not discourage the tendency. Stan, according to John Lardner, had a pulp fiction writer's mind and a taste for melodrama. He could not resist "stringing his saga with tinsel," much of which made its way into the sources, including Fleischer's biography. Stan's closest friends in the final year of his life, adds Lardner, were "the three greatest Munchausens in America — Willus Britt, a fight manager; Wilson Mizner, a literary con man; and Hype Igoe, a romantic journalist."[3]

But some things emerge from the sources with clarity: Stanley was complex, capable in polar extremes of tenderness and ferocity. On social introductions, he was shy to the point of timidity; once acquainted with a face, his transformation was electric. He could weep, said friends, at the sight of a painting on a whorehouse wall that depicted little sheep lost in a storm. He had the same reaction to piano ballads played at one of his haunts near Broadway, during his ring heyday, where singers and songwriters hung out.

Madly superstitious, he might throw a fit if someone dropped a hat on his bed or opened an umbrella at the wrong moment in his training camp. Entering the ring, he insisted upon a ritual handshake with his cornermen, always shaking last with his friend Pete "the Goat" Stone. A picture of concentration when the chips were finally down, he was all but impossible to contain in the hours preceding. Away from the ring, he was "the soul of generosity," an easy mark for any sad story that crossed his path.[4] Yet it was said by some that he had a devil tearing at his insides.

It was as leader of a bunch known as the West Sides, said Stanley, that he learned to scrap. He was, by his own admission, a tough kid who needed walloping and got it often from his father. While he had little scholarship, he was engaging, and he knew how to get from people what he wanted.

As to the scholarship, Ketchel's friend Mizner, noted above, would tell wryly of how he had once explained to Stan the theory of evolution. That evening, he came upon him studying a bowl of goldfish and muttering in consternation. Asked what was the matter, the fighter is alleged to have said, "I've been watching these damned fish for nine hours, and they haven't changed a bit."

Whether or not it happened, the story may reveal something of how Stan came across to certain observers. Certainly there is no doubt that young Ketchel was game for adventure. Enamored with tales of the James Gang and slingers of the Colt and Winchester, he departed home early to ride the rails, seeking what vestige was left of the Old West.

By Fleisher's account,[5] Stan's entrance into boxing came with a chance run-in that he had while working as a bellhop at a seamy joint in Butte called the Copper Queen. On this occasion a bouncer, known for his rough brand of humor, tripped him, sending an armload of trays and dishes flying.

When Ketchel gave the fellow a trouncing, he won the favor of owner Josh Allen, himself a fight fan, who fired the bully and hired Stan in his place. One night soon after, when he flattened a trouble-seeking customer, Stan caught the eye of Sid Lamont, a local lightweight of some reputation who saw in him the stuff of a world-beater. After Sid taught him a few basics, he got schooling in depth from Maurice Thompson, a seasoned pug who turned "workouts" into fights with no quarter given.

Soon he found himself in a Butte honky-tonk, volunteering to go four rounds with a welterweight named Jack Tracey, who was offering a sawbuck to anyone who could last the limit. It was alleged to be a dirty affair, wherein Jack had an accomplice behind a curtain who could administer, if need be, a whack on the head to a man once Tracey had him in position. Wise to the game, Stanley managed not only to give Jack a whipping, but to put him on the receiving end of his own trick for good measure.[6] Collecting the ten dollars afterward figured to be another battle, but Lamont and his boys made sure that he got it.

As word of the fight got out, Stan became the talk of the town. In succeeding months he made a fast rise,[7] relying on Lamont and his old boss Allen for training advice and help in concealing a lack of book knowledge about which he was keenly sensitive. When Stan made a game showing against Thompson in a fight that saw him fouled and badly licked, the neighborhood gained a hero.

Stanley Ketchel, who hit as hard, pound for pound, as any man alive. Fleischer counted Stan as the best all-time among the middleweights. Ketchel's bouts with Joe Thomas and Billy Papke were wars to remember (c. 1908).

A Dramatic Arrival

In 1904 he would lose another decision to Thompson, and then pull even with him in a ten-round draw at year's end. He also racked up eleven wins, all by KO. In the following year he won, but for a lone draw, all of his fights, scoring a knockout in each of 17 victories.

What Stanley lacked at this point in guile, he had in power. His right hand was devastating, and equally so his left hook, which he sometimes threw with a "shift," starting a right and then unloading the other hand with full-weight force. In 1906 he rang up wins right and left until a California newsman named R.A. Smith, seeing Stan in a Butte club, urged him to seek out a place where he would be seen better. Smith gave Ketchel a letter to make his introduction in Sacramento, and the next day the young fighter hopped a rail in that direction.

The year 1907 saw Stan hit the headlines. In a day when most men steered clear of black opposition, he would mix with anyone. At this time, a formidable African American fighter named George "KO" Brown was making his living in that California town, and he had beaten some of the best in the division. The promoter, a fellow named Inglis, wanted to see Brown against heralded "Wonder Man" Joe Thomas of San Francisco on July 4. Brown and Thomas had already fought a ten-round draw, and Inglis thought that a quick go with the young wayfarer from Montana would provide quick cash in the meantime.

When Stan opened camp, he looked crude, and George's people figured him as a tune-up. The fighters met in Sacramento on May 23. What transpired in the first three minutes did nothing to change opinion, as the favorite, boxing easily, set the tune. When the second round ended, the only pertinent question was whether George and Joe might draw a record gate weeks down the line.

Then, in the third, the gods spoke and lightning struck. The young rail-rider bounced a right hand off Brown's chin. Before the stricken man could fall, he added an uppercut to the same place. Brown went down like a building. He was out for more than ten minutes.

A Sure Enough Fightin' Fool

Stan, already jubilant over his $500 guarantee for that fight, now wanted to take Brown's place against Thomas. Inglis, too, liked the idea, though he was not overly friendly about the wad that he had just dropped on George. By now, middleweight champion Tommy Ryan[8] had retired, and Thomas was the strongest heir-claimant to the throne. Over the past couple of years, Joe had cleaned house, knocking out anyone who would go with him after the standoff with Brown.

Was Ketchel a match for Thomas? Lou Trevor, head of the committee that would organize the celebration of the nation's birth, held a conference with his fellows. "It may be just as well," he stated, "that Brown got trimmed ... because this youngster that whaled him is a sure enough fightin' fool, a slugging devil if I ever saw one." Stan did not figure to beat Thomas, but it would be a piece of action while it went, and the Michigander would go down fighting. And Ketchel's growing fan base bode well for the gate. (This following, alleges Fleischer, owed something to Stan's tiff with a thug named Bill Barton. Six feet and 200 pounds, Barton was a cruel wielder of the blackjack who patrolled the railroads and was detested by those who knew him. When he went after Ketchel, goes the story, Stan flattened him barehanded and became a hero to all who were present.)

That night Trevor's right-hand man Cal Somers found Stan in Marysville's main dance hall. Like many kids from the down side of the tracks, Ketchel loved style. Having laid out a hunk of change for a new set of threads, he was now stepping fancy with a lass from the neighborhood. Amazed at the young hobo's transformation, Somers eyed him with interest. When the music stopped, he made his bid.

"Lou wants to see you at once," he announced. "He's figuring on having you meet Joe Thomas for twenty rounds on the Fourth." Thomas, he stressed, was counted by some newsmen as being the champion already. But if Stan was going to have a chance, he would have to change his habits.

Stan shrugged. "I can't bother with Trevor tonight," he explained. First he was going to see the dance through to the end. But any man that Trevor found for an opponent — what difference did it make? — was all right.

Somers, taken aback, relayed the message. The next day, Ketchel learned that his end would be $1,000, win, lose, or draw, while the California fighter would get $2,500. The guarantee, explained the promoter, was to safeguard Stan's end of the bargain, since Thomas was "one tough hombre."

"So am I," rejoined Stan. He would go winner take all, if Joe wanted.

"Say," asked Trevor, intrigued by the attitude of this youngster, "how old are you?"

"Twenty-one," said Ketchel, "old enough to know I can lick any guy near my weight in the world. If you want to make some easy dough, have a bet on me. This Thomas bird ain't any tougher than plenty of other bimboes I've sent to the cleaners." A champion, he reasoned, was only one "until some fellow comes along and belts him down." And he was ready to do some explosive work on Independence Day.

Thomas, who had outgrown the going welterweight limit of 142 pounds, was around 150 for this fight, Stan tipping the scales at 147. After 20 rounds, when the fight was judged even, Ketchel's star had risen. Veteran observers were amazed that an established force like Thomas could be held even by a novice. And Ketchel had more than held his own — when Joe was knocked through the ropes in the 11th, only the gong had saved him. If Stan did not get the decision, he had won in a bigger way. He was the hottest name on the circuit.

Laying Waste to a Division

There was, wrote John Lardner, "a true fiendishness in the way he fought."[9] Like heavyweight champion Jack Dempsey of the following decade, he was a mild-mannered kid who turned killer when the bell released his primal instinct. After the bout in Marysville, veteran referee Billy Roche, matchmaker for James J. Coffroth's fight club in Colma, California, wired Stan with the offer of a return go that coming Labor Day, September 2. By the laws governing Colma action, this could be a "finish" fight, meaning a duration, if needed, of 45 rounds.

"I'll give you boys," he said, "fifty per cent of the house."

"Suits me," said Stan. Thomas said likewise.

Ketchel did not dispute over a single detail, something that amazed Roche, who was used to dealing with men who sought an advantage down to the last smidgen. When Roche and Thomas talked it over, Joe insisted that the fighters' split would be 75–25 his way. He also stipulated a weight limit of 150, to be met at 10 A.M. the day of the fight. Each fighter deposited $250 as a forfeit against failure to make the limit that morning.

Once they weighed, Ketchel went to a poolroom and bet the refunded money on himself at 2 to 1 on Thomas. Then he asked Coffroth what the gate receipts might total. The promoter said that he hoped for fifteen thousand. Whereupon Ketchel asked for the loser's minimum right there, so that he could bet it all! Never had the veteran dealer heard such a proposal. Amazed, he handed over the money, and Stan bet every dime. When Roche suggested that he keep back some dough to protect against hard times, he got a classic Ketchel reply: "It's all or nothing with me, sport. I never hedged in my life for marbles or money. Anyway, I'm due to win sure. There's no fighter around my weight that I can't lick inside of 45 rounds."

Roche, who refereed the fight, would say later that he never saw the like in all his years as third man in the ring. He also found Ketchel to be something to remember as a puncher. "After I had given the men their instructions," he recalled, "they went to their corners and the gong rang. Ketchel came out fast and hooked a left to the body, missing with a wild right at the same time. The punch whizzed by my ear and I plainly felt the wind of it."[10] In that instant Billy saw that Ketchel was dangerous even to a bystander.

The action soon had a pattern, Ketchel going for the body, Thomas meeting him with standup jabs and right hands. But when Thomas landed, Stan was unfazed. The war of wills continued into the ninth, when a left hook on the cheekbone sent Joe to the canvas. Wary, Thomas took the benefit of "nine" before rising.

As rounds tolled, spectators watched in admiration, and then awe. After 25, Thomas was giving ground, but he was still in it, and cagy enough to keep something in reserve. In the 29th, he caught Stan coming with a right-hand bomb. Ketchel dropped backward, his head whipping the canvas, at which point, it seemed, the contest was over. Yet slowly, with iron resolve, he made it to his feet. He lasted the round.

At that point, Roche would say, something went out of Joe. While he managed two more frames, it was now Ketchel's fight.[11] In the 32nd round, Stanley got home a left underneath and a right to the jaw, sending Thomas to the ropes in a swoon, where he hung beaten. His corner threw the towel.

As Billy recalled, "Never in my ring experience had I seen two men go at such a clip over as long a distance, and never before or since have I seen a man able to hit as hard a blow as the two Ketchel landed after thirty-two rounds.... Ketchel carried his punch longer than any man that ever breathed."[12]

It was an amazing fight, and fans wanted more. While Stan had won, each man had been down in the process, and Thomas, some imagined, would have had the advantage over a shorter distance. Thus an offer was made for a third go with a 20-round limit. "I'm willing to lick him every night in the week, if they'll ante up," replied Ketchel.

On December 12, 1907, they met in the San Francisco Seals baseball park, amidst a night storm that lent to the proceedings thunder, lightning, and rain in torrents. At one point the wind tore apart a canvas that covered the ring, and the water came down, splashing floor, fighters, referee, and press row occupants. When makeshift electric lights started going out, spectators went like monsoon refugees for the wooden grandstand.

Fighters and referee, wrote Fleischer, now "looked like phantoms struggling in the twilight of the world." But Ketchel and Thomas were oblivious to anything in the world but each other. In the first round, Ketchel dropped

Joe with a left to the head; in the second, Thomas got in licks of his own. By the end of twelve, Ketchel was emerging as the stronger man. Thomas, down in the 15th, somehow rallied to score a flash knockdown himself in the last round, with the crowd going wild at the bell. When it was over, the referee held up Ketchel's hand.

His prior knockout of Thomas had given Stan an arguable claim to the middleweight title. But the claim was disputed by several men, among them Jack "Twin" Sullivan. When Ketchel issued a challenge to Jack, he was told that he should prove himself against his twin sibling Mike, who had established himself as a prime welterweight contender.

While Stan's followers were indignant, the fighter himself took it in stride. Asked about the situation by a columnist, he remarked, on a sly note, that it reminded him of a book from which his mother had once read to him about the Civil War. In it was the tale of a man who urged all of his relatives onto the front lines while he would stay home and *pray* for victory! "Maybe," he said, "Jack Sullivan figures things that way."

When Stanley flattened Mike in one round, brother Jack, to his credit, made good. A veteran of scores of fights (some estimated a hundred) over the past decade, this other sibling figured to be a tough proposition. On May 9, 1908, ten weeks after Stan knocked out Mike, he and Ketchel met in Colma. This one was a longer affair, with Jack having good moments early. But soon Stan's attack was taking its toll. Twice Jack went down, holding his groin and claiming a foul. But referee Billy Roche, having none of it, said to him on the second occasion, "Get up and fight like a man." Sullivan did his best, but by the 20th round, he was done. Searing rights to the mid-section dropped him in a heap, and he barely beat the count. A right hand under the heart ended it.

The win strengthened Stan's hold on the title. One viable claimant, however, still disputed it. On June 4, 1908, Stan met the fighter who would become his greatest rival, a tow-headed, cherub-handsome athlete of murderous right hand punching power and day-long endurance. Known as the Illinois Thunderbolt, the man was Billy Papke.

This meeting, which would be the first of four, was set for ten rounds. They squared off in Milwaukee, each man scaling 154. It was a spirited fight from the opening. Stan had the first advantage when he floored Billy in the opening seconds with a left hook on the button. Up in a hurry, Papke showed his mettle. In the second round, each man was shaken, and Stan was on the ropes when the bell sounded.

Billy, running red from nose and mouth, kept up the attack. Hurt by a body shot in the fifth, he found Ketchel's jaw late in the round with a right hand that had the champion on one knee. In the sixth, Stan's own right had Billy down, and another doubled the Illinois fighter near the bell. The rest of the way it was a barn-burner, and only the bell stopped short a toe-to-toe in each of the last two frames. The verdict went to the champion, but Papke had earned respect. Afterward, attending physician James Frew would say that the constitution of each man had been nothing short of astounding. Papke, said Frew, was the only man he had ever examined before a fight whose heart rate was perfectly normal. It was his extraordinary condition that had enabled the challenger to stand up to Ketchel for ten rounds.[13]

On July 31, Stan defended the title against his only remaining rival, Chicago's Hugo Kelly. For two rounds, fans got a rousing show, as Kelly nailed Ketchel hard and bloodied his nose. But Stan could whack, and here it came — at the bell for round three, blood still coming from his nose, he met Kelly two-thirds of the way across the ring, where each man opened fire. As the challenger went to the body with his right hand, Ketchel let go his full-weight hook, catching Hugo on the jaw. The blow sent Kelly to his haunches, whereupon he sank back quivering, as if hit by a grenade. He was carried to his corner.

At this point the reviews of Stan's performances were verging on rhapsody. Fate, remarked W.W. Naughton, "has been kind to the Michigander in endowing him with what some one is pleased to describe as two right hands. He can hit like a piledriver with either fist, and he has such freedom of action that he is dangerous at all times."[14]

On August 18, Ketchel again met Thomas. This time the Californian played it safe in the first minute. Then, getting home his left a couple of times, he was encouraged. And then Stan erupted. A right-hand smash under the heart drained Joe of his spirit and a left hook closed his right eye. Another hook put him on the floor. Up at eight, he had little left. In the second, only Stan's blood craze made him miss, until a left hand, launched from underneath, caught Thomas on the chin with brain-wrecking force. Joe hit the floor in sections, first with his knees, then with his forehead, at last rolling onto his side, completely done.

The Sneak Attack of the Thunderbolt

There was talk at this time of Stan meeting Tommy Burns for the heavyweight title. But soon after the Thomas fight, he agreed to a rematch with Papke. They signed for a fight in California at Jim Jeffries's Athletic Club in the town of Vernon on Labor Day, September 7. Big Jeff would referee.

There was an issue as to the required weight, with Papke's corner wanting

156 at 11:00 the day of the fight and Ketchel's side preferring 158 at noon. Now able to call the shots, the champion had his way. It was also decided that winner and loser would split 60–40 on the purse. By this time, Ketchel was uncontested as the best in the world, and betting reflected it. He was installed as a 10-to-4 favorite, with even money saying that he would do it inside 15 rounds. Still, each man was an image of fighting strength in the hours leading up.

The last time, Ketchel had seized an early advantage, but he now got the surprise of his life when flaxen-haired Billy did him one better. In the day, fighters were often expected to shake hands at the bell sounding the first round. But when Ketchel extended his right hand in observance of the custom, Papke took a free swing with his left, then unloaded a right hand that caught him flush between the eyes. The punch sent Stan tumbling, breaking his nose and starting his eyes to close.

Struggling up on Queer Street, the champion furnished target practice for the rest of the round. Fighting on deep instinct, he was down three times in three minutes. Floored again in the sixth, he was all but blind.

On it went — the beating of Stanley's life. Twice, in desperation, chief second Pete lanced his face to give him momentary sight. In the twelfth, Papke drilled him with a right and Ketchel went down for a count of eight. Another right did the same, and this time Jeffries tolled nine before motioning to Stan's seconds that the fight was over.

Revenge

Ketchel did not dwell on controversy that ensued over how the fight had started. True, he had been ambushed, but he said only that he should have been ready for anything and that he was anxious to fight Papke again. It was thought that he would need six months to recuperate, yet he signed for a third match with Billy in Colma to take place on Thanksgiving Day, November 26.

The two men, noted columnist T.S. Andrews, would "put up another slashing bout at San Francisco, for neither one knows anything in a fight but to mix from the tap of the gong."[15] While each man had a measure of style, it would be mayhem when the action got hot. Pressmen across the country were pounding their keys with joy. In the days leading up, there was argument as to the logical favorite: Maybe Stan was better overall, but what had that beating taken out of him? And when had a man won back the crown after losing it?

There was also concern, among those close to him, that Stan's acquired love of high-speed motoring might spell his end before he made it to the ring. At times, recalled friend and journalist Hype Igoe in later years, Stan would pilot his high-powered Lozier down a stretch of primitive road at 80 miles an hour, oblivious to the chance he was taking with his life, or with Igoe's. But Ketchel wanted this win as he had wanted no other. He gave up the racing and took to the hills on foot, honing himself into the shape of his life.

He also had supporters among his fight brethren, including feather-weight great Abe Attell, who had worked his corner for the fight in Milwaukee. That surprise right hand from Papke in Vernon, insisted Abe, was not a duplicate of Ketchel's opening move in their first fight. Stan, though he had started fast, had not hit his man *during* the handshake. Papke's move, by contrast, was a gross foul. Seeing how Stan had mastered him the first time, Abe reasoned, he figured to win.[16]

Again, the lack of footage for some of these bouts is unfortunate. Over the years, Ketchel's side of the story, where he and Papke are concerned, has become the standard. But while Papke's own voice is seldom heard in this connection, it deserves note: "When we met in Milwaukee," he recalled before this third bout, "we shook hands as the gong sounded. Ketchel not only held my hand in a viselike grip, but he pulled me toward him and hit me flush in the face with a hard left, breaking a tooth and knocking me down. Right then, I decided I would get even for that trick.... I could have finished Ketchel much sooner, but I figured he deserved an extra dose of punishment."[17]

However the accusations might fly, betting at this time ran 10-to-7 for Billy. Hearing of it, Ketchel responded by authorizing the sale of his automobile, for as close to $3,000 as the machine would draw, and putting it down on himself. By fight time, there was no doubt as to the condition of the principals, with each hitting the scales at a nail-hard 158.

On this occasion there was no shake, and thus no chance provided for a sneak attack by either man. But once the fighting started, Ketchel was the master. While infighting was Papke's *forte*, he was beaten at it as Stan ripped him time and again, often without a counter.[18] In the fourth round, Stan drew blood from Billy's nose. In the fifth, a left to the body and a right to the jaw had Papke in trouble; two rounds later, an overhand right made him wobble.

Papke's best moment came in the ninth, when he got across a bone-shattering right to Stanley's nose that brought blood rushing. But the hope was short-lived, as Ketchel, his own claret now flying from his chin with each exertion, renewed the attack.

All but done at round's end, Papke managed a dead-game rally in the tenth. But Ketchel answered for the eleventh with the vim he had shown at the first gong. Regrettably, no footage of the fight is known to exist. Recalling the scene nearly four decades later, revered fight author Billy McCarney described it as follows: "The knockout punch was delivered as Papke was backing away from the ropes with guard down. As they separated from a clinch ... Papke stepped back with his hands handing at his sides. Quick as a flash, Ketchel took advantage of the opening, swung a left that landed flush on the jaw and down went Billy."[19] At this point, referee Jack Welsh began the count. On reaching ten, he added "eleven" as an exclamation point and tossed up the hand of the winner. Papke, thoroughly dazed, did not know for several minutes that the fight was over.

It often happens that a fighter waits years after his departure to receive full credit for what he has done. While active, he suffers by comparison with men who have gone before. Then, in two or three decades, galvanized in the public mind, his own exploits now sun-washed in reminiscence, he gains his place on the sacred hill. But this time the columnists did not wait.

Accounts the next morning sang the news that Ketchel was in command from the opening bell and near-flawless in his execution. Stan's win, it was said, "stamps him as one of the most marvelous pieces of fighting machinery that the game has ever known."[20] He overcame suspicion also, circulating for some time, that elegant living had softened him irreversibly against reaching high form again.

One more bout with Papke would take place, when he and Stan met under a blazing sun on July 5, 1909, in Colma. Like the others, it was fought with animosity. "I didn't imagine," referee Billy Roche would remark when it was done, "that two humans could stand such punishment. This country is surely breeding some healthy stock, if what I saw in the ring is a criterion." (Film footage of this fight, though it depicts constant mauling, bears out Roche's admiration. The pace would exhaust many of today's fighters well within the limit. It shows also that Stan, while he tended toward wildness, had dynamite in both hands.) Each man would shed blood in the fight, and each would break a hand. Seemingly beaten on a couple of occasions, Billy managed to rally and was still landing late in the fight. It went 20 with Ketchel getting the verdict.

Philadelphia Jack

The saga of another ring immortal began one night in Philadelphia in December of 1896 when Joseph F. Hagan, not yet 19 years of age and a truck driver by trade, climbed through the ropes to sub for an absentee named

Jack O'Brien. No one figured the kid to last, but he amazed the fans, and maybe himself, by holding up his end to the final bell. Soon after, he launched a career of his own, taking Jack's name and prefixing to it the name of his native city.

Starting in the 130s, O'Brien fought his most famous bouts within the bounds of today's middle or super-middleweight limit. A stiff hitter with each hand, he could beat a man with a vengeance when inclined, but often he let it go the limit. Primarily he was a student, like Jim Corbett and Joe Gans, leaning to the game's fine points.

In those days, many bouts in Philly went as "no decision" if they did not end in a knockout. The result is that O'Brien's genius is less evident than it might be. Then again, the record is pretty good as it stands. A four-round points edge by the great veteran Bobby Dobbs was his one loss in his first three years of campaigning. In February of 1900 he was stopped by Young Peter Jackson in 13 rounds, and the two men would be rematched in a couple of bouts five years later, O'Brien winning each time.[21]

On his best nights, Jack was amazing. Talented, game to the marrow, he would rank with the game's greatest. (Nat Fleischer rated him number 2 among the light-heavyweights and Charley Rose put him at number 3.) Suave and cerebral, he made a rather incongruous pug. He was a member of the Pennsylvania Bar Association, and a stylistic fashion piece who could make one or two changes of clothes in the course of a day. He was deemed a veritable "Dr. Jekyll and Mr. Hyde" owing to the contrast between what he did in the ring and how he handled himself in society, where he was called "the embodiment of polite accomplishments."[22]

Such was his way with the public that Jack was a virtual ambassador when he fought abroad. In 1901 and 1902 he won over fans in England and Scotland even while dropping some of their best contenders. In coming years he scored wins over some of the best in three divisions, including Joe Choynski, Al Kaufmann, Jack "Twin" Sullivan, and future heavyweight champion Tommy Burns. Late in his career, he managed to give a smart account of himself in a six-round no-decision bout with heavyweight champion Jack Johnson.

On July 23, 1904, Jack engaged Bob Fitzsimmons in a six-round no-decision bout that had each man sure he was master of the other. On October 7, he won a six-round nod over Tommy Burns in Milwaukee. In the October following, he scored a punishing knockout of young Al Kaufmann in 17 rounds, and so demand arose for a showdown with Fitzsimmons.

The freckled warrior, as some called him, was now 42 years of age. But the punch, as they say in the game, is the last thing to go, and Bob still had it. Yet as time approached, there was doubt whether it would offset an age difference between the fighters of nearly 15 years. Observers figured that Fitz might handle himself with anybody for a few rounds, but how would he fare over a scheduled 20? As the day approached, Jack was doing a brisk eight miles of roadwork, plus an hour on the bags and pull-weights, and sparring a couple of rounds to keep his ring moves sharp. By the time he wrapped up training, he was a fierce piece of machinery, impressing onlookers with a deft jab and lightning work afoot.

Indeed, it was a battle as far as it went, fought on December 20 before a roaring crowd at San Francisco's Mechanics' Pavilion. Jack, in his customary way, darted in and out, nailing Fitz to nose and mouth with blows that took a bloody toll as rounds passed. On occasion, the older man got home, but he could not hold the pace.

A warrior to the end, he drew blood from O'Brien in the tenth round and forced the action in the eleventh. Tough exchanges marked the twelfth, at which point Fitz was all but done. When he landed a couple of times in the 13th, it was his dying gasp. Sitting in his corner at the end of that round, he slumped forward and referee Ed Graney called a halt. O'Brien, seeing the great man's plight, rushed over to help revive him with a bottle of ammonia. Sitting for several minutes after, Fitz bowed his head once more and wept.

In the following year Jack would challenge Burns for the heavyweight title and come away with a 20-round draw. By 1909, however, the miles were telling. At 31 he was in his autumn. Ketchel, in the meantime, had run out of matches on the West Coast. He hired Willus Britt, a skilled publicist and negotiator and brother of world-class lightweight Jimmy Britt, as his manager. Soon he and Willus took the train back east where good fights were in the offing. It was getting harder for the champion to make the middleweight limit, but this one was worth taking. He and Jack signed to meet in a fight at Fiss, Doerr, and Carroll's horse market on East 24th Street in New York on March 26 of the following spring.

A Classic Ring Drama

"However much I enjoy a match between two good men, I believe that the most thrilling fight I ever saw was between a water buffalo and a tiger." This remark comes from the hand of author and world traveler Gilbert Forte in a piece for *Boxing and Wrestling* magazine titled "The One Who Was Best of All."[23] In this account Forte describes, as an aside, the greatest episode of sheer combat he ever witnessed. It happened when he and several companions were exploring a tiger-infested realm of India.

With the party was a domesticated water buffalo; in the thicket was a striped stalker, eyeing the little caravan and waiting its chance. Suddenly the cat appeared, advancing on the buffalo. Moving nimbly, side to side, it leaped onto the horned beast, sinking its fangs into the back of its neck. Shaken, the buffalo lowered its head, then dug into the gut of the feline with a compact jolt. Falling away, the stricken animal paused to regroup.

Clawing its way back, the tiger renewed the exchange. So the fight continued, seeming to favor the more agile competitor. Yet the buffalo, raked and bloodied, never quit finding a way to dig those mortal shots underneath. "In less than three minutes and a dozen short blows of the truly formidable horns," notes the awed writer, "the tiger lay on his back definitely dead."

The jungle episode is relevant to boxing, he adds, because it illustrates the advantage of compact blows over more flamboyant styles of attack. Likening the jolts of that buffalo to the punches of Joe Louis, he names Jack Johnson, Louis, Jack Dempsey, and Jim Jeffries as the greatest heavyweights of all time. While Forte does not mention the fight between Ketchel and Philadelphia Jack O'Brien, he might have found it to his liking.

Sometimes the real test of a fighter, once observed Nat Fleischer, "is not in having a good hand, but in playing a poor hand well."[24] When he met Ketchel, Jack had logged 14 rugged years. By now he had faded some, but he still had his wits. Throughout his career, in fact, those wits had served him well in pre-fight negotiations. It was alleged, before the Fitzsimmons fight, that prior to Jack's 1903 bout with Marvin Hart, when Marvin had come in twelve pounds over the agreed limit of 170, Jack managed to wrangle Marvin's side into forfeiting his share of the purse in the event that Marvin knocked him out! (Though the bout went six rounds to a no-decision, O'Brien was credited — to no surprise, in light of this arrangement — with a one-sided unofficial win.) But if he had been chided at times during his career for seeking, in legalistic fashion, certain concessions,[25] on this night he would show as much heart as a man can have.

The contract called for a weight of 158, with two pounds' grace allowed. That afternoon, Ketchel hit the scale at exactly the figure specified, while Jack was 160. The mutual greeting of the two men at that time was low-key, rather like the proverbial pre-storm lull, giving no indication of what would soon transpire.

"Mr. Ketchel," said O'Brien, extending a hand, "I'm glad to meet you. I didn't know you were so young and good-looking. Your remarkably fine record deceived me."

"'Lo, Jack," returned Stan, "I've heard a lot about you."

At fight time, however, the fighters presented a contrast. Ketchel, in

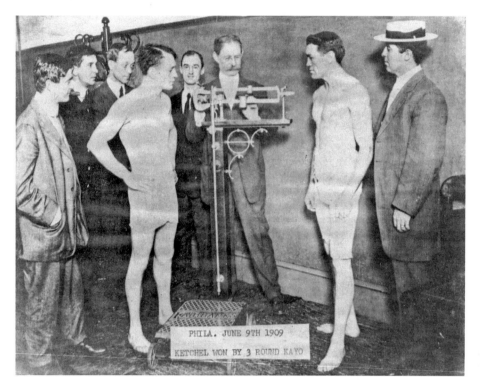

PHILA. JUNE 9TH 1909
KETCHEL WON BY 3 ROUND KAYO

Two immortals: Stan Ketchel and Philadelphia Jack O'Brien at the weigh-in preceding their second bout in June of 1909. Their first fight was called by several
journalists one of the most memorable ever fought.

bright red trunks, was a fresh picture of youth, while O'Brien seemed pale
and past his real years. Where the senior athlete was stern and collected,
Stan could scarcely hold his exuberance.

Then the bell. As it often was with Stan, there was little time wasted —
he came at Jack with bad intention. O'Brien, in classic style, relied on jab
and movement. Before the round was over, that educated left hand had
raised a welt over Ketchel's eye, and the Michigan fighter had got home a
resounding hook to the body.

On taking that hit, Jack turned to the referee, claiming a low blow, but
without success. According to Nat, who saw the weigh-in and the bout firsthand, the blow in fact was not low, and O'Brien's move was probably just
to make both the referee and Stanley wary of the possibility. (Nat adds, "I
didn't like the foxy move at all, but later in the fight, when I saw that
O'Brien was even more the lion than he was the fox, I forgave him for it.")
Jack continued his stick-and-move game in the second while Ketchel landed

again downstairs. Near the end of the round, a winging left opened a cut under Jack's right eye.

From that point it was a deadly contest, fire and ice, Ketchel supplying the heat and O'Brien meeting him with stone-cold resolve. It was Ketchel's in-close rips against O'Brien's jab, a flashing rapier that kept him in the fight longer than another man would have lasted.

"I had heard that Ketchel's dynamic onslaught was such that it could not readily be withstood," O'Brien years later would say, "but I figured I could jab his puss off.... I should have put the bum away early, but my timing was a fraction of an iota off."[26] And jab that mouth he did, at every chance. Yet Stan, when stung, would only grimace and come on, feeding crazily off each trade.

By the sixth, O'Brien had marked him up plenty, and Jack's own eyes and mouth were bleeding. Like that tiger, maybe, the Philadelphia fighter had grace and valor, but a little at a time, the life was leaving him. At round's end, blows downstairs had him stooped when he went to his corner. Amazingly, he began the seventh with a rally, but then it was Ketchel in close again.

It looked like the end in the ninth, when a hook to the body sent Jack against the ropes and to the floor. Yet he made his feet and lasted to the tenth. In the final frame Jack met Stan with little left but brazen nerve. At last Ketchel, ripping like a mad bull, sent him to the canvas with a left and right to the jaw. At nine Jack was up, trying valiantly to hold off Stanley with his left hand. He was hit to the body with both hands, and a hook to the jaw sent him down.

Dazed, he was up shakily and at the mercy of a hurricane. Stan went to the body, then brought up his right hand with everything on it, launching O'Brien in a backward fall, his head hitting a sawdust box on the ring apron. Unconscious, he did not hear the count, or the bell that stopped it at four. With that *clang* it was over. Thus the fight ended without a knockout, and went into the books as "no decision"! While newspapers roared news of its spectacular end, the bout had no official winner.

Interestingly, Fleischer would say that were the bout scored on rounds, his own verdict at the end would actually have favored O'Brien for his success early in the fight. Ketchel insisted that Willus get him a rematch. He was willing, if need be, to meet Jack in Philadelphia, and to a six-round limit. "Get me O'Brien," he snapped, swearing that he would have put Jack away last time, but for advice from his corner to "box" instead of fight. Britt, uncomfortable with the locale and with the short distance, finally relented.

Nowadays, a fighter would do nothing to jeopardize a fight on this scale. Yet a week before the return with O'Brien, Ketchel took on tough middleweight Tony Caponi in Schenectady, winning by knockout in four rounds. Ketchel's faith in himself knew no limit. Prior to this bout, recalls Fleischer, an encounter with Stan revealed to him Ketchel's confidence in the power of his own hands. Nat, who was in Philadelphia to cover the bout for a New York paper, saw Stan at Greene's hotel when Ketchel arrived. Ketchel walked over to the telegraph desk and asked for a blank form, whereupon Fleischer, knowing that Ketchel had limited writing skills, offered to lend a hand. Stan asked to send his father a wire saying that he had won the fight. When asked why, given that the bout was still four hours away, he replied that he did this as a regular policy, in order to put the old man's mind at rest. For Stan, it was not a compromise of honesty — he simply could not entertain the thought that it might not go his way.

Now, ten weeks following the first encounter with Jack, Ketchel proved his point to his own handlers. After a first round that had each man bloody, Stan overwhelmed O'Brien in the second, dropping him three times and having him helpless at the bell. Forty seconds into the third, he put the veteran on the floor with a right hand and had him out on his feet when ref Jack McGuigan intervened.

Attempting the Impossible

In time, O'Brien would be more generous in his assessment of Ketchel. Stan, he would say, was the best he ever fought, a clever attacker with punches that were, in his marvelous phrase, "like flying balls of lead." Yet there was a limit now on what Ketchel could prove at middleweight. He knew also, as did Sam Langford, that the real money lay with the big men. Given the chance, he believed, he could beat Tommy Burns, and maybe even Jack Johnson. When Johnson stopped Burns in Sydney, Ketchel figured that a payday was looming.

Stan and Jack were slated for October 16, 1909, in Colma, in a bout that has never been fully understood, but that stirred some excitement before it was done. It was, on the face of it, an absurd match, Johnson standing several inches taller and carrying at least 40 more pounds of natural body weight than did the challenger. Johnson himself would claim, in later years, that the whole event was intended merely for show, and to go the distance if at all possible.[27]

Yet when the bell rang, Ketchel did his best, carrying the fight to Jack, eating the champion's jab and getting home an occasional blow to the midsection that made him wince. For the most part, it was an exercise in futility, with Stan visiting the canvas a couple of times by his own momentum. (On one occasion, when he caught Jack with a right hand to the body, the champion responded by carrying Ketchel, when they clinched, back to the center of the ring.) In the tenth round Ketchel, game to the core, forced the action like an undersized Quixote as the crowd cheered his effort.

Feeling the impact of the little man's power, Johnson started throwing more. Stanley came out for the eleventh throwing too, and he managed once to nail Jack with a right hand high on the jaw. Johnson came back hard, but Ketchel made it to the bell. In the twelfth, Stan at last got home a right to the head that sent the Galveston Giant to the canvas.

For a second it looked as if America's David had beaten its dark Goliath. But only for a second: When Jack rose, adrenaline rushing, he caught Stanley flying at him with a blur of punches—a slashing right uppercut followed by left and right, the effort carrying him over his victim and sprawling him momentarily on the floor again. Ketchel, arms outstretched, lay dead to the world.

A Sudden End

Stan, as Harry Shaffer notes, was now veering out of orbit. He had money in his pocket, and away from center stage he maintained "a very public life of drinking, womanizing, and violence; from the saloons of Montana to the Barbary Coast ... wandering through opium dens and houses of ill repute, almost always armed and genuinely dangerous."[28] When Britt died of a heart attack days after the Johnson fight, Stan was "loose on the world" with no compass. Soon he took up with Wilson Mizner, black sheep of a prominent San Francisco family and brother of famed architect Addison Mizner.

In Wilson, the middleweight champion had not a manager but a playmate, a partner in dissipation who "poured alcohol on the flame that was Stanley Ketchel." Yet the fighter remained active. In March of 1910 he went six hard rounds in a no-decision fight with Frank Klaus, one of the greatest men of the era, at the National A.C. in Pittsburgh. The next month, he showed that he was still willing to meet bigger men when he engaged in a no-decision bout (noted in the previous chapter) with Sam Langford in Philadelphia.

While it was of short duration, likely more for show than substance, the bout set a city record of $18,750, of which Stan got 50 percent. Probably it had been agreed beforehand that the match would serve as a setup for a bigger take elsewhere. But if so, it did not keep fans from seeing some brisk action. After two rounds of sparring, Ketchel mounted a rally in the third, and each man scored hard before the frame ended. Sam, enjoying a sizeable weight advantage at 178, took the lead in the fourth, driving Stan to the ropes with punches that had him wobbly. In the final two rounds, to the thrill of the fans, Ketchel stepped it up and won the sessions going away. Thus it went into the books, as agreed, with no winner, and popular opinion ranging from a draw[29] to a Ketchel win.

On May 17, Stan knocked out Porky Flynn at the Boston Armory in the third round.[30] According to Fleischer, prior to that fight Ketchel had become involved in an argument with a wealthy Boston fan prior to the fight, and bet the man a thousand dollars, in the heat of the exchange, that he would ice Flynn inside of four rounds. When the fight was over, said Nat, Ketchel went to the beaten man's corner, picked up the water bucket and tossed it over him, then turned to the fan, seated at ringside, and demanded his money!

Ten days later, Stan met contender Willie Lewis at the National Sporting Club in New York in a bout that was supposed to go six rounds to a no-decision. Ketchel, according to "Dumb" Dan Morgan, was taking it easy in the first round, but at the round's close, Lewis gambled by landing a right-hand haymaker that broke his nose. At this point, recalled Morgan, the champion "storms to his corner, kicks the stool out of the ring, and refuses to sit down at all."[31] In the second round he buried a left into Willie's midsection and annihilated him with a right. Lewis was carried to the dressing room.

Stan's last fight would be on June 11 with Jim Smith at the National A.C. in New York. It was a tough bout with Smith on near-even terms with the champion before taking the count in the fifth.

Despite Stan's misfortune against Johnson (word had it that they actually had found a couple of his front teeth embedded in Jack's glove after the fight), he did not hold a grudge. Nor did he side automatically with Jim Jeffries, labeled by the press as a "white hope" when Jeff made an ill-advised comeback to face Jack on July 4 of that year. In fact, he found some camaraderie with Johnson, an inveterate player who shared his love of high-speed racing. Stan also harbored resentment of Jeffries for Jeff's refusal to disqualify Billy Papke for that sneak assault Billy had launched in their second fight.

* * *

Ketchel's "all or nothing" comment, noted earlier, to matchmaker Billy Roche gave vent to something deep in his constitution — a leaning to mad extremes with nothing in the middle. At times this tendency had a benign expression, as when he was asked to make a guest appearance as referee at a wrestling match during his tenure as middleweight champion: Long after the event, participant Clifford Thorne would remember the magic of meeting the fighter for the first time, prior to Thorne's contest with a comer who billed himself (borrowing the surname of a great German contemporary) as Young Hackenschmidt: "And so I met Stanley Ketchel. His hands, big and strong as a heavyweight, gripped mine like a vise. His clear eyes seemed to look at and through you as if judging and placing. He had a quick and ready smile."[32]

Asked to name a fee, Stan replied, "One thousand dollars."

Told that it was beyond anything that promoter Joe Cox could manage, he said, "Then my charge is nothing." When Thorne and Cox tried to offer the going compensation, the fighter was adamant. "*One thousand* or *nothing*," he reiterated. "As you boys can't pay, it's nothing. And I'll be glad to help you out."

But at times, the trait verged upon madness. On one occasion, he wounded his friend Pete the Goat in a moment of careless horseplay with a revolver. Then, frantic, he sailed down the road to a hospital, one arm around Pete and the other on the wheel, in a fit of near hysteria. Stan's comrade Igoe would marvel at such extremes—outlandishly generous at times, and protective of those close to him, yet crazily reckless, as when behind the wheel of his Lozier, and deadly vicious toward any who crossed him.

"I'm going to die," Stan once said to Hype, "before I'm thirty."

As it turned out, the estimate was generous. In September, Springfield, Missouri, banker and sports enthusiast Rollin P. Dickerson, a childhood acquaintance of Stan's mother Julia, made a fishing trip to Grand Rapids. Having seen some action in the Spanish American War, he was known (quite loosely) as "Colonel" in his home area. On his return, he brought Stan with him to train at his ranch near the town of Conway. Dickerson, who bore the fighter a paternal affection, wanted to see him get a needed rest on the estate. Stan's cigar habit, by now, was weighing hard on the fighter, and his night life had given him need (so surmised some) of a remedy for syphilis.

Soon Ketchel was being introduced to local society figures, and he joined the Elks Club. He became a familiar sight in Springfield, taking Dickerson's pet lion cub for walks down the street on a leather leash. At this time he began to invest in timber and farming land, and wrote to a friend that he was ready to leave the fight game behind. But one payday loomed. While at the Dickerson estate, Stan was offered $30,000 to go against formidable heavyweight Sam McVey in Paris, an offer too good to pass up.

"Get trunks ready for trip and get reservations ready," he wired to Pete the Goat in New York. Pete ran the errands, but it was not to be. While at the ranch, Stan had hit it off with Goldie, a young woman who worked the grill and fed the hired hands. Also on the premises was a man calling himself Walter Dipley, who some thought was her husband. The triangle would turn deadly.

* * *

"I'd never quit," Ketchel was once heard to say. "As long as I could get to my feet, I'd get up and [face] the enemy even if I knew the next blow was going to kill me."

But on occasion an enemy will not be faced. What exactly happened on the morning of October 15, 1910, has had more than one rendition. Roughly, it appears, it went like this: Walter Dipley came up behind Ketchel at the main ranch house with a .22 rifle and shot him in the back. The bullet struck a major blood vessel in Stan's right lung and he sank to the floor. Then, making it to his feet, he wandered to his room, located at the far end of the house, where he collapsed on the bed. He was tended by a hand named George Noland, who had been working on a new barn there on the premises. Ketchel, asking repeatedly for water, said, "I guess they got me."

When Dickerson received a phone call giving him the news, he arranged for a special train to get himself there as fast as possible. When he arrived, he asked Stan what had happened.

"I was sitting at the table," gasped the stricken fighter, "I was shot in the back by this man Hurtz [meaning Dipley]." Then he added, "Get the woman, too, for she robbed me."[33]

The wound was devastating, and the doctors whom Dickerson brought with him said that there was nothing to be done. But Stan, they thought, would be more comfortable in his remaining time if he were taken to a hospital in nearby Springfield.

Dickerson, incensed by Dipley's act, announced then, as he would repeatedly in coming days, that he was offering $5,000 reward for Stan's killer — specifying that he wanted Dipley dead, and would pay "not one cent" for him alive! His instructions were to shoot the murderer on sight. He had enough money, he maintained, to protect anyone who killed the man, and furthermore, he hoped to have Dipley's head for a trophy on his living room wall.

The train made its way to Conway, then on to Springfield. Ketchel expired at around 7 P.M. Some supposed that Walter was a jealous ranch hand who could not abide the attention that Stan showed to his lover. As it turned out, however, he and Goldie were probably in cahoots the whole time, with robbery as the real motive. When Walter was found not long afterward by a posse, he had Ketchel's wallet in his possession.[34] His real name, it was learned, was in fact Hurtz, and he had a police record. Both he and Goldie were convicted in connection with the killing, though in a second trial several years later, she was acquitted while Walter was again sentenced to life in prison. Eventually paroled in 1934, he lived until 1956.

"By God, he was a man."

Steve, as he was known to those close to him, was an icon, a flesh instance of strength and vulnerability such as one finds in the world's timeless heroes. Reading of his exploits, one may recall vibrant figures, in the sporting world and elsewhere, who embody whole eras, and even the very essence of youth itself.

"Poor Stanley Ketchel!" exclaims Jack Kofoed in a veritable hymn to the fighter, recalling his adventures and his sudden death. "Take a look at him as he stands there, fans. See the wide shoulders crawling under the skin.... See the powerful arms and slim waist.... Nature ... engined him for the battle of life. There is power and beauty in his body."[35]

Something of this feeling is captured by Ernest Hemingway in his story "The Light of the World," in which two aging prostitutes trade recollections of Steve, whom they fancy as a superman and a lover.

"I never saw a man," ventures the peroxide blonde, "as clean and as white and as beautiful as Steve Ketchel. There never was a man like that. He moved just like a tiger and he was the finest, free-est spender who ever lived."

Near the end of this scene, her companion Alice, outlandishly heavy, recalls a compliment paid to her by the fighter years earlier. In that moment her face and her voice soften, bearing witness to a bygone beauty.

"I don't care about my body," rejoins the blonde. "They can take my body. My soul belongs to Steve Ketchel. By God, he was a man."[36]

Afterword

The cave-men of the ring are extinct.
Bob Fitzsimmons

The Years Following

After Ketchel's death, his rival Papke would lay claim to the title as its rightful heir. Though this claim ended momentarily with his loss to Cyclone Johnny Thompson in Sydney in 1911, Billy renewed it after Thompson's retirement. On March 5, 1913, Frank Klaus gained widespread recognition as middleweight champion when he defeated Papke in Paris on a foul in 15 rounds.

As for the heavyweights, Jack Johnson would continue his reign until 1915, when at 37 he met 6'6" cowboy Jess Willard on a blazing summer afternoon in Havana, Cuba. Born in St. Clere, Kansas, Jess had been reared on the ranch owned by his stepfather. He was not a follower of boxing, and probably did not even see a staged bout until 1910, when he was about 28 years old. His first love was horses, even if his size made him ill-suited to the role of a rider.[1] Still, his prodigious strength made him a candidate for the role of the White Hope who would succeed Johnson.

In Jess, the sport had indeed an ironic savior. He was not clever or engaging, at least with the press; he was not even too strongly inclined to fight, once the bell rang. When he donned the gloves it was an exercise in pragmatism: "I knew that I was a big fellow and powerful strong," he would remark one day in looking back. "I just sat down and figured out that a man as big as me ought to be able to cash in on his size and that was what started me on the road to boxing."[2]

In the ring he ran hot and cold. At times, and until stung and bloodied,

178

he seemed downright timid. Over the past couple of years he had been out-performed by Luther McCarty and Gunboat Smith, and so he had not figured as the pick of the litter even where white heavyweights were concerned. Later, when opponent John "Bull" Young died after being knocked out by Jess, the fighter's ambition had all but perished.

Nor was the big Kansan thrilled with the role of a white crusader. While happy to get the title shot, he did not buy into the ideology that came with it. But images can be crafted, and when his camp brought aboard Tom Jones, a theatrical veteran and former manager of lightweight Ad Wolgast, the campaign was launched.

"Willard," intoned Tom to a Chicago reporter in days leading up to the fight, "is a God lovin' man who goes to church and teaches Sunday school. He considers it a sin to hit his fellow man but finds it a necessity to accomplish his one man crusade and ultimate goal — the defeat and abolition of Jack Johnson."[3] While this description bore little resemblance to the fighter, it tapped nicely into the going mass energy. In Jess the public saw what it longed to see — a towering, pale-skinned redeemer who might wrest the throne, and all that it conveyed in sporting virility, from a nemesis who had occupied it since December of 1908.

And so the crown did pass. Traditionally, Willard is a low-profile champion, ranked with the least formidable of the line. For reasons just noted, this is not surprising. But motivation can work wonders, and when the deal was signed, 33-year-old Jess seized the opportunity of a lifetime. In this fight (preserved on film) he appears to be no joke, a poised and determined fighter who prevails over a champion who himself looks far from finished. In a contest of good duration, he might have been a test for Jack even when the Galveston fighter was in his prime.

In later years, Johnson would call the Havana fight a fix, saying that he had been granted consideration from federal prosecutors to "lay down" against Jess. Yet ringside consensus and film evidence tell a different story. According to referee Jack Welsh, who said that he would have given the fight to Johnson on points after 20 rounds, the champion was masterful in the early going. Extant footage of the fight bears him out, as Johnson makes sudden and repeated offensives that surely could pass for a *bona fide* effort. As the rounds pass, a fairly constant pattern develops, the two men eyeing each other, feinting and studying, with an occasional punctuating trade to follow. Through it all Willard is composed, spearing Jack with a long jab and placing an occasional right hand downstairs. Still, and even past the 20th round, Johnson makes his attacks, going after Jess like a tiger after its prey. In the 26th, the challenger drives a compact right to Johnson's midriff, and a right to the jaw moments later drops Jack flat on the baking-hot canvas. According to Welsh, Johnson spent close to five minutes on his stool before feeling strong enough to leave the ring.

Part of Willard's problem is that he is remembered chiefly not for this fight, but for a very different one. Four years later, himself now 37, he would face a relative unknown named William Harrison "Jack" Dempsey, and would get one of the worst beatings ever seen in a prize ring before it was stopped at the end of three rounds. Together with baseball phenomenon Babe Ruth, Dempsey would set the tone of the Roaring Twenties, and his 1922 bout with Frenchman Georges Carpentier would make for the world's first "million-dollar gate."

The lightweight division, too, would abound in action. Battling Nelson, who gained recognition as champion with his wins over Joe Gans, would lose the title on February 22, 1910, to Ad Wolgast by a knockout in 40 savage rounds. Several years later, the division would see its outstanding fighter of the postwar period in Benjamin Leiner, known to the world as Benny Leonard.

Ranked by Nat Fleischer as the virtual equal of Gans, Leonard was another ring scientist in the mold of men like Joe himself. Never given to boast, he was nonetheless as self-assured at the opening bell, said Nat, as any man who ever stepped through the ropes. There has always been some dispute as to whether a man can be *taught* to punch, but in this case it happened. With practice Leonard developed a straight right hand as formidable as any in its day. Bright and inventive, he also took the skill of combination punching to a new level.

Old School and New

No generation, it seems, is happy with the ones that follow. Maybe the rub is inherent in human civilization: Be it work ethic or public attire, music or mores, hairstyle or athletics, each era sets its own standard and looks back, in time, upon the bright day of its own youth. Boxing is a prime example. Fighters of the new era, insisted Jim Jeffries to the last years of his life, did not train as did men of his own. "Life today," he explained three decades after his comeback effort against Jack Johnson, "is too easy for the youngsters, and that is why they don't have the stamina necessary for a ring career. I see it in every fight I attend, every one I listen to over the radio, the ones I see on the screen and the weekly amateur shows we hold here on the [Jeffries] ranch. After three or four rounds they are tired — dog tired."[4]

One can only imagine what Jeff would say about men of the present day, and especially heavyweights, who are apt to enter the ring, even for a high-profile televised bout, some thirty or forty pounds over their ideal weight.

Bob Fitzsimmons, as noted early in this book, saw that men of his own day were advanced in style beyond those of the London era. He saw, too, that these men would be surpassed in ring generalship by those who came after them. The coming stars, he believed, would face contests of shorter duration, and they might not be altogether better *fighters*. But they would be strategically wiser. In 1914, when Fitz was making his last few appearances in the ring, he was interviewed by Nat Fleischer. On being mailed afterward a copy of the piece by Nat, he added in a letter of reply that the game was changing, and that men of the kind who ruled in his day were destined to go by the way.

The cave-men of the game, explained the great three-time champion, were gone, and they would not return. Champions to come, he predicted,

> will be as children compared to the rough and ready battlers of twenty or more years ago. Fighting, like all other sports, is reaching out along lines of improvement. The men of today realize that boxing is more important than slugging.
> They are beginning to see the advantages of knowing how to block and feint, and those who still can retain their punch are the ones who will reach the top. You'll find as the years pass that fighting will become more and more scientific and championships will change hands on points and not on knockouts.[5]

In the coming decade his words had some measure of confirmation. In 1917, a clean-cut young Irishman out of Greenwich, New York, undefeated in several bouts as a professional, enlisted in the U.S. Marine Corps. While stationed in France, competing with fellow servicemen, Gene Tunney won the American Expeditionary Forces light-heavyweight championship. On returning home, he continued to rack up wins. In January of 1922 he decisioned Battling Levinsky in twelve rounds to win the American light-heavyweight title. Four months later he put that title on the line against the ferocious Harry Greb.

Did not their mortal lives overlap, one might fancy Gene as an actual reincarnation of James Corbett. A friend of Corbett in the great fighter's later days, he emulated James from the start in style and mentality. When he returned from his overseas duty, Gene was suffering from partial paralysis in his left elbow. Rather than accept this limitation, he began (much as had Corbett, many years ago) to work the weak limb overtime, chopping wood from that side only. Soon after, he went to the gym, tying his right arm fast to his side and jabbing the heavy bag until his left-hand lead, like that of James, was a thing of wonder.

Maybe the two best middleweights to succeed Stan Ketchel and his rivals were Les Darcy, a phenomenon out of Australia, and Greb. Darcy, a broad-chested 5'7" banger, laid waste to competition in his homeland, winning partial claim to the middleweight championship of the world before he was 20 years of age. Bright and amiable, yet a terror in the ring, he soon gained the Australian heavyweight title as well. Yet he died an untimely death (from complications, it appears, stemming from a case of strep throat) in 1917, at the age of 21.

Over the next few years, the division would be dominated by Greb, a two-armed hurricane ready to mix with any man alive. (Though spotting Dempsey 25 pounds, he was certain that he could outhustle Jack if given the chance.) Just shy of 28, Harry was a savvy veteran of more than 200 professional fights when he met Gene in 1922.

At this point Tunney looked like a world-beater. Yet the young Marine, unbeaten and brimming with optimism, got a bloody awakening in the opening minutes when a winging left hand from Greb shattered his nose. The remaining 14 rounds were a flaming purgatory.

Like a modern-day Scaevola, the young warrior stood it to the end, collapsing only afterward in the dressing room. Yet with Tunney no experience was a real loss. Highly astute, a quintessential learner in the ring and out, he could glean truth even from a shellacking. He would regain the title on a decision over Greb in January of the following year, after which the two men would fight three more times, each war bitterly waged with Gene's ring science gradually prevailing over Greb's all-angles attack.

So impressed was Greb with Tunney by now that he picked him to dethrone heavyweight champion Dempsey when they met. Harry's estimate proved right in September of 1926, when his rival pulled an upset, jabbing his way to a ten-round decision. Tunney would hold the title for two more years, scoring another ten-round win over Dempsey in the process, before retiring as champion in 1928.

Time, as Fleischer noted, confirmed Fitzsimmons also in his vision of the conditions under which fighters would compete. Not only did the style of boxing change, but the fights were scheduled for shorter distances and the gloves got bigger. In the late 19th century, men used skin-tight gloves, or gloves of perhaps two ounces, referring to five-ounce sparring mitts as "pillows"! In the early 20th century, gloves were commonly of that latter size, while in the day of men like Joe Louis, they commonly weighed six to eight ounces. In today's game, ten-ounce gloves for middleweights are commonplace.

* * *

What does one say, all told, about the prowess of the men who have featured in these preceding chapters? In his day, of course, each is a star of the first order. Could any of them have mixed it up, with success, against today's fighters?

Old *vs.* new, a topic never fully laid to rest, tends to produce two opposing lines of argument. Advocates of the more recent age hold that the game has improved, in its methods and training technology, with the decades, and so the curve of excellence, they imagine, has steadily risen. Indeed, it is not a new contention — Fitzsimmons, as just noted, maintained that the techniques of his day surpassed those of the bare-knucklers. Presumably he was right. What, then, of the century that has followed?

Progress, it seems, has continued. But does this mean that all the great fighters reside in times recent? Athletes in every era are a mesh of nature and environment, and if we confine our estimate of greatness to the past few decades, we ignore the bulk of talent that nature has spawned in total.

And might nurture, as well, offer something to the old guard? Consider, for one, the difference in lifestyles, then and now, and the special strength and fortitude of men who were accustomed from their youth to long hours of physical labor. Over the past half century, a conspicuous tie has emerged between poverty and ring excellence — notable, for example, in the way that some divisions have been ruled by black or Hispanic fighters in the Western hemisphere. More recently, the opening of the professional game to Eastern European and former Soviet republics has infused competitive new blood into all divisions, a breed of athlete that often has more "drive" than does its American counterpart. Nowhere is this more pronounced than in the heavyweight division, where lately these men all but own the titles awarded by major (WBA, WBC, IBF, and WBO) sanctioning bodies.

It might be added that the heavyweights, in this comparison, present a special case: In other divisions, poundage is fixed, and so the middleweight of today is no larger than the one of years ago. But premier heavyweights, over time and with sheer enlargement of the athletic pool, have gotten bigger. Of course, there were big men in the old days as well. But they were anomalies, and they were not, on average, the most impressive men in their divisions. Today, by contrast, dimensions of 6'5" and 240 pounds are common in the top twenty contenders. Some of the greatest champions (among them no less than Jack Dempsey and Joe Louis) of yesteryear did not reach even the present cruiserweight limit for their best bouts.

For this reason, I believe, some recent heavyweight champions and contenders would have had an advantage over their forebears. In fact, I will venture that some of today's less prominent titlists might have beaten men who traditionally figure high in the all-time reckoning.

This claim does not sit well with veteran fans, who resent the "champion" status and face-value records spawned in recent decades by the policies of the belt-awarding organizations. A few years ago, for example, when seven-foot, 320-pound Russian behemoth Nicolay Valuev began to approach the fabled "49 — 0" record of Rocky Marciano, certain columnists, apparently feeling that some luster would now fade from that streak, expressed their conviction that Rocky would have destroyed Valuev had the two ever been matched.

The concern, I think, was to some extent misplaced. For one thing, Marciano was a linear and *undisputed* champion, in against the best that the profession had to offer, a situation now rare in boxing's political and economic venue. Had Valuev run his record to 49 — 0 (he came close), it would not represent the same accomplishment.

At the same time, I will venture, straight across and man to man, Rocky would have had a hard time with the Russian. (In all candor, and at risk of sacrilege, I doubt that a man of Marciano's type and stature could have *reached* Valuev, let alone beaten him.) I think, too, that he would have had it tough in direct matchups with other big men like Lennox Lewis and Wladimir Klitschko. But this is separate from a more important question, namely: who, for his size, was *the better fighter*? (Marciano, scaled evenly with any of these men, would be my pick to win.)

Which man would win, head to head in a direct matchup, does not tell which is "greater," especially when one (such as Valuev, in this case) would enjoy an advantage in body weight upward of 75 percent over the other. The important question is not who would win in this contest, but which fighter is more talented. To compare Valuev directly with Marciano is about as meaningful as comparing him thus with Ray Robinson.

* * *

The classic source of praise for the old-timers, as every veteran fan knows, is Nat Fleischer. Nat ranked Fitzsimmons no less than third among the heavyweights, behind Jack Johnson and Jeffries. It may be worthwhile to see where he put the rest of this set, and to survey also a few recent opinions.

Fleischer's ratings, to which he held stubbornly even in his late years, are powerfully weighted toward men whom he saw in his youth. Extending from that time (roughly the turn of the century) to the 1960s, they involve likewise an era in which heavyweights frequently scaled less than 195 pounds. Thus they are, in the estimate of some later scribes, out of touch with the overall reality.

According to *The Ring*'s founder, fighters in the heavyweight division from the late 19th to the mid–20th century can be ranked in overall ability as follows:

1. Jack Johnson	6. Joe Louis
2. Jim Jeffries	7. Sam Langford
3. Bob Fitzsimmons	8. Gene Tunney
4. Jack Dempsey	9. Max Schmeling
5. James J. Corbett	10. Rocky Marciano

Nat's preference extended to the smaller men. He counted his friend and hero Stanley Ketchel as the best middleweight, and had Kid McCoy and Jack O'Brien as first and second among the light-heavies. He ranked Joe Walcott and Mysterious Billy Smith as the two best welters, and Gans as the number one lightweight. Battling Nelson and Kid Lavigne were at five and six. Terry McGovern and George Dixon, on Fleischer's view, ruled at feather and bantamweight.

It was not until quite late in his career that Nat offered some acknowledgment of newer fighters, naming Joe Frazier (in place of Fitzsimmons) as the most damaging body puncher among the big men. Yet again, not everyone in recent decades has thought so highly of the old guard. A well-articulated debate regarding the respective capabilities of the different generations was presented by Fleischer and Jimmy Jacobs in *The Ring* during the late 1960s. The first of these (noted in my book *A Man Among Men*) centered on the heavyweights, with Fleischer upholding men of his own time, as shown above. The second involved an argument over the most exciting fighter in any weight class.

Fleischer this time picked Jack Dempsey, the former heavyweight champion, as a "true fighting man" for the ages. Jacobs favored Ray Robinson, a dancing master whose fluid style made him the original Sugar Ray.[6] As to Ray's superiority over the older fighters, Jacobs pulled no punches. Thus, for example, he disdained Stan Ketchel as Nat's pick for the greatest middleweight, saying, "I have three Stanley Ketchel fights in my film library and that's too many." Twenty of Robinson's, he insisted, were too few.

Current Admiration of the Pioneers

And still, some historians even today are impressed with the men described in this book. Joe Gans, remarks historian Monte Cox of the International Boxing Research Organization, "was an extremely intelligent fighter who could feint his opponent out of position, but could not be feinted himself." This man, he believes, "had every asset to be considered not only as the greatest lightweight of all time but the greatest fighter of all time."

Admiration for Sam Langford, as noted earlier, continues likewise to span the generations. Sam, according to the IBRO's Clay Moyle, was conceivably the greatest fighter who ever lived. While far outsized by many of his foes, he "mixed it up with the leading heavyweights, or at least those that agreed to face him, and opponents such as Joe Jeannette, Gunboat Smith, and Harry Wills spoke in awe of his punching power."

The late Laurence Fielding, one of the most respected historians in the sport, commented[7] as follows: George Lavigne (rated by Fielding at number 8 among the lightweights) was "a good boxer and puncher [who] could wear a man down in somewhat the same way as Battling Nelson or Henry Armstrong." Bob Fitzsimmons made number one at middleweight, "a great puncher [and] a good boxer," whose knockouts of Nonpareil Jack Dempsey, James Corbett, and Peter Maher made him extraordinary.

Barbados Joe Walcott placed third among the welterweights, behind Ray Robinson and Tommy Ryan. Like Langford, said Fielding, Walcott was handicapped by his lack of stature against the big men, yet fared well in those deep waters nonetheless.

Joe Gans was number two as a lightweight, a superb boxer and puncher who stands as one of the game's true artists and pioneers. Terry McGovern, with a style similar to that of (heavyweight) Jack Dempsey, Ketchel, and Armstrong, ranked first among the bantams. McGovern, by Fielding's estimate, was unbeatable, in his prime, at his size. Sam Langford was so formidable that he was avoided even by Jack Johnson after their first meeting. As to Ketchel, "We can only guess what Stanley might have been able to achieve, if his career had not been cut short by murder."

There is much communication currently within the IBRO circle, and several other prominent members have been forthcoming in recent years with their opinions. Miles Ugarkovich, one of many in this group who has done his homework, ranks Ketchel and Fitzsimmons one and two, respectively, at middleweight, with Billy Papke number eight. Jeff Cox rates Jeffries among the elite all-time heavyweights, and has a favorable estimate of many fighters from the era. Fascinating commentary on the heroes of this time period has been provided also in articles by Mike Casey.

No reference to current opinion, in my view, is complete without a word from Tracy Callis, an IBRO historian who has given much time and thought to the virtues of the older men. To assess the game's whole talent, Tracy believes, we must reach back into the mists of the bare-knuckle and borderline stages of its evolution. His commentary pays respect time and again to men featured in this volume.

Among the heavyweights, he puts Jeffries number one, with Jack Johnson second. Among the light-heavyweights, Bob Fitzsimmons ranks second behind Gene Tunney. He names Sam Langford and Philadelphia Jack O'Brien fourth and fifth, respectively, in that division.

Tracy lists Fitzsimmons, Ketchel, and O'Brien as the three all-time best middleweights, with Sugar Ray Robinson, Nonpareil Jack Dempsey, Kid McCoy, Tommy Ryan, and Joe Walcott as the best welters. Benny Leonard and Joe Gans are his top two lightweights, and Terry McGovern tops his list as the number one bantamweight. Jimmy Barry, who fought before the turn of the century, heads his all-time flyweight division.

Pound for pound, believes Callis, the ten best ever are these:

1. Bob Fitzsimmons	6. Henry Armstrong
2. Sugar Ray Robinson	7. Stanley Ketchel
3. Nonpareil Jack Dempsey	8. Jack Dempsey
4. Sam Langford	9. Philadelphia Jack O'Brien
5. Charley Mitchell	10. Harry Greb

Fighters, and athletes generally, admits Tracy, may well get measurably bigger, faster, and stronger with time. They may enjoy the benefit of evolving technique. But this, he argues, does not always translate into better ringmanship. To give each era its due, he believes, we must take into account subtle factors that bear in every age upon athletic performance: "Different periods of history impart certain attitudes and practices due to the 'temper of the times,' and the conditions under which ... people live. Athletic skills are affected by mental conditioning and discipline as well as physical attitudes and techniques. Consequently, performance peaks and ebbs in different periods of history and fighters are better in some periods than they are in others."[8]

* * *

So the argument continues. Excellence in boxing is no doubt a function, in part, of the times. And modern fighters, to be sure, have some advantage over their predecessors. But I am inclined to agree with Tracy that advantages exist on each side: Hard times forge hard bodies and willing souls.

By the same token, the sheer frequency with which men fight will bear on their skills of survival. It is the fistic equivalent of natural selection —

when men have to enter the ring two or three times a month, they either get very good at handling themselves or they fall by the way. On this point, the older fighters get the nod.

In a related vein, we might consider the impact on the game of cultural supply and demand: The advent of television, maintained Fleischer late in his career, had made a decisive impact on the way that men plied their trade.[9] Basic ring technique, said Nat, had not changed appreciably since about 1940. But crucial points of skill were on the wane. Feinting, for one, raised to a fine art by the earlier men, was now practically lost. Telecast sponsors instead wanted *action*— as a result, more aggressive fighters were now gaining the limelight as promoters shunned displays of ring craft for a "pell-mell mix" that drew a wider, albeit less discerning, audience. In the going arena, observed Nat, a high-level contest of boxing might get boos and catcalls owing to demand for violence of a simpler kind!

In the end, it is hard to know which fighting generation is the best.[10] Indeed, "best" in this context may be a doubly gray area, since different eras involve different forms of the sport itself. But regardless of the verdict, the men who have gone before are not diminished in what they accomplish by those who come after. They are worthy of the admiration that they inspire, in much the way that mathematicians and proto-scientists of long ago deserve praise comparable to that of their intellectual descendants. Greatness in every era, and in every human enterprise, owes to the pioneering genius that precedes it. In the men whose exploits are described in this volume is an ancestry of which the sport can be proud.

Chapter Notes

Introduction

1. James Boswell, *Journal of a Tour to the Hebrides* (London: Penguin Books, 1984). This work is reprinted in one volume with Johnson's classic *Journey to the Western Islands.*

2. See discussion, for example, Appendix II in Kelly Nicholson, *A Man Among Men* (Salt Lake City: Homeward Bound, 2002).

3. *Police News*, December 26, 1891.

4. *Cleveland Tab*, November 1999. For an entertaining statement (cited also by Carney) on the subject by heavyweight champion Jack Dempsey, see chapter 4 of Roger Kahn, *A Flame of Pure Fire* (San Diego: Harcourt, 1999).

5. Bob Fitzsimmons, *Physical Culture and Self-Defense* (Philadelphia: Drexel Biddle Publisher, 1901), pages 98–99.

6. See, for example, the comment of ring scribe John Lardner in regard to Fleischer's treatment of Ketchel. Lardner's remarks are noted in chapter 8 ahead.

Chapter I

1. This is the first stanza of "The Rough Road," apparently anonymous and reprinted in George T. Pardy, "Famous Fighting Codes," *The Ring*, March 1942, pages 20 and following.

2. Alexander Johnston, *TEN— and Out!* (New York: Ives Washburn, Publisher, 1947), page 1. This book had its first printing in 1927.

3. Homer, *The Iliad* (New York: Farrar, Straus and Giroux, 1994). Robert Fitzgerald, translator. See Book XXIII, pages 550–51. These men are Achaeans (members of a united Greek force invading Troy), who take part in games honoring a fallen comrade.

4. Virgil, *The Aeneid* (New York: Vintage Classics, 1983). Robert Fitzgerald, translator. See Book V, page 141.

5. See Bob Mee, *Bare Fists: The History of Bare-Knuckle Prize-Fighting* (Woodstock: Overlook Press, 2001), pages 3 and following.

6. Quoted in *Bare Fists*, page 5.

7. See the Prologue to Elliott Gorn's *The Manly Art: Bare-Knuckle Prize-Fighting in America* (Ithaca, NY: Cornell University Press, 1986).

8. This quote, which appeared in Pierce's *Boxiana*, is reprinted in Art Collins, "The Cover Story," *The Ring*, January 1950, page 18.

9. Quoted by Johnston, *Ten — and Out!*, page 3.

10. A summary of these rules and Broughton's is contained in Appendix B of Kevin R. Smith's *Black Genesis* (Lincoln, Nebraska: iUniverse, 2003).

11. In the royal hierarchy, this title ranks above that of earl or count and below that of duke.

12. Bill Doherty, "My Recollections of the Marquess of Queensberry," *The Ring*, October 1936, page 29.

13. *The Manly Art*, page 224.

14. See Donovan's memoir *The Roosevelt That I Know* (New York: B.W. Dodge, 1909), page 44.

15. Arthur T. Lumley, "John L. as I Knew Him," *The Ring*, May 1934, page 38.

16. Quoted in Sullivan's autobiography *I Can Lick Any Sonofabitch in the House!* (New York: Proteus, 1980), page 65. This material had its first printing in 1892, shortly before Sullivan's fight with James Corbett in New Orleans.

17. Quoted in Sullivan's autobiography, page 99.

18. See also Mee's discussion in chapter 3 of *Bare Fists*.

19. See Mee's account in chapter 13.

20. Donoghue's recollection is contained in the second chapter of Nat Fleischer's *"Gentleman Jim": The Story of James J. Corbett* (New York: C.J. O'Brien, 1942).

21. Sun Tzu, *The Art of War* (New York: Barnes and Noble Classics, 2003). Lionel Giles, translator. See, for example, passages 1.18 and 11.19.

22. See James J. Corbett, *The Roar of the Crowd* (New York: Grosset and Dunlap, 1925).

23. *The Roosevelt That I Know*, page 145.

24. *The Roar of the Crowd*, page 116.

25. Thus, remembers Corbett, "I put a peg in that," saving the fact for future reference (*The Roar of the Crowd*, page 121).

26. *The Roosevelt That I Know*, page 177.

27. Donald Barr Chidsey, *John the Great* (Garden City, NY: Doubleday, Doran, 1942), page 211.

28. This quote appears in Fitzsimmons's *Physical Culture and Self-Defense* (London: Drexel Biddle, 1901).

29. Quoted in George T. Pardy, "Famous Fighting Codes," *The Ring*, March 1942, pages 20 and following.

30. Quoted in the *Mirror of Life*, March 31, 1897.

Chapter II

1. Biddy Bishop, "Kid Lavigne Greatest Lightweight of All Time," *The Ring*, May 1928, pages 4 and following. Bishop worked in Lavigne's camp for some of his biggest fights.

2. This comment appears in the April 23, 1963, edition of the *Saginaw News*.

3. This comment is made by Chiesi in his newspaper column "Sport Tales," dated June 1, 1956.

4. *Boston Herald*, March 2, 1889. While the bout, it is noted, went over four hours, neither man was severely punished.

5. *Brooklyn Daily Eagle*, October 17, 1894.

6. *New York Journal*, June 1, 1895.

7. See details in the chapter ahead.

8. This incident is noted by publisher Stan Weston in his piece "The Fighter Who Couldn't Be Hit," *Boxing and Wrestling*, March 1955.

9. Igoe refers apparently to a bout held on December 18, 1893, ruled a draw after eight rounds.

10. Nat Fleischer, "Griffo, Ring's Cleverest Boxer," *The Ring*, May 1934, page 16.

11. See Nat Fleischer's "Memories," *The Ring*, March 1953, pp. 26 and following.

12. Jack Kofoed, "The Saginaw Kid," *Fight Stories*, February 1931, page 15.

13. *Police Gazette*, October 1895.

14. Comments attributed to O'Rourke in this section were first printed around 1925.

15. Joe Woodman, "Fights I Cannot Forget," *The Ring*, July 1955, pp. 28 and following.

16. This claim is reported by George B. Underwood, in a column titled "'Greatest Fight I Ever Saw'— When Lavigne Met Joe Walcott," published from appearances in a newspaper of 1920 or shortly after. It is contained in the *Antekprizering* archival package.

17. See the chapter on Walcott ahead.

18. "The Saginaw Kid," page 6.

19. *Sioux City Journal*, January 10, 1897.

20. *Sioux City Journal*, March 28, 1897.

21. *San Francisco Examiner*, October 27, 1897.

22. *San Francisco Chronicle*, October 30, 1897.

23. *Sioux City Journal*, February 27, 1898.
24. *Brooklyn Daily Eagle*, March 18, 1898.
25. *Milwaukee Evening Wisconsin*, September 29, 1898.
26. *Police Gazette*, July 1899.
27. *Brooklyn Daily Eagle*, October 7, 1899.
28. *Milwaukee Evening Wisconsin*, June 26, 1900.
29. This comment appears in a 1913 edition of the *New York World*.

Chapter III

1. Richard K. Fox, *Bob Fitzsimmons: His Life and Battles* (New York: Richard K. Fox, Franklin Square, 1897), page 7.
2. William James, *The Varieties of Religious Experience* (New York: Barnes and Noble Classics, 2004), page 262. This work was first published around 1910.
3. Quoted in Christopher Tobin, *Fitzsimmons: Boxing's First Triple World Champion* (Timaru, New Zealand: David A. Jack and C.P. Tobin, 2000), page 10.
4. *Physical Culture and Self-Defense*, page 104.
5. Quoted by Gilbert Odd in *The Fighting Blacksmith: The Story of Bob Fitzsimmons* (London: Pelham Books, 1976), page 35.
6. The remark is noted by Nat Fleischer in *50 Years at Ringside* (NY: Fleet, 1958), page 241.
7. Quoted in Pember W. Rocap and William H. Rocap, *Remembering Bob Fitzsimmons* (Wayne, ME: Archives Press, 2001), page 4. This volume consists of a series of pieces on Fitzsimmons penned by William Rocap for the *Philadelphia Public Ledger* in the fall of 1917, together with updated commentaries by his nephew Pember in 2001.
8. *Remembering Bob Fitzsimmons*, pages 11–12.
9. Here is one of those cases where sources conflict: Older accounts identify Fitzsimmons's opponent with the more famous Slade, while more recent ones, including that of Adam Pollack, hold that it was the brother.

10. According to Gilbert Odd, this meeting was a pantomime staged for the purpose of making Fitzsimmons a betting favorite in the fight upcoming; see chapter 3 of *The Fighting Blacksmith*. Adam Pollack, whose research on this era of Bob's career is painstaking, lists four-round exhibitions for the two men in November of 1888 and a five-round knockout win by Fitzsimmons on January 19 of the following year.
11. Opinion on this point was divided. According to the *Sydney Referee* of February 12, 1890, Fitzsimmons slid off his chair in the corner after being counted out, and was still dazed afterward in the dressing room. Tobin, sharing the view of Rocap and other writers, sees it otherwise, saying that the flutter of fast cash made Bob take a dive, going down from "a weak right push on the jaw," whereupon he lay "winking and grinning" as he was counted out" (page 12). Fox, who also leans this way, notes that Fitzsimmons was then in financial straits and might have been pressured into the deal (*Bob Fitzsimmons*, chapter 10).
12. Richard K. Fox, *Life and Battles of Jack Dempsey* (Franklin Square, New York: Richard K. Fox), page 7.
13. This remark is related by Stan Weston in "Jack Dempsey, the Nonpareil," *Boxing Illustrated Wrestling News*, April 1961, pp. 28 and following.
14. Forbes's account is described by Weston in the article just noted.
15. See Fox's account, pp. 72 and following.
16. *San Francisco Call*, May 30, 1890.
17. *Milwaukee Evening Wisconsin*, January 15, 1891.
18. *Milwaukee Evening Wisconsin*, January 15, 1891.
19. *Bob Fitzsimmons: His Life and Battles*, page 16.
20. Quoted by Matt Donnellon, *The Irish Champion Peter Maher* (Victoria, BC: Trafford, 2008), page 87.
21. See chapter 5 of The *Fighting Blacksmith*.
22. *Portland Oregonian*, February 18, 1891.

23. This woman appears to be Fitzsimmons's first wife Louisa. It is believed by most researchers that "Alice Jones" was Louisa's stage name. See, for example, Keith Robinson, *Lanky Bob* (Victoria, BC: Trafford, 2008), page 448.

24. See *Bob Fitzsimmons*, chapter 22.

25. *The Fighting Blacksmith*, page 84.

26. This meeting was attended by a Captain Glori, a former police officer who had been Fitzsimmons's friend and negotiator before Julian arrived on the scene, and by Brady and Fitzsimmons himself.

27. Clarence Riodan, "I Saw the Ring's Most Unusual Spectacle," *Boxing and Wrestling*, August 1956, pp. 16 and following.

28. See chapters 4 and 6 of *A Man Among Men*.

29. This quote is taken from the first of a series of installments bearing the title "Fighters I've Met" by Sharkey that appeared in the *Evening Herald* in 1917. It is reprinted in the June 27, 2005, issue of the *IBRO Journal*, pp. 15 and following.

30. See Weston, "Sailor with the Loaded Fists."

31. According to Sharkey, onlookers with timepieces told him later that the fight, ten count included, had lasted a total of 26 seconds ("Fighters I've Met," page 19).

32. See Sharkey's account in the September 12, 2005, issue of the *IBRO Journal*, page 18. Corbett recalls the fight in chapter 14 of *The Roar of the Crowd*. Corbett would say later that he appealed to the referee to end the bout owing to his opponent's rough tactics, at which point the bout was stopped by the attending police chief to prevent a riot; Sharkey would say that Corbett looked directly to the cop, hoping to halt the action and escape being knocked out.

33. The promotional group, centered in New York and called the National Athletic Club, had in its membership Sharkey himself and his manager Dan Lynch (*The Fighting Blacksmith*, page 125).

34. For detailed commentary and conflicting versions of what happened in this affair, see chapter 9 of Odd's *The Fighting Blacksmith*. Pollack's research, which is painstaking, makes it evident that Bob all but literally mopped the floor with his opponent until the time of Earp's call.

35. Fitzsimmons, said Sam Austin, sporting editor of the *Police Gazette*, emerged from this fight "the better man and the conqueror," and was judged by everyone on the scene as being "loser upon a technicality [at] worst." (Quoted by Fox, page 100.)

36. Quoted by Fox in *Bob Fitzsimmons*, pp. 97–98.

37. According to Leo N. Miletich, some 25,000 people were at Chicago's City Hall Park to hear bulletins from telegraphers, and 8,000 were present at New York's Herald Square. See the concluding portion of his book *Dan Stuart's Fistic Carnival* (College Station: Texas A&M Press, 1994).

38. *Milwaukee Evening Wisconsin*, October 5, 1895.

39. See chapter 23 of Hugh Fullerton, *Two Fisted Jeff* (Chicago: Consolidated Book Publishers, 1929).

40. It is worth note that a news column of that period includes the comment that "Fitzsimmons is bitter at the treatment according him by Corbett after the Sullivan fight" (*Milwaukee Evening Wisconsin*, October 11, 1892).

41. See *The Roosevelt That I Know*, chapter 11.

42. *Milwaukee Evening Wisconsin*, November 30, 1895.

43. *Galveston Daily News*, March 15, 1897.

44. *San Francisco Chronicle*, March 6, 1897.

45. *Galveston Daily News*, March 15, 1897.

46. *Sacramento Bee*, March 20, 1897.

47. *Chicago Inter-Ocean*, March 17, 1897.

48. *Ibid.*

49. Robert H. Davis, *"Ruby Robert"— Alias Bob Fitzsimmons* (New York: George H. Doran, 1926), page 45. By Davis's own admission, which is worth noting, prior to this time he had not seen a single prizefight in his life.

50. Gertrude Phillips, "The Influence of Women at Boxing Bouts," *The Ring*, February 15, 1922, page 5. This 16-page item was the inaugural issue of what would become known as the "Bible of Boxing."

51. Thomas T. Williams, "The Heavyweight Championship Battle," contained as chapter 20 in *Physical Culture and Self Defense*, page 149.

52. *The Roar of the Crowd*, page 265.

53. This remark was made by Corbett in his subsequent account, published by the *New York Journal* with the title "The Fight of the Century" and containing an album of 81 photos connected with the bout. Corbett also noted in this statement that he had lost one of his teeth as early as the third round, when he caught "a left-hander under the jaw."

54. *Mirror of Life*, March 31, 1897. "Mentally," concludes this observation, "Mrs. Fitzsimmons is a stronger character than her husband. He yields to her in everything with a sort of dog-like affection and fidelity."

55. *Portland Oregonian*, March 23, 1897.

56. *San Francisco Chronicle*, March 18, 1897.

57. George Engel, "Haymakers," *The Ring*, December 1932, pp. 4 and following. As Engel notes, the punch landed on what had earlier been called Broughton's Mark.

58. Both the Siler and Muldoon comments are contained in "The Fight of the Century."

59. This was Corbett's claim (*The Roar of the Crowd*, page 266), which may be the source from which others have drawn.

60. *Ibid.*

61. Davis, *"Ruby Robert,"* page 94.

62. This story, featured in more than one source, is recalled by Pardy in "The Slugging Blacksmith," Street and Smith's *Sport Story* magazine, August 1937, pp. 47 and following.

63. See A.D. Phillips, "Fights and Fighters," *The Ring*, October 1931, pp. 29 and following.

64. This incident is noted by Davis in chapter 8 of *"Ruby Robert"* and recalled

by him also in an article entitled "Bob Fitzsimmons and the Leadville Blacksmith," *Boxing and Wrestling*, April 1958, pp. 24 and following.)

65. With this, notes Davis, "He got to his feet, tipped his that and sauntered away with the grace of a thrashing machine" (*Ibid.*, page 61).

66. This is noted by Odd, who is among the most meticulous of historians. Other writers have attributed the comment to Bob in connection with one or the other of his fights with Jeffries.

67. See *Physical Culture and Self-Defense*, page 173.

68. This quote is contained in Odd's account, page 182.

69. This song, which has Fitz dropping each man with "his wallop, his wallop, his wallop," is sung to the tune of Gilbert and Sullivan's "Tit-Willow" from *The Mikado*. (See the conclusion of this chapter.)

70. See *Two Fisted Jeff*, pp. 219–20.

71. *The Fighting Blacksmith*, page 217.

72. Quoted in *Remembering Bob Fitzsimmons*, page 53.

73. *"Ruby Robert,"* page 77.

74. Recalled in a column by Frank G. Menke, *The Sporting News*, January 20, 1944.

75. Reprinted in Edward Van Every, "When Fitz Made Comeback Bid," *The Ring*, March 1951, pp. 28 and following.

Chapter IV

1. Nat Fleischer, *The Three Colored Aces: Story of George Dixon, Joe Gans, Joe Walcott and Several Contemporaries*, vol. 3 of *Black Dynamite: The Story of the Negro in the Prize Ring from 1782 to 1938* (New York: Ring Athletic Library, 1938), page 196.

2. *Baltimore Morning Herald*, February 27, 1900.

3. This remark comes from Fleischer, who maintains that Dixon and Joe met the same night that Walcott scored these two wins. While there are slight discrepancies between Fleischer's account and the current record, it is worth mention that Dixon did box a four-round draw

with the noted Walter Edgerton in Phila-delphia on October 29, thus making it a plausible time for the two men to become acquainted.

4. *The Three Colored Aces*, page 225.

5. This quote appears in an undated photocopy fragment of a piece authored by Doc Almy in an issue of *The Veteran Boxer*.

6. See, for example, See Michael Glick, "If You Can't Beat 'Em Fair — Fool 'Em!," *Boxing Illustrated Wrestling News*, September 1959, pp. 37 and following.

7. This statement, from a New York news columnist, is dated April 4 and is contained in *The Three Colored Aces*, chapter 18.

8. "Memories," page 25.

9. *Portland Oregonian*, February 24, 1900.

10. *Portland Oregonian*, May 6, 1900.

11. *Milwaukee Evening Wisconsin*, August 28, 1900.

12. See *The Three Colored Aces*, chapter 20.

13. *Police Gazette*, July 26, 1901.

14. *The Three Colored Aces*, pp. 249–50.

15. *Milwaukee Free Press*, December 19, 1901.

16. According to Fleischer (though current records do not list it), the two men met a second time, with Walcott making a desperate effort to even the score, and being held to a draw over 20 rounds. Walcott, maintains Nat, was still quite formidable at the time he met up with the Kid, and despite his regard for Joe, he says also that the title should have passed hands at that point. Contrary to what some imagine, he insists, "the Kid won his title on the square and retained it gallantly in the second encounter" (*The Three Colored Aces*, page 255).

17. Editors, "Solved ... the Mystery of the Missing Champion," *Boxing and Wrestling*, January 1956, pages 22 and following.

Chapter V

1. Tony Canzoneri, "The Greatest Lightweights of All Time," *Boxing and Wrestling*, January 1957, pages 25 and following.

2. *Milwaukee Free Press*, August 5, 1906.

3. See Ted Carroll, "Joe Gans ... The Mystic Hero," *The Ring*, June 1961, pages 24 and following.

4. Norman Mailer, "Ego," contained in David Halberstam, ed., *The Best American Sports Writing of the Century* (Boston: Houghton Mifflin, 1999), page 715. This piece was reprinted from an issue of *Life* magazine.

5. Colleen Aycock and Mark Scott, *Joe Gans: A Biography of the First African American World Boxing Champion* (Jefferson, NC: McFarland, 2008), page 39. For relevant commentary see also chapter 18, "The Old Master's Legacy."

6. *The Three Colored Aces*, page 130.

7. According to Aycock and Scott, however, the bout was initially declared a draw, and Dobbs got the decision only when the referee, bowing to "local pressure," awarded it to him.

8. *San Francisco Chronicle*, September 9, 1907. For a rich collection of Gans commentary, see Monte Cox, "Joe Gans, The Old Master," at coxscorner.tripod.com.

9. *Police Gazette*, May 6, 1899. According to one rumor, Joe had stuffed himself with some two dozen doughnuts earlier in the day, and paid a terrible price when the action heated up.

10. August 19, 1899.

11. *San Francisco Chronicle*, June 28, 1902.

12. It may be that the injury was even more severe than some sources have made out. According to the *San Francisco Chronicle* of March 24, 1900, "Gans' eye was [dislodged] from its socket." The *Chicago Times-Herald* of that date reported the same thing, though this detail seems a little doubtful, given how soon the fighter was in action again.

13. In fact, some accounts have Gans lying down to Hawkins, Erne, and Mc-Govern, and agreeing to let up (see the section ahead) Jimmy Britt. See Charles Samuels, *The Magnificent Rube: The Life and Gaudy Times of Tex Rickard* (New

York: McGraw-Hill, 1957). For corroborating opinion, see discussion by veteran referee George Siler in his book *Inside Facts on Pugilism* (Chicago: Laird and Lee, 1907), and the recent work by Aycock and Scott.

14. See *The Three Colored Aces*, page 155.

15. The *Boston Globe* reported that "The decision was not well received by many of the spectators" who saw it as Joe's fight, and featherweight champion Young Corbett would recall a couple of years later that "Gans mastered him and outpunched him all the way" (October 1, 1906).

16. See Ritchie's commentary in Peter Heller, *In This Corner...!: 42 World Champions Tell Their Stories* (New York: Da Capo, 1994), pp. 18 and following.

17. According to Aycock and Scott, Al Herford told Gans (and virtually coerced him) in advance to let Britt "make a good showing" in order to cash in on some betting action. For an extensive account of this fight, and the injustice connected with it, see chapter 9 of the Gans biography.

18. See Pardy's "When the Lights Went Out," *The Ring*, October 1939, page 40.

19. *San Francisco Chronicle*, January 20, 1906.

20. July 24, 1906.

21. See chapter XVIII of Nelson's own *Life, Battles and Career of Battling Nelson* (Hegewisch, IL: [s.n.], 1908).

22. London's account is reprinted in the Nelson autobiography.

23. *Ibid.*, page 178.

24. This opinion is attributed to an unnamed writer on pp. 108–09 of *The Magnificent Rube*.

25. Nelson's autobiography, completed shortly after his third bout with Gans in 1908, details his encounters with five black fighters under a section entitled "My Ring Experiences with the Negro Population."

26. This comment is noted in the *Police Gazette*, July, 1906. The author of the column, it may be noted, expresses reservation as to its genuineness.

27. Milwaukee *Evening Wisconsin*, July 27, 1906.

28. *Baltimore American*, August 20, 1906.

29. *Baltimore American*, August 23, 1906.

30. *Ibid.* On this occasion Nelson also vowed that neither he nor Gans would do any fouling, a prediction that ran sadly afoul of the truth, as it turned out.

31. *Baltimore American*, August 27, 1906.

32. *Baltimore American*, August 23, 1906.

33. *Baltimore American*, August 24, 1906. Among other things, this column notes that an examination given only 15 minutes after his workout recorded a pulse rate of 72.

34. *The Magnificent Rube*, page 110.

35. *Life, Battles, and Career*, page 117.

36. This comment, part of stretch excerpted from Nelson's autobiography, is contained in "My Fight with Joe Gans," *Boxing and Wrestling*, November 1957, pp. 34 and following.

37. *San Francisco Chronicle*, September 4, 1906.

38. *Chicago Record Herald*, January 2, 1907.

39. Whether or not the injury was real, it appears that Britt was outclassed from the start. "At no stage in the short fight, notes the *San Francisco Chronicle*, "did the Californian ... have a chance. Gans ... was winning all the way" (September 10, 1907).

40. Noted in *The Sporting News*, December 14, 1944.

41. Smyth's account is reprinted in *Life, Battles, and Career*, pages 227 and following.

42. *Chicago Sunday Examiner*, September 20, 1908. These statements appear also in Nelson's autobiography.

43. In fact, according to the *New York Daily Herald*, Gans dropped White four times in the bout, and the British fighter was saved twice by the bell (March 13, 1909).

44. Lenny's recollection of Gans, with whom he worked more than 500 rounds, is detailed in Johnny Brannigan's "This

Was Joe Gans," *Boxing Illustrated Wrestling News*, August 1960, pp. 20 and following.

45. This remark, in a column authored by Ed Stone, is from a newspaper dated 1956 and contained in the Gans files available through Harry Shaffer's Antiquities of the Prize Ring.

46. *Ibid.*

47. Brannigan, "This Was Joe Gans," pages 22 and following.

Chapter VI

1. *The Magnificent Rube*, page 87.

2. There were, observes Nat Fleischer, "more amateur teams at that time in Brooklyn than there are politicians in New York today." See Fleischer's *"Terrible Terry": The Brooklyn Terror* (New York: C.J. O'Brien, 1943), page 5. Information in the first few pages of this chapter is taken largely from this source.

3. McGovern has traditionally been credited with a one-round knockout, on this date, of a fighter named Jack Shea. But according to the next day's account, he and Snee, each scaling 110, met in a bout scheduled for ten rounds, and "for three rounds ... made matters lively" with Terry having the better of it in a fight marred by fouling on each side. In the fourth, the referee awarded the bout to Johnny by disqualification (*Brooklyn Daily Eagle*, April 4, 1897).

4. This statement comes from McGovern's *How to Box to Win*, reprinted with materials from other celebrity authors in *How to Box* (Chicago: Stein Publishing House, 1931), page 52.

5. Thus, for example, Henry Besterman became Harry Lewis, Ugo Micheli was Hugo Kelly, and Otto Husine took the moniker of Young Mahoney.

6. *The Roosevelt That I Know*, page 233.

7. As Fleischer notes, she did better to see it in this fashion, as women were still *persona non grata* at most prizefights.

8. "George Dixon Greatest," Tom O'Rourke, *The Ring*, October 1936, page 35.

9. *The Three Colored Aces*, pp. 65–67.

10. By now this weight had been declared the official featherweight limit.

11. *Milwaukee Evening Wisconsin*, January 6, 1900.

12. *Police Gazette*, January 27, 1900.

13. *Portland Oregonian*, January 10, 1900.

14. *Milwaukee Evening Wisconsin*, January 10, 1900.

15. *Portland Oregonian*, January 14, 1900.

16. The Veteran, "I Remember When — ," *The Ring*, March 1942, pages 28 and following.

17. "Terrible Terry," page 43.

18. *Life, Battles, and Career of Battling Nelson*, page 147.

19. Samuels, *The Magnificent Rube*, page 11.

Chapter VII

1. Stan Weston, "Sam Langford Was Great," *Boxing and Wrestling*, May 1956, pp. 30 and following.

2. Rick Scurti, "The 5 Greatest Fighters Who Ever Lived," *Boxing Digest*, August 2003, pp. 56 and following.

3. Don Elbaum, Robert Cassidy, et al., "The 100 Greatest Punchers of All-Time!" *The Ring Yearbook*, 2003 edition (Ambler, PA: London, 2003). This volume names Joe Louis as the number one, and Jimmy Wilde, Archie Moore, and Sandy Saddler as the three following Langford.

4. Recalled from a private conversation with Sam by A.J. Liebling, *The Sweet Science* (New York: North Point, page 265).

5. See Harman Nichols and Oscar Fraley, "The Boston Tar Baby," *True Boxing Yearbook* 1952, pp. 24 and following.

6. This quotation comes from a photocopied issue of a London publication printed by Health and Strength, titled *The Life and Battles of Sam Langford*. It appears to date from about 1909.

7. *Ibid.*

8. Clay Moyle, *Sam Langford: Boxing's Greatest Uncrowned Champion* (Seattle: Bennett & Hastings, 2007), page 3.

9. This scenario is related by Weston, "Sam Langford Was Great." The remainder of the chapter draws from multiple sources.

10. Robert R. Richards, "The Amazing Langford!," *Fight Stories*, Winter 1948-49, page 30.

11. See Runyan's "Jack Johnson Could Fight," pp. 14–15, in Johnson's *Jack Johnson in the Ring and Out* (New York: Citadel Press, 1992).

12. This statement comes from an extensive article in the London *Health and Strength* titled "The Life and Battles of Sam Langford." It appears to date from about 1908, when Sam was 22 years old.

13. This quotation comes from an untitled photocopy source in an interview called "Tar Baby: An Interview with Sam Langford" and appears to have been published well after Sam's fighting days were over.

14. *In the Ring and Out*, page 52.

15. This comment, quite famous as a piece of fight coverage, is excerpted in Fleischer's book *The Heavyweight Championship* (New York: Putnam's, 1949), pp. 141–42.

16. This statement is attributed to Jeannette in the premier issue of *Boxing Illustrated Wrestling News* (November 1958) in an article, included at the expense of a production delay, by the publishers after they had received late-breaking news of Joe's death.

17. This story is recounted in "The Amazing Langford," page 47.

18. *50 Years at Ringside*, page 77.

19. *Ibid.*, page 78.

20. Again, a column much quoted, found reprinted in multiple sources, including W.C. Heinz, *The Fireside Book of Boxing* (New York: Simon & Schuster, 1961), pages 256 and following.

21. Quoted by the renowned columnist TAD (T.A. Dorgan) in a preface statement to Johnson's autobiography.

22. Engel, "Haymakers," page 4.

23. This claim is made by Johnston in *Ten—and Out!*, page 195.

24. This anecdote is related by Johnston, page 194.

25. This quotation comes from the earlier cited "Tar Baby" interview.

26. This portion of the chapter is taken primarily from Laney's "Two Visits with Sam Langford," contained in Heinz, ed., *The Fireside Book of Boxing*, pp. 226 and following.

27. This material originally appeared as two separate columns in the *New York Herald Tribune*.

28. Heinz, ed., *The Fireside Book of Boxing*, page 227.

Chapter VIII

1. Nat Fleischer, *"The Michigan Assassin": The Saga of Stanley Ketchel* (New York: C.J. O'Brien, 1946), page 5.

2. More than one spelling of this last name has been reported.

3. See John Lardner, "Ketchel Was a Wild Man," *True Boxing Yearbook*, 1957. This piece had first run in a regular issue of *True* magazine three years earlier.

4. *50 Years at Ringside*, page 64.

5. See chapter 1 of *"The Michigan Assassin."*

6. So claimed Ketchel—it is a neat piece of drama, though here again one might remember Lardner's literary caution.

7. Exactly when some fighters of this era made their debuts is often unclear. The Cyber Boxing Zone lists a May 2, 1904, one-round knockout of "Kid Tracy" as Stan's first fight, while there is note elsewhere of a knockout in 24 rounds over a Mose LaFontaine, or LaFontise, in Butte on August 8, 1903, as Stan's actual ring debut.

8. According to Fleischer (though the bout is not listed in current records), Ketchel got an early taste of the big time in 1904 when he volunteered to box four rounds with Ryan when the great champion was on tour. By this account, Ryan's manager Jack Curley, on meeting Stan, accepted his offer with a twinge of regret, figuring that the innocent-looking kid was in for a pasting. As it turned out, claimed Fleischer, Ryan got more than he bargained for, as Stan's ferocity prompted

Curley to cut the rounds to reduce the action.

9. "Ketchel Was a Wild Man," pp. 6 and following.

10. Roche's account is contained in chapter 5 of Fleischer's book.

11. By his own recollection, Roche leaned over the ropes between rounds at about this time and remarked, "This fellow Ketchel isn't a man — he's a fighting devil!"

12. *"The Michigan Assassin,"* page 42.

13. This observation was recalled and printed after the second Ketchel-Papke fight in the *Milwaukee Evening Wisconsin,* September 12, 1908.

14. This remark was made by Naughton also in the August 2 *San Francisco Examiner.*

15. They would, noted T.S. Andrews in the *Milwaukee Evening Wisconsin* of September 19, "put up another slashing bout at San Francisco, for neither one knows anything in a fight but to mix from the tap of the gong."

16. *Milwaukee Free Press,* November 22, 1908.

17. This statement from the *Milwaukee Evening Wisconsin* of October 12, 1908, is contained in Harry Shaffer's article "The Color Line, Mayhem, and Madness: The Last Days of Stanley Ketchel, Part II," in the November 2005 issue of *Boxing Collector's News.*

18. The winner, notes the *Milwaukee Evening Wisconsin* of November 27, in a representative description, "fought the best fight of his career, boxing well, blocking in a way that, at times, made Papke appear like a beginner at the game, landing stiff punches to the body ... and in no way suffering himself."

19. Billy McCarney, "Holiday Fights," *The Ring,* December 1948, page 25.

20. *Milwaukee Free Press,* November 29, 1908.

21. Jack won the first of these latter bouts on March 25, 1905, on a foul when Jackson felled him with a right hand on the break, thus violating a pre-fight agreement. He met Jackson in a savage 10-round fight two weeks later, winning by

decision. By one account, "The Philadelphian scored first blood in the sixth round, and had Jackson groggy late in the fight though he was unable to put his man away" (*Milwaukee Evening Wisconsin,* April 8, 1905). An account in the *Milwaukee Free Press* is more favorable to Jackson, but by each account the fight was a barnburner.

22. *Police Gazette,* November 1905.

23. Gilbert Forte, "The One Who Was Best of All," *Boxing and Wrestling,* March 1955. Forte, who was born in 1876, describes in this piece his personal observations of heavyweight champions from John L. Sullivan to the present day.

24. *"The Michigan Assassin,"* page 68.

25. *Police Gazette,* November 1905.

26. Recalled by Liebling in *The Sweet Science,* page 3.

27. See, for example, Jack Johnson, "How Ketchel Tried to Double Cross Me," *Boxing and Wrestling,* July 1957, pages 14 and following.

28. Shaffer, "The Color Line."

29. This was Fleischer's own view, as he recorded it in the *New York Press.*

30. *50 Years at Ringside,* page 79.

31. "'Dumb Dan,' the Fighter's Man," Jack Mahon, *True Boxing Yearbook,* 1952, page 62.

32. Clifford L. Thorne, "Human Side of Ketchel," *The Ring,* January 1936, page 24.

33. According to Igoe, he made only one request while there, asking to be taken home to his mother. In a short time he was comatose, and he died hours later.

34. This detail is alleged by Lardner. According to Igoe's account, Dipley made off with two $1,000 bills that Ketchel had in his pocket, as well as a five-carat diamond ring that he was wearing on his finger.

35. Jack Kofoed, "The Michigan Assassin: Part III," *Fight Stories,* May 1929, pages 46 and following.

36. Reprinted in *The Complete Short Stories of Ernest Hemingway* (New York: Scribner's, 2003), pp. 292 and following.

Afterword

1. Jim Mace, "Jess Willard — Heavyweight Champion of the World," cyberboxingzone.com April 10, 2005.

2. Quoted in Graeme Kent, *The Great White Hopes* (Hereford, UK: Sutton, 2005), page 206.

3. Quoted in Stan Weston's "Jess Willard: The 'Public Be Damned' Fighter," *Boxing and Wrestling*, August 1956, pages 24 and following.

4. T.W. McNeil, "Jeffries Retains Interest in Boxing," *The Ring*, June 1941, pages 17 and following. Jeffries would hold much the same opinion nine years later, when interviewed by his friend Fleischer in a four-part *Ring* interview.

5. This statement, which is reprinted in more than one source, is noted by Fleischer in chapter 24 of *50 Years at Ringside*.

6. Jimmy Jacobs, "'Sugar' Ray Robinson was Truly Unique," *The Ring*, March 1969, pp. 31 and following. For a recent piece that pays respect to boxing by weight divisions over several time periods, see Gavin Evans, "The Best Eras in Boxing History," *The Ring*, August 2008, pp. 79 and following.

7. Fielding, a veteran observer and member of the International Boxing Research Organization, supplied these remarks in a private correspondence.

8. Tracy Callis, "The Greatest Fighters of All Time," *Cyberboxingzone*, September 21, 2004. See related discussion in Appendix II of my book *A Man Among Men*.

9. Gilbert Rogin, "Mr. Boxing, Himself," originally published in *The Ring* magazine around the year 1962. This article, which is in large part an interview, is reprinted in the December 20, 2007, issue of the *IBRO Journal*.

10. Readers who wish to pursue the issue of boxing across generations may want to explore a recent work by Mike Silver titled *The Arc of Boxing: The Rise and Decline of the Sweet Science*. Boxing, argues Silver, was at its apex in roughly the era of the 1920s and '30s, and many of today's elite stars would have been surpassed by relatively inconspicuous fighters of that day.

Bibliography

Books

Anderson, Dave. *In the Corner: Great Boxing Trainers Talk About Their Art.* New York: William Morrow, 1991.

Ashe, Arthur. *A Hard Road to Glory: The African-American Athlete in Boxing.* New York: Amistad, 1993.

Aycock, Colleen, and Mark Scott. *Joe Gans: A Biography of the First African American World Boxing Champion.* Jefferson, NC: McFarland, 2008.

Brown, Gene, Arleen Keylin, and Daniel Lundy, eds. *Great Moments in Sports History.* New York: New York Times, 1984.

Cavanaugh, Jack. *Tunney: Boxing's Brainiest Champ and His Upset of the Great Jack Dempsey.* New York: Random House, 2007.

Chidsey, Donald Barr. *John the Great.* New York: Doubleday, Doran, 1942.

Corbett, James J. *The Roar of the Crowd.* New York: Grosset and Dunlap, 1925.

Davis, Robert H. *"Ruby Robert"— Alias Bob Fitzsimmons.* New York: Doran, 1926.

Dempsey, Jack. *Dempsey: By the Man Himself.* As told to Bob Considine and Bill Slocum. New York: Simon & Schuster, 1960.

Donnellon, Matt. *The Irish Champion Peter Maher.* Victoria, BC: Trafford, 2008.

Donovan, Mike. *The Roosevelt That I Know.* New York: B.W. Dodge, 1909.

Fitzsimmons, Bob. *Physical Culture and Self-Defense.* Philadelphia: Drexel Biddle, 1901.

Fleischer, Nat. *Black Dynamite: The Story of the Negro in the Prize Ring from 1782 to 1938.* Vols. 3 and 4. New York: Ring Athletic Library, 1938 and following.

_____. *50 Years at Ringside.* New York: Fleet, 1958.

_____. *"Gentleman Jim": The Story of James J. Corbett.* New York: C.J. O'Brien, 1942.

_____. *The Heavyweight Championship.* New York: Putnam's, 1949.

_____. *Leonard the Magnificent.* Norwalk, CT: O'Brien Suburban Press, 1947.

_____. *"The Michigan Assassin": The Saga of Stanley Ketchel.* New York: C.J. O'Brien, 1946.

_____. *The Ring Record Book.* New York: The Ring Bookshop, 1950 and editions following.

_____. *"Terrible Terry": The Brooklyn Terror.* New York: C.J. O'Brien, 1943.

_____, and Sam André. *A Pictorial History of Boxing.* New York: Bonanza Books, 1959.

Fox, Richard K. *Bob Fitzsimmons: His Life and Battles.* New York: Richard K. Fox, Franklin Square, 1897.

_____. *Life and Battles of Jack Dempsey.* New York: Richard K. Fox, Franklin Square, 1889.

Fullerton, Hugh. *Two Fisted Jeff.* Chicago: Consolidated, 1929.

Gorn, Elliott. *The Manly Art: Bare-Knuckle Prize Fighting in America.* Ithaca, NY: Cornell University Press, 1986.

Graffis, Herbert, ed. *Esquire's First Sports Reader*. New York: A.S. Barnes, 1945.

Halberstam, David, ed. *The Best American Sports Writing of the Century*. Boston: Houghton Mifflin, 1999.

Heinz, W.C., ed. *The Fireside Book of Boxing*. New York: Simon & Schuster, 1961.

_____, and Nathan Ward, eds. *The Book of Boxing*. Kingston, New York: Total Sports Publishing, 1999.

Heller, Peter. *In This Corner...!: 42 World Champions Tell Their Stories*. New York: Da Capo, 1994.

Hemingway, Ernest. *The Complete Short Stories of Ernest Hemingway*. New York: Scribner's, 2003.

Homer. *The Iliad*. Robert Fitzgerald, translator. New York: Farrar, Straus, and Giroux, 1994.

Isenberg, Michael T. *John L. Sullivan and His America*. Chicago: University of Illinois Press, 1994.

Jackson, Holbrook. *The Eighteen Nineties*. 1913. London: Penguin, 1950.

James, William. *The Varieties of Religious Experience*. New York: Barnes and Noble Classics, 2004.

Jeffries, James J. *My Life and Battles*. Edited and illustrated by R. Edgren. New York: Ringside, 1910.

Johnson, Jack. *Jack Johnson in the Ring and Out*. 1927. New York: Citadel Press, 1992.

Johnson, Samuel, and James Boswell. *A Journey to the Western Islands* and *Journal of a Tour to the Hebrides*. 1 vol. 1786. London: Penguin Books, 1984.

Johnston, Alexander. *Ten — and Out!* 3rd ed. New York: Ives Washburn, 1947.

Kahn, Roger. *A Flame of Pure Fire: Jack Dempsey and the Roaring 20s*. San Diego: Harcourt, 1999.

Kent, Graeme. *The Great White Hopes*. Hereford, UK: Sutton, 2005.

Lardner, Rex. *The Legendary Champions*. New York: American Heritage Press, 1972.

Liebling, A.J. *The Sweet Science*. New York: North Point Press, 2004.

Lotierzo, Frank, and Tom Donelson. *Viewing Boxing from Ringside*. New York: Writers Club Press, 2002.

Lowe, Benjamin. *The Beauty of Sport*. Englewood Cliffs, NJ: Prentice Hall, 1977.

McConaughy, J.W. *Big Jim Jeffries and His Twelve Greatest Ring Battles*. New York: Sinclair, 1910.

McGovern, Terry, et al. *How to Box: 4 Books in One*. Chicago: Stein Publishing House, 1931. (This volume brings together material authored by McGovern, James J. Corbett, G.E. and A.R. Keeley, and J. Gardner Smith that was previously published by the *New York Evening World*.)

Mee, Bob. *Bare Fists: The History of Bare-Knuckle Prize-Fighting*. Woodstock: Overlook Press, 2001.

Miletich, Leo N. *Dan Stuart's Fistic Carnival*. College Station: Texas A&M Press, 1994.

Moyle, Clay. *Sam Langford: Boxing's Greatest Uncrowned Champion*. Seattle: Bennett & Hastings, 2007.

Myler, Patrick. *Gentleman Jim Corbett*. London: Robson Books, 1998.

Naughton, W.W. *Heavyweight Champions*. San Francisco: John Kitchen, Jr., 1910.

Nelson, Oscar. *Life, Battles and Career of Battling Nelson*. Hegeswisch, IL: [s.n.], 1908.

Nicholson, Kelly. *A Man Among Men: The Life and Ring Battles of Jim Jeffries*. Salt Lake City: Homeward Bound, 2002.

Odd, Gilbert. *The Fighting Blacksmith: The Story of Bob Fitzsimmons*. London: Pelham Books, 1976.

_____. *The Great Champions*. London: Hamlyn Publishing Group, 1974.

O'Farrell, Dick. *How to Box*. Sydney: Frank Johnson, Publisher, undated.

Pollack, Adam. *In the Ring with Bob Fitzsimmons*. Iowa City, IA: Win By KO Publishers, 2007.

Rice, Edward, and John Durant. *Come Out Fighting*. Cincinnati: Zebra Picture Books, 1946.

Robinson, Charles M. *The Men Who Wear the Star: The Story of the Texas Rangers*. New York: Random House, 2000.

Robinson, Keith. *Lanky Bob*. Victoria, BC: Trafford, 2008.

Rocap, William H., and Pember Rocap. *Remembering Bob Fitzsimmons*. Wayne, ME: Archives Press, 2001.

Samuels, Charles. The *Magnificent Rube: The Life and Gaudy Times of Tex Rickard*. New York: McGraw-Hill, 1957.

Siler, George. *Inside Facts on Pugilism*. Chicago: Laird and Lee, 1907.

Silver, Mike. *The Arc of Boxing: The Rise and Decline of the Sweet Science*. Jefferson, NC: McFarland, 2008.

Smith, Kevin R. *Black Genesis*. Lincoln, NE: iUniverse, 2003.

Sullivan, John L. *I Can Lick Any Sonofabitch in the House!* 1892. London: Proteus, 1980. Original title *Life and Reminiscences of a Nineteenth Century Gladiator*.

Sun Tzu. *The Art of War*. Lionel Giles, translator. New York: Barnes and Noble Classics, 2003.

Swanwick, Raymond. *Les Darcy: Australia's Golden Boy of Boxing*. Sydney: Ure Smith Pty. Limited, 1965.

Tobin, Christopher. *Fitzsimmons: Boxing's First Triple World Champion*. Timaru, New Zealand: David A. Jack and C. Tobin, 2000).

Virgil. *The Aeneid*. Robert Fitzgerald, translator. New York: Vintage Classics, 1983. Webb, Dale. *Prize Fighter: The Life and Times of Bob Fitzsimmons*. Edinburgh: Mainstream, 2001.

Willoughby, David. *The Super Athlete: A Record of the Limits of Human Strength, Speed and Stamina*. New York: A.S. Barnes, 1970.

Periodical Articles and Website Sources

Almy, Doc. "Champion of Champions." *The Ring* 30, no. 5 (June 1951): pp. 6ff.

Anselmo, Philip. "The Heavyweight Division: 1958 and Today." *Boxing Digest* 40, no. 10 (November-December 2008): pp. 12ff.

Austin, Sam. "First Fight Movies." *The Ring* 12, no. 3 (April 1933): pp. 10ff.

Barton, George. "Durable Dane Greatest Marathon Fighter." *The Ring* 32, no. 9 (November 1953): pp. 26ff.

Bishop, Biddy. "Kid Lavigne Greatest Lightweight of All Time." *The Ring* 7, no. 4 (May 1928): pp. 4ff.

Bodenrader, Ted. "10 Heavyweight Fights That Transcended Boxing." *World Boxing* 34, no. 3 (November 2002): pp. 68ff.

Borden, Ed. "Gentleman Jim Corbett." *Boxing and Wrestling* 1, no. 9 (December 1951): pp. 10ff.

_____. "How They Felt: Jim Corbett and Bob Fitzsimmons Cover Their Own Fight." *Boxing and Wrestling* 7, no. 6 (February 1957). This feature includes reprint of by-line statements of each man published in the *San Francisco Examiner* the day after their Carson City fight in 1897.

Bragen, Sam. "Jim Jeffries vs. Bob Fitzsimmons." *Boxing and Wrestling* 7, no. 9 (May 1957): pp. 19ff. This feature reprints a story written shortly after the second Jeffries-Fitzsimmons fight in 1902.

Brannigan, Johnny. "Bloodbath on a Barge." *Boxing Illustrated Wrestling News* 4, no. 12 (December 1962): pp. 32ff.

_____. "Feud of the Champions." *Boxing Illustrated Wrestling News* 2, no. 12 (December 1960): pp. 22ff.

_____. "This Was Joe Gans." *Boxing Illustrated* 2, no. 8 (August 1960): pp. 20ff.

Buck, Al. "Where Are the Iron Men?" *The Ring* 28, no. 11 (December 1949): pp. 23ff.

Callis, Tracy. "Athletes—Bigger, Faster, and Stronger—Are They Better?" *WAIL!* June 1998, cyberboxingzone.com.

_____. "Battling Nelson: Always Battered, Seldom Beaten." *WAIL!* February 2006, cyberboxingzone.com.

_____. "Bob Fitzsimmons, 'Pound for Pound—the Greatest Ever.'" *WAIL!* June 1999, cyberboxingzone.com.

_____. "The Greatest Fighters of All Time." September 21, 2004, cyberboxingzone.com.

_____. "Jim Jeffries ... 'Warhorse of Yesteryear.'" *WAIL!* April 2001, cyberboxingzone.com.

_____. "Joe Choynski ... 'Clever, Shifty,

and Explosive.'" *WAIL!* May 2002, cyberboxingzone.com.
_____. "Ranking the All-Time Boxing Greats." *WAIL!* July 1998, cyberboxing zone.com.
Canzoneri, Tony. "The Greatest Lightweights of All Time." *Boxing and Wrestling* 7, no. 5 (January 1957): pp. 25ff.
Carney, Jim, Jr. "What's the Power Source for Boxing's Big Hitters?" *Cleveland Tab*, November 1999.
Carroll, Ted. "Jack Johnson Best." *The Ring* 27, no. 4 (May 1948): pp. 24ff.
_____. "Joe Gans ... The Mystic Hero." *The Ring* 40, no. 5 (June 1961): pp. 24ff.
_____. "Old vs. New: Present-Day Rulers Compare Favorably." *The Ring* 28, no. 11 (December 1949): pp. 12ff.
_____. "TV Vexing Issue." *The Ring* 30, no. 5 (June 1951): pp. 3ff.
Casey, Mike. "Blood, Guts and Greatness: The Incredible Kid Lavigne." *IBRO Journal*, no. 96 (December 20, 2007): pp. 9ff.
_____. "Gene Tunney: The King of Cool." *IBRO Journal*, no. 98 (June 15, 2008): pp. 29ff.
_____. "The Seminal Master: Why Jack Johnson Would Be King Today." *IBRO Journal*, no. 98 (June 15, 2008): pp. 48ff.
_____. "The $10,000 Glass of Sherry: When Young Griffo Fell Off the Wagon." *IBRO Journal*, no. 97 (March 12, 2008): pp. 31ff.
Collins, Art. "The Cover Story." *The Ring* 28, no. 12 (January 1950): pp. 18ff.
"Coronation at Rushcutters Bay." *Boxing Illustrated Wrestling News* 3, no. 4 (April 1961): pp. 20ff.
Cox, Monte. "Cox's Corner/Joe Gans' Championship Years: Setting the Record Straight." *IBRO Journal*, no. 82 (June 23, 2004): pp. 18ff.
_____. "James J. Corbett: Turning Point in Pugilism." *IBRO Journal*, no. 97 (March 12, 2008): pp. 25ff.
_____. "Joe Gans, The Old Master." coxs corner.tripod.com.
_____. "Joe Gans: Was He the Greatest?" *IBRO Journal*, no. 83 (September 22, 2004): pp. 18ff.
Daniel, Daniel M. "Battling Nelson's Surprise Victory." *The Ring* 23, no. 8 (September 1944): pp. 20ff.
_____. "How Would Old Timers Have Fared on TV?" *The Ring Annual* 1954, pp. 18ff.
Davis, Albert. "Bob Fitzsimmons and the Leadville Blacksmith." *Boxing and Wrestling* 8, no. 7 (April 1958).
"The Day the Michigan Assassin Was Licked." *Boxing Life* 1, no. 1 (March 1953): pp. 48ff. This article was originally published in the July 1952 issue of *Men* magazine.
"Dempsey: 'I Was Afraid of Sam Langford.'" *Boxing Illustrated Wrestling News* 2, no. 8.
DeRougomont, R.R. "The Ten Greats of All Time." *Boxing and Wrestling* 6, no. 4 (December 1955): pp. 27.
Diamond, Wilf. "The Hectic Life of the Harum-Scarum Kid." *Boxing and Wrestling* 7, no. 5 (January 1957): pp. 27ff.
Doherty, Bill. "My Recollections of the Marquess of Queensberry." *The Ring* 15, no. 9 (October 1936): pp. 29ff.
Dorgan, John L. "When Dixon Lost His Crown." *The Ring* 10, no. 10 (November 1931): page 14.
Dorgan, Tad. "When Sullivan Hit the Deck: The great man's darkest hour." *Boxing and Wrestling* 7, no. 9 (May 1957): pp. 41ff.
Elbaum, Don, Robert Cassidy, et al. "The 100 Greatest Punchers of All-Time!" *The Ring Yearbook 2003* 72, no. 10.
Engel, George. "Haymakers." *The Ring* 11, no. 11 (December 1932): pp. 4ff.
Evans, Gavin. "The Best Eras in Boxing History." *The Ring* 87, no. 9 (August 2008): pp. 79ff.
_____. "Ten Moments That Changed Boxing." *The Ring* 88, no. 12 (October 2008): pp. 61ff.
"Famous Fights Recalled." *The Ring* 10, no. 9 (October 1931). Includes note and illustrations of Young Griffo vs. Horace Leeds.
Fleischer, Nat. "Big Jim Reminisces." *The Ring* 29, no. 7 (August 1950): pp. 20ff.
_____. "Big Jim Reminisces." *The Ring* 29, no. 8 (September 1950): pp. 18ff.

_____. "Clay Pulled Corkscrew." *The Ring* 44, no. 8 (September 1965): pp. 8ff.

_____. "40 Experts Pick Jack Dempsey as All Time Great." *The Ring* 41, no. 11 (December 1962): pp. 6ff.

_____. "Gentleman Jim." *The Ring* 12, no. 3 (April 1933): pp. 2ff. This piece is followed by several pages of lavish illustrations in a memorial section featured shortly after Corbett's passing.

_____. "Great Moments in Ring History." *The Ring* 28, no. 3 (April 1949): pp. 28ff.

_____. "Griffo, Ring's Cleverest Boxer." *The Ring* 13, no. 4 (May 1934): pp. 16ff.

_____. "Jim Jeffries Talks About Great Fighters of His Era." *The Ring* 29, no. 9 (October 1950): pp. 24ff.

_____. "Jim Jeffries Talks About Old Days with Fleischer." *The Ring* 29, no. 6 (July 1950): pp. 4ff. This installment is the first in a four-part interview with Jeffries, the next three of which follow in order of publication.

_____. "Memories." *The Ring* 28, no. 10 (November 1949): pp. 26ff.

_____. "Memories." *The Ring* 32, no. 2 (March 1953): pp. 26ff.

_____. "The Perfect Boxer." *The Ring* 40, no. 10 (November 1961): pp. 20ff.

_____, and Jim Jacobs. "Fleischer vs. Jacobs in Return Match." *The Ring* 48, no. 2 (March 1969): pp. 27ff.

_____, and _____. "Fleischer vs. Jacobs: The Great Debate." *The Ring* 47, no. 2 (March 1968): pp. 21ff.

Forte, Gilbert. "The One Who Was Best of All." *Boxing and Wrestling* 5, no. 8 (March 1955): pp. 24ff.

Franklin, George. "George 'Kid' Lavigne." *Boxing Illustrated Wrestling News* 1, no. 9 (September 1959): pp. 22ff.

"The Furious Fights Between Stanley Ketchel and Joe Thomas." *Boxing Illustrated Wrestling News* 2, no. 3, pp. 34ff.

Furniss, Harold, ed. *Famous Fights Past and Present* 1, no. 11 (c. 1900). This periodical, selling for one penny, was printed and published by Furniss. The issue includes an installment from an ongoing feature describing the 39-round fight between John L. Sullivan and England's Charley Mitchell.

"Gentleman Jim Corbett." *Boxing and Wrestling* 1, no. 9 (December 1951): pp. 10ff.

Glick, Michael A. "If You Can't Beat 'Em — Fool 'Em!" *Boxing Illustrated Wrestling News* 1, no. 9 (September 1959): pp. 36ff.

_____. "Mystery at Rushcutters Bay: Johnson vs. Burns." *Boxing Illustrated Wrestling News* 1, no. 1 (November 1958): pp. 29ff.

_____. "Tom Sharkey Was a Victim of His Times." *Boxing Illustrated Wrestling News* 1, no. 8 (August 1959): pp. 10ff.

Golding, Luis. "The Fight That Will Never Die." *Boxing and Wrestling* 7, no. 6 (February 1957): pp. 14ff.

_____. "The Slave Who Became Heavyweight Champion." *Boxing and Wrestling* 7, no. 11 (July 1957): pp. 16ff.

Griffin, Marcus. "The Bluff That Saved Ketchel." *Boxing and Wrestling* 7, no. 9 (May 1957): pp. 22ff.

Gruenwald, Max. "The Irresistible Fighting Machine." *Boxing and Wrestling* 6, no. 9 (May 1956): pp. 24ff.

Heinz, W.C. "The Catcher No Hero." *The Ring* 30, no. 8 (September 1951): pp. 25ff.

Henessey, Hal. "Just How Dangerous Is Boxing?" *Boxing Illustrated Wrestling News* 3, no. 8 (January 1961): pp. 26ff.

Igoe, Hype. "20-Round Fights Back in US." *The Ring* 18, no. 9 (October 1939): pp. 15ff. Jacobs, Jimmy. "Don't Tell Me Jack Johnson Took a Dive!" *Boxing Illustrated Wrestling News* 3, no. 11 (November 1961): pp. 40ff.

_____. "'Sugar' Ray Robinson Was Truly Unique." *The Ring* 48, no. 2 (March 1969): pp. 31ff.

Jennings, Sidney. "Johnson Didn't Dump It!" *Boxing* 1, no. 2 (May 1953): pp. 28ff.

Johnson, Irene. "Jack Johnson Was a Fine Gentleman." *Boxing and Wrestling* 7, no. 6 (February 1957): pp. 30ff.

Johnson, Jack. "A Champ Recalls." *The Ring* 25, no. 6 (July 1946): pp. 20ff.

_____. "How Ketchel Tried to Double Cross Me." *Boxing and Wrestling* 7, no. 11 (July 1957): pp. 14ff. This feature reprints a story composed by Johnson a number of years earlier for publication elsewhere.

Jones, Jersey. "Help Wanted — Male." *The Ring* 28, no. 5 (June 1949): pp. 6ff.

_____. "Rocky Another Jeff?" *The Ring* 33, no. 9 (October 1954): pp. 8ff.

_____. "Sailor Tom." *The Ring* 32, no. 6 (July 1953): pp. 12ff.

_____. "Wyatt Earp — Referee." *The Ring* 37, no. 3 (April 1958): pp. 20ff.

Kofoed, Jack. "Jack Dempsey — The Nonpareil." *Fight Stories* 1, no. 5 (October 1928).

_____. "Jack Dempsey — The Nonpareil: Part II." *Fight Stories* 1, no. 6 (November 1928).

_____. "Jack Dempsey — The Nonpareil: Part III." *Fight Stories* 1, no. 7 (December 1928).

_____. "The Michigan Assassin." *Fight Stories* 1, no. 10 (March 1929).

_____. "The Michigan Assassin: Part II." *Fight Stories* 1, no. 11 (April 1929).

_____. "The Michigan Assassin: Part III." *Fight Stories* 1, no. 12 (May 1929).

_____. "The Michigan Assassin: Part IV." *Fight Stories* 2, no. 1 (June 1929).

_____. "The Saginaw Kid: Part I." *Fight Stories* 3, no. 9 (February 1931): pp. 5ff.

_____. "The Saginaw Kid: Part II." *Fight Stories* 3, no. 10 (March 1931): pp. 71ff.

Laine, Sam. "The Passing of Joe Jeanette." *Boxing Illustrated Wrestling News* 1, no. 1 (November 1958): pp. 33ff.

Lardner, John. "Ketchel Was a Wild Man." *True Magazine Boxing Yearbook* (1957): pp. 6ff.

_____. "The Life and Loves of the Real McCoy." *True Magazine Boxing Yearbook* (1957): pp. 14 ff.

Lewis, Christine. "George LaBlanche: The Lawrence, MA Years." *IBRO Journal*, no. 101 (March 2009): pp. 54 ff.

"The Life of Bob Fitzsimmons." *Boxing and Wrestling* 7, no. 11 (July 1957): pp. 30ff.

"The Life of Stanley Ketchel." *Boxing and Wrestling* 8, no. 1 (September 1957): pp. 36ff. Pictorial with captions.

Lumley, Arthur T. "John L. as I Knew Him." *The Ring* 13, no. 4 (May 1934): pp. 38ff.

Mace, Jim. "Jess Willard — Heavyweight Champion of the World." cyberboxing zone.-com, April 10, 2005.

Magriel, Paul. "The Life and Times of John L. Sullivan." *Boxing and Wrestling* 8, no. 7 (April 1958): pp. 32ff.

Mahon, Jack. "'Dumb Dan,' the Fighter's Man." *True Boxing Yearbook* (1952): pp. 40ff.

Mayer, Al. "When Jack Johnson Clobbered Luis Firpo." *Boxing and Wrestling* 7, no. 11 (July 1957): pp. 28ff.

McCallum, John. "The Saga of Jack Johnson." *True Magazine Boxing Yearbook* (1953).

McCarney, Billy. "Holiday Fights." *The Ring* 27, no. 11 (December 1948): pp. 24ff.

McClellan, Harvey. "The Cowboy Crushed." *The Ring* 20, no. 11 (December 1941): pp. 17ff.

"McGrath, Sharkey's Manager, Passes Away at Seventy-eight." *The Ring* 29, no. 3 (April 1950): page 35ff.

McNiel, T.W. "Jeffries Retains Interest in Boxing." *The Ring* 20, no. 5 (June 1941): pp. 17ff.

_____. "The Punch That Made Willard a Champion." *The Ring* 18, no. 9 (October 1939): pp. 19ff.

Miller, Bill. "The Jew in Boxing." *The Ring* 11, no. 11 (December 1932): pp. 8ff.

Moyle, Clay. "Sam Langford ... Rare Photos and Facts." *Boxing Collectors' News*, no. 211 (March 2006): pp. 6ff.

Mulcahey, Mike. "Tommy Ryan." *Boxing Digest* 51, no. 2 (February 2009): pp. 40ff.

Myler, Thomas. "Jack 'The Nonpareil' Dempsey." *Boxing Digest* 40, no. 6 (August 2008): pp. 30ff.

Nagler, Barney. "No Short Cut to Success." *The Ring* 31, no. 8 (September 1952): pp. 3ff.

Naughton, W.W. "The Battle of the Iron Men." *Boxing and Wrestling* 7, no. 11 (July 1957): pp. 24ff.

Nelson, Oscar. "My Fight with Joe Gans." *Boxing and Wrestling* 8, no. 2 (November 1957): pp. 34ff.

Nichols, Harman W., and Oscar Fraley. "The Boston Tar Baby." *True Boxing Yearbook* (1952): pp 24ff.

Nicolaisen, Steve. "You Couldn't Make It Up." *Boxing Monthly* 20, no. 6 (October 2008): pp. 26ff.

O'Rourke, Tom. "George Dixon Greatest, Says O'Rourke." *The Ring* 15, no. 9 (October 1936): pp. 34ff.

Pardy, George T. "Battlers of the Irish Brigade." *The Ring* 13, no. 4 (May 1934): pp. 14ff.

_____. "Famous Fighting Codes." *The Ring* 21, no. 2 (March 1942): pp. 20ff.

_____. "The Slugging Blacksmith." *Sport Story* (August 1937): pp. 47ff.

_____. "When the Lights Went Out." *The Ring* 18, no. 9 (October 1939): pp. 30ff.

Patrick, Toby. "When the Strongest Man in the World Fought the Ring Champion." *Boxing and Wrestling* 5, no. 10 (June 1955): pp. 34ff.

Pegg, Harry. "Fistic Carnival of Champions in New Orleans." *Boxiana Review 1972*, pp. 21ff. Pepper, Mike. "The Ten Deadliest Punches Ever Thrown." *Boxing and Wrestling* 5, no. 10 (June 1955): pp. 30ff.

_____. "To Destination and Return." *Boxiana Review 1972*, pp. 8ff.

Pete, Roland. "The Extraordinary Mr. Langford." *Boxing and Wrestling* 8, no. 3 (December 1957): pp. 24ff.

Phillips, A.D. "Drawing the Color Line." *The Ring* 11, no. 4 (May 1932): page 38.

_____. "Fights and Fighters." *The Ring* 10, no. 9 (October 1931): pp. 29ff.

Phillips, Gertrude. "The Influence of Women at Boxing Bouts." *The Ring* 1, no. 1 (February 15, 1922).

Ribalow, Harold U. "Jack Johnson — 'The First King.'" *Boxing Illustrated Wrestling News* 8, no. 6 (June 1966): pp. 16ff.

_____. "Sam Langford — The Boston Tar-Baby." *Boxing Illustrated* 9, no. 1 (January 1967): pp. 23ff.

Richards, Robert. "The Amazing Langford!" *Fight Stories* 9, no. 3 (Winter 1948–49): pp. 30ff.

Rickard, Tex. "Abe Attell was the Greatest." *Boxing and Wrestling* 7, no. 11 (August 1957): pp. 30ff.

The Ring Staff. "The Big Round." *The Ring* 30, no. 4 (May 1951): pp. 10ff.

Ringside Reporter. "The Sullivan-Kilrain Fight." *Boxing Illustrated Wrestling News* 1, no. 5 (April 1959).

Riodan, Clarence. "I Saw the Ring's Most Unusual Spectacle." *Boxing and Wrestling* 6, no. 12 (August 1956): pp. 16ff.

Rogin, Gilbert. "Mr. Boxing, Himself." *IBRO Journal*, no. 96 (December 20, 2007): pp. 22ff. This article, which quotes Fleisher extensively, was originally published in *The Ring* circa 1962.

Santoro, Al. "Big Jim Jeffries." *Eagle* 34 (May 1946): pp. 12ff.

Scurti, Rick. "5 Greatest Fighters." *Boxing Digest* 45, no. 7 (August 2003): pp. 56ff.

Shaffer, Harry. "The Color Line, Mayhem, and Madness: The Last Days of Stanley Ketchel, Part II." *Boxing Collectors' News*, no. 203 (November 2005): pp. 6ff.

_____. "Life in the Fast Lane: The Last Days of Stanley Ketchel, Part I." *Boxing Collectors' News*, no. 202 (May 2005): pp. 6ff.

Sharkey, Tom. "Fighters I've Met." *IBRO Journal*, no. 86 (June 27, 2005): pp. 15ff.

Sherry, Mike. "Greatest Fights of the Century." *Boxing and Wrestling* 5, no. 12 (August 1955): pp. 36ff.

_____. "Kid McCoy vs. Tom Sharkey." *Boxing and Wrestling* 5, no. 8 (March 1955): pp. 34ff.

"Solved ... the Mystery of the Missing Champion." *Boxing and Wrestling* 6, no. 4 (January 1956): pp. 22ff.

"Some Punch!" *The Ring* 30, no. 7 (August 1951): pp. 26ff.

Stradley, Don. "The Art of the Cheat: Boxing's Long and Sordid Tradition." *The Ring* 88, no. 6 (May 2009): pp. 86ff.

_____. "The Tumultuous Life and Times of Terry McGovern." *The Ring* 88, no. 13 (December 2009): pp. 78ff.

Stump, Al. "All Jeff Had Was His Fists." *Boxing Illustrated Wrestling News* 1, no. 6 (May 1959): pp. 10ff.

Sullivan, John L. "How It Feels to Win the Heavyweight Championship." *Boxing and Wrestling* 7, no. 7 (April 1957): pp. 14ff. This feature excerpts, with added illustration, a part of Sullivan's 1892 autobiography.

Thorne, Clifford L. "Human Side of

Ketchel." *The Ring* 14, no. 12 (January 1936): p. 24.

Thornton, Robert J. "Complete History of the Middleweight Division." *Boxing and Wrestling* 8, no. 7 (April 1958): pp. 26ff.

_____. "The Lightweights: A Complete History." *Boxing Illustrated Wrestling News* 3, no. 3 (March 1961): pp. 30ff.

_____. "Special Heavyweight Section." *Boxing Illustrated Wrestling News* 1, no. 8 (August 1959): pp. 17.

Van Every, Edward. "When Fitz Made Comeback Bid." *The Ring* 30, no. 2 (March 1951): pp. 28 ff.

The Veteran. "The Battle of Maspeth." *Boxing and Wrestling* 1, no. 10 (January 1952): pp. 8ff.

_____. "I Remember When — ." *The Ring* 21, no. 2 (March 1942): pp. 28ff.

Waldrop, Dennis. "The Man Young Griffo Wanted to Tear Apart." *Boxing and Wrestling* 7, no. 9 (May 1957): pp. 42ff.

Weider, Joseph. "The Fight Game's KO Kings." *Boxing and Wrestling* 1, no. 9 (December 1951): pp. 12ff.

Weinberg, S. Kirson, and Henry Around. "The Occupational Culture of the Boxer." *The American Journal of Sociology* 57 (March 1952): pp. 460ff.

Weston, Stanley. "The Accidental Fighter: How Jim Jeffries Was Discovered." *Boxing and Wrestling* 7, no. 2 (October 1956): pp. 26ff.

_____. "Battling Nelson: The Durable Dane." *Boxing and Wrestling* 5, no. 2 (August 1954): pp. 28ff.

_____. "A Century of Lightweight Champions." *Boxing and Wrestling* 4, no. 4 (August 1953): pp. 24ff.

_____. "The Cowpoke Who Became a Legend." *Boxing and Wrestling* 7, no. 9 (May 1957): pp. 30ff.

_____. "The Fighter Who Couldn't Be Hit." *Boxing and Wrestling* 5, no. 8 (March 1955): pp. 30ff.

_____. "Greatest Fights of the Century: Joe Gans vs. Elbows McFadden." *Boxing and Wrestling* 6, no. 11 (July 1956): pp. 32.

_____. "Jack Dempsey, the Nonpareil."

Boxing Illustrated Wrestling News 3, no. 4 (April 1961): p. 28ff.

_____. "James J. Jeffries: They Called Him the Man with the Concrete Jaw!" *Boxing and Wrestling* 1, no. 12 (March-April 1952): pp. 20ff.

_____. "Jess Willard: The 'Public Be Damned' Champion." *Boxing and Wrestling* 6, no. 12 (August 1956): pp. 24ff.

_____. "Jim Jeffries in Pictures: Flashback in Photos of a Great Fighter." *Boxing and Wrestling* 7, no. 6 (February 1957): pp. 20ff.

_____. "Kid McCoy vs. Jim Stewart." *Boxing and Wrestling* 7, no. 3 (November 1956): pp. 34ff.

_____. "Sailor with the Loaded Fists." *Boxing and Wrestling* 8, no. 2 (November 1957): pp. 20ff.

_____. "Sam Langford Was Great." *Boxing and Wrestling* 6, no. 9 (May 1956): pp. 30ff.

_____. "Stanley Ketchel." *Boxing Illustrated Wrestling News* 2, no. 10 (October 1960): pp. 33ff.

_____. "The Tex Rickard Story." *Boxing and Wrestling* 1, no. 12 (March-April 1952): pp. 30ff. This installment, part of a series of articles on Rickard, discusses his promotion of the Johnson-Jeffries fight.

_____. "This Was the Real McCoy: Part 1." *Boxing Illustrated Wrestling News* 3, no. 1 (January 1961): pp. 20ff.

_____. "This Was the Real McCoy: Part 2." *Boxing Illustrated Wrestling News* 3, no. 2 (February 1961): pp. 20ff.

_____. "When the Turf Ran Red at Chichester." *Boxing and Wrestling* 7, no. 7 (April 1957): pp. 30ff.

Williams, Billy. "Getting Soft?" *The Ring* 29, no. 8 (September 1950): pp. 9ff.

Wise, Bill. "When the Boilermaker Knocked Out Ruby Robert." *Boxing Annual* (1966): pp. 22ff.

Woodbury, Vincent. "The True Wyatt Earp." *The Ring* 11, no. 4 (May 1932): pp. 39ff.

Woodman, Joe. "Fights I Cannot Forget." *The Ring* 34, no. 6 (July 1955): pp. 28ff.

* * *

In addition to the above sources, I wish to note those contained in the archive resources of Harry and Raven Shaffer, proprietors of Antiquities of the Prize Ring. Cited explicitly in this book, thanks often to Harry and Raven, are eyewitness accounts and editorial statements spanning several decades from the *Australian Bulletin, Baltimore American, Baltimore Morning Herald, Boston Globe, Boston Herald, Boston Press, Brooklyn Daily Eagle, Burbank Daily News, Chicago Inter-Ocean, Chicago Record, Chicago Sunday Examiner, Chicago Times-Herald, Chicago Tribune, Cleveland Tab, Galveston Daily News, Grand Rapids Herald, London Health and Strength, Milwaukee Free Press, Milwaukee Evening Wisconsin, Mirror of Life, New York Daily Herald, New York Journal, New York Press, New York Times, New York Tribune, New York World, Philadelphia Evening Bulletin, Police Gazette, Police News, Portland Oregonian, Sacramento Bee, Saginaw News, San Francisco Bulletin, San Francisco Call, San Francisco Chronicle, San Francisco Examiner, Seattle Times, Sioux City Journal, Sport Story, The Sporting News,* and *Sydney Referee.* Included in Harry's materials, as well, were rare magazine pieces cited herein.

Also of value has been the quarterly *Journal* of the International Boxing Research Organization. On this note, I state again my gratitude to Clay Moyle, Monte Cox, and other members of IBRO who provided such generous help with regard to certain fighters featured in this book. Clay's biography of Sam Langford has filled a gap that has existed in boxing literature for the past hundred years. Monte's commentary on the Joe Gans chapter was apt and much appreciated. My debt to Tracy Callis once again (as was true in regard to my biography of James J. Jeffries) challenges my powers of expression. Tracy has combed this volume on countless occasions, providing ceaseless encouragement and pointing out with painstaking care the places where revision of an item or a phrase was needed. His keen eye and attention to detail in the past year have been a blessing.

Index

Numbers in **bold italics** indicate pages with photographs.